Smollett's Women

SMOLLETT'S WOMEN

A Study in an Eighteenth-Century Masculine Sensibility

ROBERT D. SPECTOR

Contributions to the
Study of World Literature,
Number 56

GREENWOOD PRESS
Westport, Connecticut
London

Library of Congress Cataloging-in-Publication Data

Spector, Robert Donald.
    Smollett's women : a study in an eighteenth-century masculine
sensibility / Robert D. Spector.
      p. cm.—(Contributions to the study of world literature,
ISSN 0738-9345 ; no. 56)
    Includes bibliographical references and index.
    ISBN 0-313-28790-2 (alk. paper)
    1. Smollett, Tobias George, 1721-1771—Characters—Women.
2. Women and literature—England—History—18th century.
3. Masculinity (Psychology) in literature. I. Title. II. Series.
PR3698.W6S6 1994
823'.6—dc20   93-49538

British Library Cataloguing in Publication Data is available.

Library of Congress Catalog Card Number: 93-49538
ISBN: 0-313-28790-2
ISSN: 0738-9345

First published in 1994

Greenwood Press, 88 Post Road West, Westport, CT 06881
An imprint of Greenwood Publishing Group, Inc.

Printed in the United States of America

The paper used in this book complies with the
Permanent Paper Standard issued by the National
Information Standards Organization (Z39.48-1984).

10 9 8 7 6 5 4 3 2

Contents

Smollett's Women

1

Shaping Forces: Society, Personality, and Literary Tradition

Eighteenth-century England was a man's world. Englishmen did not pretend otherwise, nor would it have occurred to them to do so. They accepted their position as part of the natural order. Men governed the nation, made and dispensed its laws, and controlled its pursestrings. They wholeheartedly embraced as their national symbol the figure of John Bull, a lusty, blunt and gruff, beef-eating yeoman whose very name suggests the stereotypical ideal of male potency. More than a mere caricature to be employed for polemical purposes on the international scene, this dominating national self-image revealed the values and principles that motivated the British nation. According to the historian Linda Colley:

There was a sense . . . in which the British conceived of themselves as an essentially "masculine" culture—bluff, forthright, rational, down to earth to the extent of being philistine—caught up in an eternal rivalry with an essentially "effeminate" France—subtle, intellectually devious, preoccupied with high fashion, fine cuisine and etiquette, and so obsessed with sex that boudoir politics was bound to direct it.[1]

Such attitudes assured the marginalization of women in public life. Exclusion, perhaps, would be a better word. In the arts, with the exception of literature, women were virtually nonexistent; few names, indeed, have made their way into the histories of painting, sculpture, music, or architecture for the period. Even in literature their contributions were and continued to be for a long time either denigrated or ignored. Until almost the end of the century, women writers drew scornful comments from male contemporaries. The writing "misses" of Gothic tales at the end of the century remained targets for scathing comments that rated their work on a par with that of printers' devils. The very character of a female author was the object of suspicion. All but ostracized from the arts, women were no more present in the judiciary, politics, science, industry, or business. They simply had no place in the public world of eighteenth-century men whose very retreats from their labors—clubs, taverns, and coffeehouses— were sanctuaries free of the presence of the female sex.

If one's self-image helps determine success in life, eighteenth-century women were clearly doomed to failure. Wherever they turned in their society, they found themselves portrayed as weak and defenseless creatures, occupied mainly with the most frivolous activities, and dependent, like pets or children, upon men for support and guidance. Their silliness called for gentle chiding; their extravagance demanded sterner reproaches; and their emotional excesses, particularly suggestive of sexual feelings, called forth the severest rebukes. Periodicals and conduct books especially present a clear and no doubt dependable view of the image of women, an image created by men but generally shared by both sexes in the society. As early as Joseph Addison and Richard Steele's *Spectator*, periodical writers portray the female sex as attractive but essentially weak-minded, victims of foolishness, fashion, and vanity, the perfect targets for the new consumerism that Englishmen saw as a threat to the national character. Lord Chesterfield would keep women from business affairs since he regarded them as "children of a larger growth." Jonathan Swift dismissed the sex as mindless, while Lady Mary Wortley Montagu, with obvious frustration, plainly enunciates the general assessment of her sisterhood: "Folly is reckoned our proper sphere."[2]

So it must have been. Even those who were friendly to the sex and concerned with their welfare still believed that women were an inferior species in need of male protection, defense even, from male predators since they lacked the qualities to thrive in a masculine world. John Dunton's *Athenian Mercury*, particularly appreciative of the talents of female writers, nevertheless in more worldly matters saw women in conventional social and religious terms.[3] In the *Connoisseur* George Colman and Bonnell Thornton, writers concerned with championing women authors, repeatedly take the sex to task for behavior best described as immature and childish. Ridiculing women's use of cosmetics, the *Connoisseur* focuses on female vanity, the dangers of their emotionalism, and their petty concerns for gambling and party-going.[4] The effect of this paternalistic image may be seen even in the work of one of the strongest and most daring women writers of the period, Eliza Haywood, whose *Female Spectator* proves no less patronizing toward women than the works of the male writers already cited. Indeed, it is difficult to distinguish between Haywood's treatment of her sex and the advice offered in a conduct book, *The Ladies Calling*, that admonished a woman "to live in a submissive selflessness consonant with her congenital incapacities."[5] Although written seventy years after the conduct book, the interests in Haywood's courtesy periodical do not differ essentially from those of her male predecessor. Her topics are "love and marriage, parent-child relationships, female education, moral and social decorum";[6] her views, despite her reputation as a scandalous writer, prove as conventional as those in *The Ladies Calling*, and, indeed, differ little from those of the host of male courtesy writers who preceded her.

If someone like Haywood could be influenced by the pervasive male view of women in the prints, the evidence suggests that she was not alone even among the strongest in her sex. Elizabeth Brophy has demonstrated how the conduct books shaped women's own view of themselves—whether in terms of their natural abilities, their emotional and intellectual weaknesses, or the dangers of their being overeducated.[7] Looking at women's writing about themselves and their sex, it is difficult to distinguish how much of the portrait plays up to male expectations, how much in various subtle ways attempts to undermine the masculine view, or how much represents an acceptance of male definitions of womanhood.[8] Even the many fine women novelists of the century, "rediscovered" by feminist critics and publishers, indicate the enormous pressures on them to conform personally and professionally to male and indeed female expectations of women and their subject matter. Whatever may be traced to genuine gender differences, social conventions, and marketplace demands, these women were constantly made aware of their sex and limitations on it.[9] For example, whatever her considerable abilities as a translator, Elizabeth Carter could be comically but nonetheless seriously praised by Samuel Johnson on her equally fine ability to make a pudding. For all her intellectual talents, Carter, and many others like her, had to know that in the world of men they had a limited and very well-defined sphere.

Given this paternalistic view of women's character—whose very virtues appear designed to serve men's needs—the sphere for female activity would have to be extremely circumscribed in its boundaries. Women, after all, had inherent weaknesses, limited powers of reasoning, and emotions too easily stirred by the vapors from the womb. Men seriously regarded women as incompetent to perform the important tasks of society, too frivolous and whimsical to be trusted in serious endeavor: on the great stage of the world, men were intended to be performers, while women were intended to remain silently and respectfully behind the curtain until called upon by men.[10] From this point of view, women appear not simply inferior to men but creatures of a different order on nature's chain of being.[11]

Yet the very things that men felt kept women naturally out of the larger political and social scene made them very special in another sphere of life, one important for men's comfort, security, fortunes, and progeny. Those qualities of charitableness, compassion, submissiveness, and piety were icons of the household.[12] Women in the domestic setting served a masculine society as totems of family values, of stability, of purity, of concern, and of loyalty. Affectionate marriages replacing the traditional contract alliances suggest men's recognition that they had to satisfy their emotional needs through matrimony. Certainly there was greater gratification in the romantic relationship than in the bleak ties of a loveless arrangement.[13] Superficially, at least, it would seem there was some kind of triumph for womanhood in this new companionate marriage and its implications for greater authority at least in the household. It would seem not a bad trade-off for women who generally conceded their intellectual inferiority to men.[14] It did, after all, give women more sway in household matters than they had ever had before.[15] It allowed them to act with enough guile to "reign . . . by insinuating ways" so long as they maintained their customary "mildness and cheerfulness."[16]

For many women the development of the affectionate marriage, the regal control over the household, and the idealization of womanhood that accompanied it must certainly have been gratifying whatever the cost in having to deny the full intellect and sexuality of one's nature. For such women, words like William Alexander's in 1779 would have sounded comforting rather than annoying: "As women are, in polished society, weak and incapable of self-defence, the laws of this country have supplied this defect, and formed a kind of barrier around them, by rendering their persons so sacred and inviolable, that even death is, in several cases, the consequence of taking improper advantage of that weakness."[17] Whatever their feelings, as the eighteenth century progressed, more and more the sphere of women became clearly the domestic workplace,[18] and woman was idealized by man until she lost all truly human qualities except those required to serve men's needs.

Surely, however, there were women who would have recognized what Janet Todd labels as "belittling idealization" in Alexander's words. Sheryl O'Donnell describes such views as "patriarchal notions of women as highly venerated inferior beings." Companionate marriage itself, Ruth Perry suggests, may be "interpretable as a more thoroughgoing psychological appropriation of women to serve the emotional needs of men," a harsh judgment but not altogether untrue.[19] Not all eighteenth-century women could have found pleasure in the notion that marriage was the be-all and end-all of their existence. As far back as Millamant in William Congreve's *Way of the World*, the drawbacks of the marital state provided material for a woman's lament; Charlotte Lennox's Arabella in *The Female Quixote* most assuredly recognized the effects marriage could have on women,[20] a good example of the rage that seethed beneath women's forced surface complacency. Domestic idealism could have had little appeal to the unmarried woman without prospects or to the intellectual female expected to hide her learning from an easily affronted male ego. Knowledge that domestic duties rated above intellectual interests could hardly have pleased the Bluestockings, however well they learned to play the game of self-effacement in a male society.[21] Still, early and late in the long years from 1660 to 1800, female voices of protest were limited in a patriarchal society, and no great chorus joined such soloists as Mary Astell, Lady Mary Wortley Montagu, and Mary Wollstonecraft.

If the companionate marriage undoubtedly brought greater passion to the marital state itself, it did nothing to enlarge the sense and possibility of female sexuality in the general society. In fact, in some ways the marriage of affection demanded new or increased insistence on female chastity before and after the wedding. To be sure, the double standard in sexual matters readily accepted that men bring sexual experience to the marriage bed. With the view of the woman's superior morality, her idealization as a symbol of maternal tenderness, and her embodiment of Christian virtues, however, came a demand for purity, both physical and mental. Idealization merely brought the upper- and middle-class woman to a point where she was expected to deny her genuine emotions—either to suppress her passions or, at least, pretend that they did not exist. None of this, of course, applied to women of the lower orders. They were regarded as morally and socially inferior, not in control of their passions, and natural game for the male sex-hunter, particularly of the established classes.[22]

No better example of the double standard exists than the marital relationship of Samuel Johnson's friends, the Thrales. Henry Thrale, the brewer, carried on illicit relationships throughout his marriage to Hester Thrale. As a consequence of his behavior, he suffered repeated venereal ailments, the treatment of which became, in part, his wife's responsibility even during a pregnancy. Still, no one in their society, and even Hester Thrale's twentieth-century male biographer, found Henry Thrale's conduct appalling. Indeed, like other males in their circle (Boswell, of course, is a good example), Henry Thrale no doubt wore his suffering as a sign of the nobility of his virility. His friends looked upon such manhood, if not the consequence, as admirable. Yet, when her husband died and Mrs. Thrale married Gabriel Piozzi, an Italian musician, she scandalized her circle of friends—including the novelist Fanny Burney—not simply because Piozzi was an Italian Catholic and a musician, but because in choosing him despite these drawbacks she had displayed a passion unbecoming to a woman of her times. She had placed her romantic feelings, her sexual desires, above the common sense expected of the now desexualized respectable woman.[23]

In every way society had made women citizens of another country. The double standard allowed men to cheat freely on their wives while demanding impeccable fidelity from them. For upper-class men to foist bastards on lower-class women, including their own household servants, brought neither shame nor embarrassment to them. If they chose to pay for the upkeep of these children, that was evidence of their generosity. If idealization had made married women beings devoid of normal human emotions, the very laws of their country turned them into chattel, the property of their husbands. Let a woman fall from grace, and it required a miracle or at least a generous-hearted novelist to rescue her from utter destruction. Once having yielded to her passions, she was regarded as proper prey for all other males in her society. Even at the lower levels of society, the disparity of the sexes is evident, for example, in such a thing as the notorious practice of wife-selling in the period. Despite a recent attempt to apologize for it as a poor man's system of divorce and to show that women frequently found satisfaction in it,[24] the fact remains that it was the selling of wives and not husbands that characterized the procedure.

Like the very system that excluded women from the public sphere, the terms of more personal relationships removed women from intimate relationships with men. Given the circumstances of women in eighteenth-century society, it is not remarkable that they cut such poor figures in the novels of the period. One way or another, they were perceived by male writers as stereotypes: idealized heroines, fallen figures, comic and grotesque old maids, bluestockings, sexy servants, and the like. It would require the talents and sensitivity of the most unusual male writer—or, indeed, female—to get beyond the façade and thus create as well-rounded female characters as the believable heroes of eighteenth-century fiction.

Very much a part of that male-dominated world of eighteenth-century England, Tobias Smollett could be expected to regard women from that limited perspective. Indeed, it would be difficult to name a writer in the period more likely to display an example of the masculine sensibility. Even more than Henry Fielding, the contemporary novelist that he most resembles, Smollett wrote fiction that has, from his own time to the present, appealed largely to male readers. Whether in his personal life, his attitude toward women in the real world, his generic literary interests, or the interrelationships among them, the forces shaping Smollett's novels led naturally to the minor roles played by caricatured women in his writing.

Clearly, from whatever point of view it has been written, critical opinion has consistently denied Smollett's ability to deal with women and their emotions. Feminist critics find his work insignificant for their purposes, contrast his blindness to female sensitivities with Samuel Richardson's awareness of women's feelings, and charge him with a lack of understanding and respect for the opposite sex.[25] More traditional evaluations of Smollett's treatment, from early on and regardless of the gender of the writers, prove equally dismissive of his talent for dealing with women, their feelings, or their relationships with men. When Smollett's female characters are not being ignored, they are discussed for their eccentricities, their absence of reality, or their evidence of the author's paternalistic attitudes.[26] Their very presence in Smollett's work and their treatment are attributed to the writer's need to satisfy public taste rather than to any genuine personal interest in them.[27] Whether as stereotypical idealized heroines or comic grotesques, Smollett's women are seen only in terms of the roles they serve to satisfy his heroes' needs.[28]

Certainly, neither in his life nor his fiction does Smollett display the kind of sensitivity to women's emotions that would permit him to create heroines that go much beyond the idealization that makes their sexual passions anything more than a convenience to gratify their husbands' desires. If he achieves a sense of sympathy for the situation of fallen women in a character like Miss Williams in *Roderick Random,* her tale and its emotions are largely written to formulaic stereotypes. The distance between the fictional conventions in her story and the more revealing inset of "Memoirs of a Lady of Quality" in *Peregrine Pickle* reveals the contrast between masculine assumptions and genuine feminine sensitivities. Smollett feels most secure in his comic or grotesque female characters because they depend—despite his superior skills—on conventional stereotypes that protect him from having to go too deeply into their emotions. After all, tender sensibility toward women should hardly be expected from a novelist capable of repeatedly harsh treatment of Jews (with the exception of Joshua in *Ferdinand Count Fathom*) and of blacks in both *Roderick Random* and *Humphry Clinker.* The wonder of it is that Smollett—for all his limitations—managed to create so much variety in his female characters of all types. That fact suggests the importance of talent and the effects of function in fiction.

Smollett's limitations begin with his personal experience. Some sense of what can be expected in Smollett's female characters, especially his heroines, becomes evident in an examination of his actual relationships and associations with women. Although the time has long passed when simple biographical criticism could be freely used to explain works of literature, that does not mean that an author's life is so distinct from his or her writing that biographical material cannot contribute to a better understanding of how and why the writer's fiction takes the shape that it does. The author's interests, values, and experiences, after all, account for choice in subject matter, methods of presentation, and objects of focus. If, for example, a writer regards women in a particular way, that attitude is likely to affect his or her treatment of female characters. If a writer concentrates on a hero rather than a heroine's activities and interests, then it is likely to be the hero who dominates the work while women play minor or subsidiary roles. For Smollett especially, since he relied so much on his own experiences and sought to bring to his fiction a genuine sense of the actual world as he perceived it, the facts of his biography as they bear upon his relationships to women seem appropriate.[29]

Given Smollett's dependence on experience and his relations with women, it is not surprising that he chooses the picaresque mode for his novels, that he emphasizes the adventures of a single male character, and that he uses his fictional women primarily as adjuncts to the interests of his heroes. Smollett's biography, particularly his personal and emotional relationships with women, discloses a strongly male personality, even for an eighteenth-century man, that forecasts the manner in which female characters appear in his novels—novels, after all, entitled *Roderick Random* and *Peregrine Pickle* rather than *Pamela* or *Clarissa*.

Judged by what we know of Smollett's relationship to his wife, he was a man who, if he had romantic passion, managed very well to control any expression of it. At a time when a new order of familial connections had become well established and affection between marital partners was the norm, Smollett's biography and work reflect no real tendency to an open expression of romantic feelings toward Nancy (Anne) Lassells, the West Indian heiress whom he married in about 1743. That very doubt about their wedding date suggests the manner in which Smollett chose to expose his personal feelings to the world. The same vagueness marks the place of their marriage, and Smollett's earliest biographers—those, after all, closest to the evidence and one a good friend—could provide no help on the matter and had to resort to creating imaginary details about it and about Anne herself.[30] Like the idealized heroines of romance, Smollett's wife, as presented by him, seems little more than a fictional construction existing for the role she played in the life of the hero.

Smollett's taciturnity about his most intimate relationship with a woman seems to mask what strongly appears to have been a good marriage. No evidence of other women—before or during their marriage—exists anywhere in Smollett's biography, an absence that perhaps helps account for the lack of any concreteness in his portrayal of the emotional lives of most of his heroines. Certainly Smollett never indicates any dissatisfaction with their relationship. The one statement in a letter to Robert Barclay in 1744 that enigmatically expresses Smollett's uncertain state at the time may refer, as Lewis Knapp suggests,[31] to Smollett's financial insecurity. Characteristically, Smollett holds back on the details. Smollett himself, years later in his Will, provides a clear picture of how he regarded Anne. Although Knapp says of the document, "Through the legal terminology of [it] there burns the flame of . . . his true affection for his wife,"[32] its formality speaks more to her generosity than to any strong emotion on his part. The novelist who could readily give vent to passions of anger and revenge in both life and fiction could not easily find words to describe the romantic emotions of love. Unlike Henry Mackenzie, his fellow Scots novelist, Smollett could not employ the vocabulary of a man of feeling. Even in his Will he can come up with no stronger language than "my dear Wife Anne Smollett." When Dr. Giovanni Gentili, after Smollett's death, summarized the life of the Smolletts as one of "perfect harmony,"[33] he appears to be seeing the relationship through Smollett's own stoical sensibility.

That same stoicism did not characterize Anne. The few documents of hers we have reveal not only an intelligent and informed woman but also strong emotional relationship in their marriage despite her husband's inability ever to find appropriate words to describe it. Surely, for all that is known of Smollett's emotional outbursts of anger with others, he apparently knew well enough not to vent his spleen against his wife, or, at least, she knew well enough how to deal with him in a marriage that gives no evidence that he ever lost her affection.[34] Like Smollett, she could explode when circumstances called for it, but unlike him she could find a tender phrase to express her feelings of love and did not hesitate to do so. In a letter to Archibald Hamilton in 1773, she displays a fairly close familiarity with her husband's work and a good understanding of literature. Protective of her husband's reputation, she pushes, ultimately successfully, for a monument to his memory. She asks that his books be sent to her. She bemoans "how much that Dear Man Suffered" while he wrote *Humphry Clinker* during his final illness and how ill-used he was by his publisher. For her he was "my dear Smollett," and, as their friend Robert Graham wrote in a prologue to a play for her benefit, she was capable of weeping for the loss of "Smollet [sic] [who] once was mine!"[35] Only once does Smollett himself provide a picture of their blissful marriage. In an undated fragment of a letter, he writes: "Many a time do I stop my task and betake me to a game of romps with Betty [Elizabeth, his daughter], while my wife looks on smiling and longing in her heart to join in the sport; then back to the cursed round of duty."[36] The "round of duty" is Smollett's, not Anne's, and she remains, like women of her time, an appendage to her husband.

In Smollett's letters, poetry, and *Travels Through France and Italy*, the same picture emerges. Perhaps it is unfair to use his letters as evidence. Smollett was too busy to concern himself with writing letters, and generally they are perfunctory and business-like, hardly the place to expect much emotional expression, let alone romantic effusions. If any were ever written to Anne herself, they no longer exist. References to her are few: regards to a family member and friends, a comment about selling part of her estate, the puzzling remark to Barclay perhaps about his trepidations about marriage, and a comment on her health. In a letter to Richard Smith, an American admirer, in 1763, however, Smollett summarizes his life and describes his marriage. To be sure, it would be remarkable if Smollett displayed his emotions in a letter to a stranger. Nevertheless, his comment illustrates again his characteristic coldness in his references to Anne: "I married, very young, a native of Jamaica, a young Lady well known and universally respected, under the name of Miss Nancy Lassells; and by her I enjoy a comfortable tho' moderate estate in that Island."[37]

The coldness of Smollett's language and what he chooses to say are a remarkable foreshadowing of the descriptive terms in his Will. Even in a letter to his friend Alexander Reid after the Smolletts had lost their only child, Smollett, while speaking of his grief in a half a sentence, ignores altogether the impact on Anne and only later speaks of his wife as "en-joy[ing] pretty good Health."[38]

Not even in poetry supposedly addressed to Anne does Smollett manage to convey romantic emotion. His novels show him to be passionate—about injustice, personal grievance, stupidity, and the like. In the poem *Tears of Scotland* on the outrageous treatment of the Scots after the Battle of Culloden, he does not hold back on his feelings, and in "Ode to Leven-Water" in *Humphry Clinker* he bursts forth into sentimental nostalgia. And yet neither "A Declaration in Love: Ode to Blue-Ey'd Ann" nor his "Pastoral Ballad" (both published in his *British Magazine* in 1760) rises above the genre pieces conventional in his period or offers anything resembling deep emotion. The ode, probably a "relic of his courtship,"[39] seems rescued from a pile of old papers to serve as a filler in his new magazine. The ballad, a stock piece, has no merit other than the fact that it is probably Smollett's. Neither has the strength or passion that suggests genuine emotion. Nor was it likely that Smollett's poems would be open declarations of his deepest romantic feelings. When Lord George Lyttelton published his openly sentimental monody on the death of his wife, Smollett responded with a savage parody in *Peregrine Pickle*. Smollett was no Lyttelton, nor was he like the later Dante Gabriel Rossetti, who cast the manuscript of his poems into the grave of his wife, Elizabeth Siddall. If Roderick Random's two poems to the heroine of his novel (225–27) or the poet Melopoyn's, in which Roderick substitutes her name for the character's, were inspired by Smollett's feelings for Anne (and the novel was, after all, written only a few years after their marriage), it would be a sign of his sentiments, romantic feelings that he otherwise managed to keep well hidden.

For Smollett, women—even the woman to whom he was closest—were attendant upon men just as the heroines of his novels served to fill out men's stories and adventures. They were observed, when they were observed, from the outside. Consider the role that Anne plays in *Travels Through France and Italy*. Although she was present throughout the journey, she seems barely to exist. According to Knapp, the references to Anne in the *Travels* "indicate that the novelist was warmly devoted to his Ann."[40] In a paternalistic way that is true, but it is even more to the point to note that the small role that she plays in the work serves the purposes of the artist, the male traveler who is the focus of the book's attention.

To begin with, it is odd to suggest that Smollett expresses any great feelings toward his wife when she appears briefly in only four of the letters. Even in those letters her purpose is to describe the hero's character and intentions. Smollett begins the *Travels* by explaining that the journey has been spurred by his concern for his wife: "My wife earnestly begged I would convey her from a country where every object served to nourish her grief: I was in hopes that a succession of new scenes would engage her attention, and gradually call off her mind from a series of painful reflections"(2). Smollett, of course, is referring to the death of their daughter. While he also expresses his own grief, without identifying it, the effect of his passage is to indicate Anne's dependence on him.

It is a dependence that becomes the theme of his further references to her in the work. She becomes his measure for describing the inadequacy of the inns in Boulogne (78). Her health provides the explanation of their not eating in the "public ordinary" (71). On a gondola trip to Genoa, Anne serves to make up part of the traveling troupe (205). Commenting on the severity of his fit of coughing, he uses his wife's terror to underscore the severity of his condition (298). In the longest reference to Anne, she becomes the conventional heroine of eighteenth-century fiction. Recounting their misadventure on the road to Florence—one brought on by his own obstinacy—Anne might well be Narcissa in *Roderick Random* or Aurelia in *Sir Launcelot Greaves* at a more advanced age. After a five-mile walk, poor Anne—"my wife a delicate creature, who had scarce ever walked a mile in her life"—is in such a state that Smollett is "obliged to support my wife, who wept in silence, half dead with terror and fatigue" (301). Perhaps it should be recalled that Anne Smollett, born in the same year as her husband, survived him by twenty years and managed to care for herself long after he was dead—hardly a delicate and defenseless flower. It is also worth noting that all the evidence indicates that she was a woman of sharp intelligence and clearly not lacking in knowledge. Yet in the *Travels*, according to Smollett's account, she appears without opinions on art, architecture, men, and manners.

Smollett's strong masculine sensibility so evident in his marital relationship was bound to affect his treatment of female characters in his novels. That same sensibility apparently influenced his relationship with women in the society outside his home, and that, too, would help account for his fictional approach to members of the other sex, especially limiting his ability to go beneath the surface of his female characters to develop their emotions and to understand their sensibilities. No other major male writer in the period seems so restricted in his association with women, particularly in social situations.

It is not that Smollett was unsociable. The naïve response to Smollett's affability in company expressed by his contemporary William Robertson, the eminent Scottish historian, who expressed surprise that the author had none of the coarseness of his fictional characters,[41] is typical of how the novelist's reputation at the time and subsequently suffered from identification with the rough and tumble heroes of his stories. As the well-documented account of his social life in Chelsea demonstrates, Smollett participated fully in a wide range of activities in his community. No doubt Anne Smollett played a role in these. Nevertheless, women provided a negligible part of that social life. In the standard biography of Smollett, there is a remarkable absence of female names in the index. Whether for business or pleasure, Smollett's involvement was generally with men, and the focus of his pleasurable activities was in the coffeehouses and taverns. Don Saltero's, the Rainbow, and Forrest's figure large in Smollett's daily life. When ill-health curtailed his social engagements, what he most deplored was being "obliged to give up all the pleasures of society, at least those of tavern society, to which you know I have been always addicted."[42] Such society had little room for women.

To appreciate fully the isolation of Smollett from the world of women, it is helpful to contrast his relationships with those of Samuel Richardson. To be sure, Richardson's female associations were probably the most pronounced of any of the eighteenth-century male novelists, but the difference between the two men in that regard helps explain the sensibility that characterizes the treatment of women in their novels. Richardson felt comfortable in the company of women. During the early 1750s "his closest association [was] with literary ladies." He boasted of his intimate ties to them, his visits to them, his friendships with them. As Mrs. Barbauld pointed out in her introduction to his correspondence, he was truly dependent "on a circle of female admirers."[43]

In the letters of the two authors, the differences in their temperaments are especially pronounced. Smollett's collected letters include a single offering to a female correspondent, the duchess of Hamilton, and its purpose is merely to seek her help in his attempt to gain the consulship of Nice.[44] By contrast, women dominate even Richardson's selected letters: women number almost half the recipients and by far the greater number of letters are written to them. Whether they were young or old, related to friends or altogether new acquaintances, Richardson could address women on easy and familiar terms. He did not hesitate to ask their advice on his fictional creations.[45] It is impossible to imagine Smollett following Richardson's practice of sending a "finely bound copy, with interleaved pages for corrections" of *Pamela* to Astraea and Minerva Hill for their corrections; offering installments of *Clarissa* to his "new friend Sarah Wescomb . . . [for] corrections and observations"; calling on Mrs. Delany for suggestions on *Clarissa*; or gratefully accepting Lady Bradshaigh's marginalia in volumes of both *Pamela* and *Clarissa*.[46] It hardly seems surprising that the experiences of the two writers should lead to the fictional approach to women resulting in one's having written two novels bearing the heroines' names as their titles and the other having written five novels in which women's existence relates mainly to men's fortunes.

If Smollett's real-life relations with women made it unlikely for him to approach them in his fiction with great understanding of their emotions or to treat the sentiment of love in sexual relationships with any great degree of insight, his insistence upon strong masculine values insured that his work would bear a decidedly masculine perspective. His identification with such protagonists as Roderick Random and Peregrine Pickle can be attested to by the stance he takes everywhere in his life and work. In his willingness to excuse his heroes' dissolute sexual conduct, no less than in his celebration of their physical triumphs and eagerness to battle over whatever they regarded as personal slights, Smollett revealed his admiration for the manly values of his time. Women in his fiction could expect only passing interest, their fortunes tied to the adventures of the men in their world.

Dealing with male behavior on the public scene, Smollett displayed a strong distaste for anything that suggested less than heroic and manly conduct. To be sure, he might show leniency toward two of the fallen figures of the Seven Years' War as he responded to their disgrace in the pages of his periodical, the *Critical Review*. However, the treatment of both Admiral John Byng and Lord George Sackville owed more to Smollett's politics than to his approval of their activities under fire. The Tory sympathies of his review protected them because Smollett's concern lay with the political advantages that their cases gave him in his struggle against a Whig administration.[47] Admiral Charles Knowles was less fortunate; his wartime behavior drew Smollett's full wrath as a writer. Reviewing Knowles's pamphlet that sought to vindicate his conduct at the battle of Rochefort in 1757, Smollett lashes out at what he regards as Knowles's unmanliness. Smollett's severe attack brought Knowles's libel action and provided the author with an opportunity to display what he regarded as manly behavior when he confessed to writing the article and thereby brought about the acquittal of Archibald Hamilton, printer and publisher of the review, but sent Smollett himself to jail on charges of libel when truth itself was still considered no defense.[48]

Taking on another military man, Sir John Cope, whose retreat at Prestonpans from the Highlanders in the Jacobite Rebellion in 1745 unleashed Smollett's poetic disdain, Smollett linked the general's misconduct to what he regarded as sexual perversion. The charges of homosexuality in Smollett's *Advice* were as daring at that time as they were scurrilous, but they appear to be another example of Smollett's proclamation of his own masculinity even as Alexander Pope's defamatory comments on Lord Hervey in *An Epistle to Dr. Arbuthnot*, Smollett's model, had been that poet's attempt to display his masculine superiority by deriding Hervey's suspected bisexuality.[49] But whatever Smollett's purpose, the sensibility exhibited clearly foreshadows the approach likely to be made to the more sensitive and delicate treatment of love and women's emotions in Smollett's novels.

The novels, indeed, everywhere display Smollett's desire to show his truly masculine views of his world. His attacks on homosexuality and whatever he regards as sexual deviation surely place him in the persons of his male heroes in his fiction. Throughout his writing Smollett was aroused by his personal emotions.[50] When Roderick responds to the homosexuality of Captain Whiffle in *Roderick Random*, not only the character-narrator but clearly the author himself is appalled by what is being described. From his first meeting with Captain Whiffle, who is "lolling on his couch with a languishing air" and applying "a smelling-bottle to his nose," through an account of his affected speech and manners, to his demands for a ridiculous dress code, and finally to "his maintaining a correspondence with his surgeon, not fit to be named," Roderick presents, as Smollett's persona, a stereotypical portrait of homosexuality (197ff). Roderick's disdain and feeling of insecurity in Whiffle's presence clearly reflect Smollett's own feelings, a sense of a threat to his masculinity.

Smollett makes the point even more directly in his hero's experiences with Earl Strutwell. Falsely described by a scholar as "the first account of homosexuality in European fiction since that of Petronius,"[51] it nevertheless presents a genuine expression of the novelist's own view of the subject not common to such narrative point of view in the period. Not only does Strutwell's discussion of the subject make Roderick uneasy and fearful that he may be mistaken for a homosexual—"infected with this spurious and sordid desire"—but the quotation that he chooses to describe it identifies the hero's views with those of Smollett himself. To express his "utter detestation and abhorrence of it," he borrows lines from Smollett's *Advice*:

Eternal infamy the wretch confound
Who planted first, this vice on British ground!
A vice! that 'spite of sense and nature reigns,
And poisons genial love, and manhood stains! (310–11)

That threat to manhood repeatedly recurs in the work of a novelist determined to view the world in conventionally (and for him normal) masculine terms—those terms that see women as existing as objects for men's desire. In *Peregrine Pickle* the hero is appalled by what he regards as the unnatural conduct of an Italian count and German baron whom he meets on the Grand Tour. In response to their homosexual activities, Perry—in the words of the third-person narrator, clearly Smollett—"entertained a just detestation for all such abominable practices, [and] was incensed" (242). Equally abhorrent to the novelist were the threats of sexual ambiguity posed by transvestites and hermaphrodites. For all the comic intentions of Perry in persuading the foolish painter Pallet to attend a masquerade dressed as a woman in *Peregrine Pickle*, it suggests a broader satire than that aimed simply at unnatural sexual activities and raises questions, unintended by the novelist, about the meaning of being a woman in Smollett's society.[52] The episode itself quickly loses its humor in an air of uneasiness that reflects the author's own discomfort with the subject.

It is the same kind of uneasiness that characterizes the use of the castrato in *Humphry Clinker*, another of the sexual aberrations that ruffled the composure of the determinedly masculine novelist. As James Carson has pointed out, it is Matt Bramble, Smollett's hero and counterpart in the novel, who regards the female characters' infatuation with the singer Tenducci as a sign of their attraction to what he considers "unnatural" and dangerous.[53] For Smollett a deviation from the sexual norm posed a threat to his idealized views of women and sex. Indeed, sex itself in a natural romantic attachment was for Smollett a subject to be kept at a distance, and unusual sex threatened his conventional notions of male sexuality.

In the fullest discussion of Smollett's sexuality, Robert Day challenges the simple view of the novelist's sexual imagination. Day's account thoroughly covers Smollett's expressed fears of uncommon sexuality. However, as he examines Smollett's work and its preoccupation with the buttocks, Day suggests "a deeply buried homosexual-excremental myth [that] furnishes the motive power for Smollett's fiction."[54] At this distance in time, it is impossible to argue with any certainty what processes evolved from Smollett's psyche, and the evidence of what Smollett believed deep within his unconscious seems irretrievable past a certain level. But Day does disclose in Smollett's writing the kind of fear of any sexuality that runs counter to the accepted conventions of his masculine world, fears that men in Smollett's time responded to with more and more emphatic assertions of their masculinity. Certainly, behind that male bravado lies an obvious fear of seeing women as anything other than submissive creatures for masculine comfort so that a writer like Smollett, even when describing the consummation of the wedding night, portrays his heroes not as sharing sexual delight with their brides, but approaching them in the bridal bed as though their sole purpose was to provide a tasty feast.

Surely for all the portrayal of women as objects of male sexual desire, there runs beneath the description a constant sense of uneasiness about men's sexuality. The social distance between men and women made the female sex alien territory. All the conventional notions seem a means for controlling that difference, an expression of fear of the unknown covered by a kind of boyish boastfulness. Smollett's response to women seems typical. When Trunnion in *Peregrine Pickle* speaks of women, his voice plainly conveys Smollett's own doubts—doubts unlikely to permit the full creation of female characters:

He compared a woman to a great gun loaded with fire, brimstone and noise, which being violently heated, will bounce and fly, and play the devil, if you don't take special care of her breechings. He said she was like a hurricane that never blows from one quarter, but veers about to all points of the compass: he likened her to a painted galley curiously rigged, with a leak in her hold, which her husband would never be able to stop. He observed that her inclinations were like the Bay of

Biscay; for why? because you may heave your deep sea lead long enough, without ever reaching bottom. (15)

It is an unwitting expression of men's feelings of sexual inadequacy and recognition of men's fear of female dominance. It expresses the writer's own view of women as a threat to the masculine social order.[55] As Smollett the novelist knew, the only way to deal with the situation was through the use of comedy, exaggeration, or idealization in portraying women. The danger comes in recognizing woman's full humanity. Use a comic figure like Commodore Trunnion to describe her sexuality, and it is reduced to a harmless joke.

Given his temperament, personality, and relations with women, Smollett inevitably created a kind of fiction not easily accessible to fashioning female characters with genuine emotional depth or sensitivity. If it were possible to shape the materials of popular romance in such a way that it could convey realistic female sensibility, as his contemporary Richardson succeeded in doing, Smollett's open hostility to the genre itself prevented his finding the appropriate means in his novels. Of all the major novelists in his period, he was the most determinedly antipathetic to the romance genre.[56] In a period of generic transformation as the traditional romance was being absorbed into the evolving novel,[57] Smollett stubbornly rejected most of its conventions, especially the amorous interests of the romance, while holding on to its counterpart, the picaresque. His strongly masculine nature rebuffed the expressiveness of tender emotions, any indulgence in pathos. Fearful of sentiment, he regarded its use as somehow unmanly, something to be turned to comedy, the material for humor.[58] Approaching the subject of love—the fundamental material of romance—Smollett never permitted his head to be governed by his heart.[59] As the old romances moved toward the "sexual romanticism" of the next century,[60] Smollett was the foremost novelist opposing the change.

To be sure, as a professional writer, Smollett could neglect neither the public taste for romance nor the use that it might provide for his fiction. He could not ignore what other novelists found more comfortable in the superficial effects provided by the romance.[61] Yet for the convenience that he found in the genre for the happy endings in his novels and whatever sentimental details he employed to placate his audience's taste, he generally undercuts the romantic sensibility of such material or merely finds it serviceable in shaping his plots.[62] In the fullest treatment of the subject—an analysis of Smollett's play on romance in *Humphry Clinker*—Sheridan Baker provides a detailed description of what he regards as Smollett's "comic romance,"[63] which in itself is a form of antiromance.

What is most apparent in Baker's assessment and in Smollett's work as a whole is the fact that the novelist rarely uses romance as a means for exploring the inner emotions associated with the experience of love in his female characters, except as a device for evoking scatological or satiric humor. For Smollett the fictional view is externalized; emotion is seen from the outside or through action. While the technique can successfully convey violent and angry emotions, it denies insight into the more tender passions of love associated with the romance. Seen from the outside, especially from a male perspective, it tends to turn women into either stereotypes or comic characters.

Smollett's sources of fictional inspiration—the drama and the picaresque—merely reinforce the externality of his point of view, a difficult vision to allow a portrayal of the inner life of characters, especially females, when the narrative voice is that of a man. In his dependence on drama for his characterization, Smollett severely limits his possibilities. His effectiveness is most likely to come with his heroic central figures, those whose existence dominates the attention on the stage. Smollett displays a good knowledge of drama, not only Elizabethan and Jacobean plays, but also of acting techniques and theories.[64] On the whole, the effect is potentially beneficial for creating his heroes and his comic and grotesque minor characters, but it is less propitious in achieving characterization going beyond the surface of "external physical reaction to depict the emotional states of his characters." He depends on acting theories that offer a "grammar of the passions" and that in fiction prove especially formulaic and stereotypical. As keys to the passions, the acting formulas from Smollett's period serve well enough to convey the activities and movements of his typically picaresque narratives, but are unlikely to produce the kind of sensitivity required of his heroines, particularly since their conduct lacks a sense of reality that might only be achieved by an examination of their feelings.

Smollett gravitates naturally to the picaresque, a genre strongly masculine in its interests, intent on action, yielding to emotion mainly in the form of anger, and rejecting the warmer sentiments of love. Occasionally a woman writer like Aphra Behn handles the material or a male author like Defoe develops a female picara rather than the rambunctious, brawling, hard-headed picaro typical of the genre. Still, from *Lazarillo de Tormes* and *Guzmán de Alfarache* through *Gil Blas* the picaresque bears a male identity; clearly it appeals to Smollett as evident in his translation of Le Sage's work and his comments on narrative theory in *Roderick Random* and *Ferdinand Count Fathom*. Despite questions raised about the extent of the picaresque in the entirety of his work and despite the suggestion that his writing indicates a decline in the genre, Smollett depends on it as a narrative base, employs it in his techniques of characterization, and maintains its point of view and/or its attitudes throughout his career.[65]

As Smollett himself makes clear in his theoretical statements, the picaresque focuses intensely on its hero or antihero. He is omnipresent in the action. He provides a vehicle for satirizing a corrupt society. Other characters exist only in relation to his and the satirical needs. In no way does the picaro display the emotions of a man of feeling unless for the purposes of deceiving others. Given the nature of the genre, love interests can only serve an ancillary role, and women are merely appendages to the hero's needs. Even sex, as one critic has noted, is for the most part portrayed as no more than the hero's "successful evacuation." With the heroine, who is there for the purposes of Smollett's hero, her "side of the sexual equation is not well sustained . . . either by her perpetual presence or by her vitality as a character."[66] Interested as he is in adventure and satire, Smollett could not care less about that female side of the equation. His use of the picaresque, like that of the drama, along with his antiromantic views and nature, make it remarkable that Smollett should create as much variety and interest as he does in his female characters. And yet, whether fallen women, comics or grotesques, and even heroines, they emerge with a peculiar kind of vitality and certainly play significant functional roles in his novels.

2

Heroines

With all that has been said about Smollett's views of and experiences with women, it should be obvious that his greatest difficulty in creating female characters would come in his development of his heroines. Critics, generally failing to make distinctions among Smollett's women, have consistently declared his efforts a failure. Whether attributing his inability to the grossness in his own character that prevented him from making the essential purity of his heroines interesting, or simply disposing of his treatment with dismissive comments about his awkward techniques, or merely noting his lack of interest in romance, they have concluded that Smollett's women "count for little or nothing." They are depicted as tiresome, unexciting, "pasteboard caricature[s] of an ideal."[1] Even when his treatment of heroines has been offered as evidence of unexpected virtue in Smollett's own character, the praise is diluted by depicting it as "a sincere if somewhat sentimental idealization of woman."[2]

Yet in some ways, from the perspective of eighteenth-century attitudes toward women, Smollett's heroines have a peculiar sort of realism, however repugnant from a modern point of view. To rebuke him for the asexual nature of their characters is to ignore what his age demanded of women.[3] Samuel Johnson, responding to Boswell's comment on the harshness of judging a woman for a single "deviation from chastity," expressed a common view of his contemporaries: "Why, no, Sir, it is the greatest principle which she is taught. When she has given up that principle, she has given up every notion of female honour and virtue, which are all included in chastity."[4] As the epitome of sexual virtue, pure in body and mind, Smollett's heroines represented the highest ideals of eighteenth-century society.[5] Whether in real life or fiction, even the sentimental romances, heroines were denied sexual feelings. The very protection of her virtue from aggressive male attackers symbolized a woman's upholding

the values of a patriarchal society.[6] Sexual expression—the province of
the lower social orders—stood beyond the pale for heroines, who naturally
belonged to the upper classes.[7] Smollett's Presbyterian upbringing merely
reinforced the sexual values of his age, one in which open discussion of
sex belonged to such scandalous literature as John Cleland's *Fanny Hill*.[8]

But not only in matters of sexuality did the views of Smollett's society
proscribe, or at least inhibit the possibility of, interesting fictional heroines.
Smollett's physical descriptions of them reflect the stereotypical notions
of his time. In appearance and conduct they were cut from a pattern that
was intended to create a model of perfection whose only faults were evidence of their greater delicacy and tenderness, expressed in emotional
outbursts of tears and fainting fits appealing to the masculine strengths of
their heroes. What could an honest writer do to give life to women trained
to be ornaments in society and educated to satisfy the needs of men? Even
a periodical like *The Lady's Magazine* (1770–94), intent on bringing
knowledge to women and insistent on their rights to education, focused
on morals and manners. Despite its arguments for women's intellectual
gifts, it disdained to offer articles on politics and the slave trade. Its editor
feared any tendency toward indecency and scandal and worried about the
stimulation of the readers' passions. Like Smollett's own heroines, they
required protection from the realities of a harsh world and were especially
treated to practical advice on household matters,[9] holding to the domestic
sphere of women's domain.

For all that, Smollett's heroines play a significant role in his novels, and
in his use of them and through some suggestive techniques he makes them
more than the cardboard cutouts that they have been portrayed as being.
Dependent on their functions in the novels, they become quite distinguishable from one another. If Aurelia in *Greaves* is a figure of perfection, she
fits neatly within the fable of a Quixotic hero's adventures. Narcissa in
Roderick Random yields to Roderick only on her own terms. Whatever
Serafina's angelic nature in *Fathom*, she thwarts the antihero while other
women fall before his wiles and the wisest men are taken in by his ruses.
Lydia in *Humphry Clinker* displays an intuitive intelligence that makes
her judgment of her mysterious lover superior to that of her more worldly
uncle and brother. In Emilia in *Peregrine Pickle* Smollett comes close to
creating a heroine to rival the intelligent and witty women in Restoration
comedy. For all their patterned characteristics, Smollett's heroines present
features of a uniqueness that separates them not only from each other but
also from the fictional stereotypes of the period.

To be sure, Smollett uses his heroines in subservience to the adventures
of his heroes. Nevertheless, they emerge as the means for bringing coher-
ence to his plots. If they satisfy Smollett's desire for happy endings to his
novels, they perform, even in that role, in different ways. Serafina helps
defeat Fathom; Lydia's steadfastness yields victory in her romantic quest;

and both Narcissa and Emilia subdue the wanton lust of their heroes. While using the devices of the romance that he detests, Smollett in various ways satirizes its conventions in his heroines' happy triumphs.[10] Throughout all five of his novels, they serve to reinforce Smollett's themes.[11] Even in his treatment of their sexuality, if the novelist is more reticent than modern taste would like, he still suggests their sensuousness and, as one source notes, "make[s] us feel that these girls have well-rounded bodies under their clothes."[12] Emilia's heaving bosom may come to us through her lover Peregrine's eyes, but it remains the heaving bosom of a woman of passion. It signals the reader that Smollett's heroines have a depth that goes beyond surface appearances. Smollett's sensibility is indeed masculine, and all the factors that have been discussed indicate the difficulties he had to overcome to create female characters with some verisimilitude. Nevertheless, his attention to what his stories demanded and his own talents do produce heroines that hold the reader's interest and offer a reminder of the dangers of oversimplifying and generalizing about other historical periods and literature.

There is no better place to seek an author's concept of a heroine's character than in that writer's creation of heroic tragedy. As it turns out, for Smollett that was the very point at which he attempted to start his career. When he first came to London in 1739, he brought along the completed manuscript of *The Regicide*, a play that he sought unsuccessfully to have produced for the next eight years and that he finally had to settle for publishing with a bitter attack on the theatrical establishment that had rejected it. It seems never to have occurred to Smollett that the sole responsibility for the failure to bring his drama to the boards resided in his inadequacies as a playwright. Neither in his own time nor in all the years since its publication has *The Regicide* found a reader willing to share Smollett's high regard for his own play.[13] Smollett's one and only heroic tragedy is an example of what has now become a notoriously weak genre according to literary opinion. Its excesses in diction, gesture, and characterization—even amid the genre's popularity during the Restoration—made it an easy target for burlesque. By Smollett's time, although such work continued with regularity on the stage, its exaggerated conduct and rhetoric made its sentiments less than fashionable. If, as Shadwell noted in his epilogue to *The Virtuoso*, the genre's characteristic deification of its heroines appealed to a female audience, its features otherwise had become more comical than tragic to sophisticated audiences. With little talent for the tragic, at any rate, Smollett, whether in drama or fiction, seems always to emphasize the worst characteristics of tragic writing, often unintentionally permitting his comic vision to create laughter where none appears intended.

Still, in *The Regicide* Eleanora *does* present a good starting point for a discussion of Smollett's romantic heroines in his novels. Her idealization reflects both Smollett's knowledge of generic demands and his natural response to the expectations of behavior and demeanor from a woman of good character. No matter what her status in life, Smollett's good woman is essentially a creature of passion whose problem always is in maintaining proper control of her emotions. Consider what happens to poor Miss Williams in *Roderick Random* when she permits her feelings to overcome her good sense. Narcissa, the heroine in the same novel, must conduct herself under the strictest rules of decorum lest she be swept away by the hero's impetuous nature and behavior. Surely, Emilia in *Peregrine Pickle* must carefully balance her heart's desire and her head's direction if she is to hold off the assault of the headstrong hero until her triumphant moment. For both Lydia in *Humphry Clinker* and Serafina in *Fathom* common sense and emotional stability are required to carry them through long separations that test their attachments to their lovers. Smollett indicates in *The Regicide* what he regards as the requisite fortitude to guide a woman's nature through temptations and to permit her to confront intelligently choices in divided loyalties.

As the daughter of Angus, the king's most devoted servant, Eleanora knows from the outset what familial and patriotic fealty demand of her when Stuart, whom she loves, attempts to usurp the throne. Although from her very first appearance—"In all the pride of dazzling charms array'd" (146)—she reflects Smollett's belief that a heroine must be beautiful beyond all other virtues, Eleanora for a variety of reasons comes across as a more fully realized woman than those in most of his fiction. Perhaps the sense of greater depth in her character, despite the exaggerations of the generic conventions in language and expression and the tendency toward stereotype that marks all Smollett's characterization in the play,[14] results from the more serious situation that she confronts in comparison with the problems Smollett's more conventional heroines face. After all, her actions reflect the torments of affairs that affect the state itself. Perhaps, too—and this is an important point in judging Smollett's treatment of women throughout his work—the difference in what genres and subgenres permit in character development contributes most significantly to how a figure comes through to an audience. In *The Regicide*, Eleanora's voice is a constantly recurring force, requiring no intermediary to explain it in awkward, embarrassed, indeed masculine terms. For the heroines in Smollett's novels, the voices are generally muted or transformed. It is difficult to imagine Narcissa's voice from the scraps provided by the male narrator-protagonist; when she speaks in a letter, no matter how emotional the content, her tones are modulated by the demands of feminine decorum. If Aurelia, the paragon in *Sir Launcelot Greaves*, has a distinctive voice, it is inaudible amid the satiric notes. Serafina, who speaks more frequently in *Fathom*, ranges between romance and satire, varying between melodrama and ethereal idealization, and thus lacks a very real sound of her own.

Unlike most of Smollett's fictional heroines—Lydia is an exception—Eleanora speaks without intermediary. To be sure, it does not hurt in setting her character when her father recalls to her those traits that she has inherited from her mother: "Thy mother's soul / In purity excell'd the snowy fleece / That clothes our northern hills!—her youthful charms, / Her artless blush, her looks serenely sweet, / Her dignity of mien, and smiles of love, / Survive in thee"(154). It helps, too, to suggest her stature, when Dunbar, who loves her as she cannot love him, having earlier noted her dazzling beauty, praises the "heroic maid!," describes the manner in which she attempted to hold off physically the traitorous opposition, and then gave her life in the king's cause (200). But these are like footnotes to Eleanora's text—too often stylized and artificial, but always more revealing of her genuine emotions and clearer in delineating her conflicts than a narrator's commentary could manage. It is almost as though the form itself forces Smollett to go deeper into the female character and to empathize through his impersonation.

Certainly he shows more respect for Eleanora than for his other heroines—even as she foreshadows most of their characteristics: beauty, good sense, and, most especially, fidelity. Despite the pathos of much of her language, she demonstrates skill and understanding in dealing with the men around her. With Dunbar, whom she actually regards with sisterly affection for all his demands on her for love and commitment, she emerges as wiser and more experienced. As he speaks of love and passion, she thwarts him with language: "O youth beware! / Let not the flow'ry scenes of joy and peace, / That faithless passion to the view presents, / Ensnare thee into woe!"(146). She cools his ardor, thanking him for his attentions, acknowledging, as all the world does, his virtues, but concluding with, "tho' my heart / Denies thee love, thy virtues have acquired / Th' esteem of Eleanora"(147).

Indeed, for all its bombastic diction and artificial striking of poses, the heroic drama, which allows the heroine to engage in debate (unusual for Smollett's female characters in his novels), brings forth a more fully realized woman in the interests and language of the idealized Eleanora than Smollett's narrative technique develops in his fiction. Eleanora struggles to understand her own emotions. Why should she still be attracted to the deceitful Stuart who has betrayed her love for "the charms / Of treacherous ambition!" (149)? She surely is not weaker than he. Not even her former attachment to him blinds her to the fact that once he has broken his word to her, she can no longer trust him. Contrasting his nature with Dunbar's, Eleanora makes clear, as Shakespeare's Cleopatra does to Antony and Othello to Desdemona, that betrayal is not a failure in behavior but a character flaw.

Capable of rebuking Stuart for his falsity, aware of the justice of her father's arguments on behalf of Dunbar's superior qualities to those of her former lover, still Eleanora cannot deny her own emotions. The dramatic work permits Smollett to put this clearly in her own words in a fashion that he is uncomfortable with in his novels. Her quandary—not to be resolved and thus making her situation more interesting—comes forth plainly in her words to Dunbar:

> My judgment, weak and erring as it is,
> Too well discerns on whom I would bestow
> My love and my esteem. But, trust me, youth,
> Thou little know'st how hard it is to wean
> The mind from darling habits long indug'd! (172)

These are not the casual words of a simple young woman. Here, certainly, she appears too mature for Dunbar. For all of what Stuart does to her right up to the end of his life, she continues to have feelings for him too deep to be rooted out without destroying what has attracted her to him. Love may be inexplicable, but here Smollett has handled it better—in his very first chance—than he manages to do anywhere in his later work. Whatever its failures, *The Regicide* deals honestly with its heroine's emotions. A recent critic has suggested that Dunbar's failure to gain Eleanora's heart results from the young hero's impetuous nature.[15] With all the patience in the world, Dunbar did not have a chance; the sexual attraction that motivates love simply did not exist in Eleanora's feelings for him. Smollett himself clearly understood, and his heroine's words make plain, that where love is concerned explanations are neither necessary nor helpful. If Eleanora possesses many of the characteristics of Smollett's fictional heroines, the genre she exists in gives her a dimension not easily available in the kind of novels that Smollett wrote.

Drama, indeed, whether tragic or comic, proved most propitious for Smollett in creating heroines. Ironically, one of his most attractive, one close to possessing a sense of a real flesh and blood woman, appears in a work little read, little noted, and generally otherwise undeserving of regard. Harriet, Smollett's heroine in *The Reprisal; or the Tars of Old England* (1757), labeled by him a two-act comedy but actually a flimsy farce, draws her breath clearly from Smollett's familiarity with Restoration comedy. (Restoration comedy is also the source of the most effective heroine in his novels: Emelia in *Peregrine Pickle*, the second edition of which appeared in the year following his comedy.) Although Smollett's dramatic talents rank nowhere in a class with such dramatists as Congreve, Wycherely, or Vanbrugh, the novelist does manage to imitate their neatly fash-

ioned female characters whose saucy manners and clever tongues permit
them to survive in the dangerous world of masculine wiles and snares.

Along with her fiancé Heartly and his servant Brush, Harriet falls cap-
tive to Champignon, commander of a French frigate, who has illegally
seized their pleasure boat. Smollett clearly establishes her beauty, not only
through the comments of Heartly and Brush, but also in the desire of the
foolish French commander to win her favor and the willingness of his two
foreign officers—a Scot and an Irishman—to come to her rescue. Smollett
does not neglect the characteristic feminine weaknesses of his heroines as
he permits her on a couple of occasions to yield to expressions purportedly
designed to reveal her feminine daintiness. Worried about Heartly's safety
as he goes off to seek help, she responds with trepidation to the noises of
scuffling aboard ship. Later she sounds the "heroine's" note of distress as
she and Brush await their rescue: "O Brush! Brush! how my little heart
palpitates with fear and suspense!" (235). In both instances, however, she
recovers swiftly and with her customary sharpness takes over the situation
from the truly frightened servant. She teases him about his fear of dying
at sea and rebukes him: "Hang fear, Brush, and pluck up your courage"
(232). When he suggests to her that his concern is not for himself, but for
her, she openly laughs at his pretenses.

In every way, Harriet is at least the equal of the men in the play.
Throughout the silly misadventure, the series of comedy of errors that
constitutes Smollett's propagandistic piece attacking the French adversar-
ies at the beginning of the Seven Years' War, Harriet is a solid figure of
good sense. She shows herself to be witty, courageous, resourceful, and
sound. Capable of early role-playing as Heartly's sister to protect her from
Champignon, she proves an adept schemer in helping design their escape
after the French commander discovers her true relationship to Heartly.
As Oclabber, the Irish lieutenant in the French service, notes, Harriet is
"a very sensible young woman!" (225).

Nothing better illustrates Harriet's good sense and intelligence than her
dealings with the foolish but rapacious Champignon. First, with solid argument, she speaks clearly to the illegality of his action: "Nothing can be
more disgraceful than what you have done . . . .You have carried off an
unarmed boat, contrary to the law of nations; and rifled the passengers,
in opposition to the dictates of justice and humanity—I should be glad to
know what a common robber could do worse?"(215). An expert in international law could not have put it better, but, of course, it has no effect
on the stupid French commander (the object of Smollett's scorn), who is
driven by his desire for Harriet. She is at her best as she wittily parries
his assaults. Moving from false compliments to the would-be lover to
clever verbal play in both speech and song—little of which Champignon
understands or is intended to as the butt of Smollett's humor—Harriet
keeps him off balance until her rescuers arrive. Smollett's technique, as it

does with Emilia in *Peregrine Pickle*, captures some of the genuine wit of a Restoration heroine, and it makes the reader wish that he had employed it more freely with his other fictional heroines.

When Smollett uses his heroines simply as idealizations of womanhood in his novels, no matter what roles they play in the narratives or however significantly they serve his heroes, as women they prove no less caricatures than the other stock types that play ancillary parts in his fiction. Whatever their differences in contributing to structure or their thematic functions, Narcissa in *Roderick Random*, Serafina in *Fathom*, and Aurelia in *Greaves* are, as women, ultimately close to interchangeable parts in Smollett's creation of female perfection. Only when he plays upon Restoration concepts of a heroine with Emilia in *Peregrine Pickle* or takes advantage of the possibilities of the epistolary form with Lydia in *Clinker* does Smollett truly break free of his own conventional notions of the heroic female. Still, beginning with Narcissa there are little distinctions among even the most conventional heroines that suggest the effects of formal considerations on art and indicate how aesthetic demands influence the most seemingly predictable sensibility of an author.

Not until halfway through *Roderick Random* does Narcissa, the heroine of Smollett's first novel, appear. Then, having established her relationship to the eponymous hero, she vanishes for the next hundred pages, transformed into a totemic name to be conjured up at moments of the hero's extreme sexual waywardness or moral bankruptcy as though to defend his imperilled soul. Like two significant male characters, Roderick's loyal friend Hugh Strap and the hero's benevolent uncle Lieutenant Bowling, who also depart for long stretches in the novel, Narcissa functions less as a character than as a fictional device—a means for giving direction and meaning to the plot and for permitting the discovery of aspects of Roderick's character hidden in the hero's struggle for survival in a harsh, picaresque world.

Smollett uses Strap to save Roderick at times of financial despair, to boost the hero's spirits when he faces the ugliest cynicism of society, and to demonstrate the existence of the main character's too often obscured benevolence. Bowling rescues Roderick from precarious situations and offers opportunities for the hero's expression of warmth, tenderness, and familial feelings otherwise lost in a narrative that emphasizes his emotional ferociousness. In Narcissa Smollett creates a romantic balance to the picaresque harshness of the novel. She plainly presents an idealized masculine view of womanhood—a chastity unsullied by any sexuality not clearly associated with marriage and familial considerations and related solely to the one object of her adoration—a promised security, comfort, and happiness for a male partner who, once sated in his appetite for a variety of sexual gratifications, can settle into the sanctity of marriage and retire from combat with the real world. Narcissa represents the end of the quest for a knight without the scruples of Galahad as he goes through the adventures of a world in which sexual conquests provide temporary satisfactions for his very masculine needs.[16]

As Smollett views the role of woman here in offering connubial bliss, there is small likelihood that he can develop Narcissa as a realistic female character. Hoping to appeal to female readers through his romantic interest, and unable to convey the emotions of love, particularly since he is limited by his first-person masculine perspective, he is unable to present Narcissa as anything more than a flat character. She functions mainly to capture those whose curiosity is stirred by the happy endings of sentimental romance, and she exists, although the romance narrative jars harshly with the picaresque elements in the fiction, to give some direction to Smollett's otherwise loosely structured plot. Smollett's most effective tool as a writer was caricature, best adapted to his comic creations, but unfortunately generally leaving the impression only of its exaggeration when used to fashion his idealized heroines.[17] Narcissa's purpose in the novel is to serve as a distant goal throughout Roderick's adventures, to suggest that there is more to him than the reckless young man embroiled in ceaseless battles and various attempts to gain advantage in the material world. Narcissa acts to demonstrate Roderick's ultimate worthiness as a hero; her "humaneness" (219) rescues him from the meaner side of his spirit and helps resolve his inner conflicts embroiled by his passions.[18]

Smollett's idealization of Narcissa—seen mainly through Roderick's eyes, but not solely—is apparent in descriptions of her conduct and physical attributes. Preparatory to her first appearances, Smollett uses Mrs. Sagely's account of Narcissa to circumvent the narrowness of Roderick's first-person point of view. According to the old woman responsible for introducing Roderick to the household of Narcissa's eccentric and difficult aunt, the young woman's saintliness is evident in her beauty and behavior: "a very lovely creature [who] humours her aunt often to the prejudice of her own health, by sitting up with her whole nights together" (216). Roderick witnesses Narcissa in action that supports Mrs. Sagely's claims. As Narcissa's aunt experiences one of her hallucinations, only the young lady's musical charms can soothe the woman. With great aplomb, Narcissa plays the harpsichord and, with a voice "sweet and melodious," calms her aunt into submissiveness (222).

Nowhere is Narcissa's idealized treatment more evident than in Roderick's physical description of her, where she emerges less a woman than the stereotypical romantic heroine who is fashioned only by a man's imagination:

So much sweetness appeared in the countenance and carriage of this amiable apparition, that my heart was captivated at first sight.... Her age seemed to be seventeen, her stature tall, her shape unexceptionable, her hair, that fell down upon her ivory neck in ringlets, black as jet; her arched eyebrows of the same colour; her eyes piercing, yet tender; her lips of the consistence and hue of cherries; her complexion clear, delicate and healthy; her aspect noble, ingen'ous and humane; and the whole so ravishingly delightful, that it was impossible for any creature, endued with sensibility, to see without admiring, and admire without loving her to excess! (219)

Without a blemish to mar her beauty, a sign of faded acne, or a hint of fault, Narcissa comes forth from those romances that Smollett scorns in the preface to his novel. Of course, there is no suggestion here of how Narcissa feels about Roderick. To be sure, the first-person point of view would make that difficult to ascertain. But she is not there for herself, but for Roderick, and for him she is an "idol of adoration."

For all his idealization of Narcissa Roderick is a man of passion, and Smollett contrasts their behavior in a way that anticipates Roderick's conduct after he has been separated from her. In her aunt's house, he expresses his feelings for her, and they are less than virtuous: "Inglorious as my station was [he is acting the role of servant], I became blind to my own unworthiness, and even conceived hopes of one day enjoying this amiable creature, whose affability greatly encouraged these presumptuous thoughts" (222). Despite the sexual innuendos in Roderick's thoughts, nothing in Narcissa's behavior gives license to them. Her purity is such that when she recognizes that his love poems are addressed to her, "her behaviour, which, though always benevolent to me, was henceforth more reserved and less cheerful" (227).

Like any heroine of romance, her chastity presents a temptation for villainy, and when it comes from Sir Timothy, who attacks her but is thwarted by Roderick, Smollett's description of the scene comes directly from romance narratives, but is filled, at the same time, with unintended irony. Roderick's language, describing the scene, has all the clichés of such tales, and Narcissa's manner of defense, as she swoons, belongs to the genre of sentimental romance: "[Sir Timothy] actually offered violence to this pattern of innocence and beauty. But heaven would not suffer so much goodness to be violated. . . . What were the emotions of my soul, when I beheld Narcissa, almost sinking beneath the brutal force of this satyr!" Despite Roderick's noble language and sentiments here, when, after he has rescued her, she swoons again, he behaves in a hardly more acceptable fashion than Sir Timothy: "My soul was thrilled with tumultuous joy, at finding the object of my dearest wishes within my arms; and while she lay insensible, I could not refrain from applying my cheek to her's, and ravishing a kiss" (229).

His conduct provides an index to his own sexuality ("ravishing" is a strong word for the context), and that is not to be denied after they are separated. To be sure, Narcissa, during their separation, hovers over the narrative like an unseen presence, but she is in the Holy Land, and Roderick's adventures are in the real and secular world. Her name recurs with sacred force each time he falls, but in her absence his sexuality cannot be denied and his eye, fixed on the main chance, when fortune beckons, through marriage of convenience, cannot be turned away. While in her household, he can deny himself the pleasure offered by the cook and dairy maid; he notes, "but at present, my soul was engrossed by Narcissa, and I could not bear the thoughts of doing any thing derogatory of the passion I entertained for her" (228). Apart from her he has no such compunctions. Oddly enough, or perhaps naturally enough, his masculinity never permits him to conceive that Narcissa is enjoying another attachment.

Episode after episode reveals that Narcissa is some noble idea that will be fulfilled in the future. Like Fielding's Tom Jones, Roderick cannot renounce the invitation to take a woman to bed. In the very first incident after his separation from Narcissa, he takes advantage of a capuchin monk's providing him with a young girl at an inn. While sharply critical of the capuchin's hypocrisy, he does not recognize his own when at the conclusion of the sexual encounter, he sighs, "In vain did my reason suggest the respect I owed to my dear mistress Narcissa, the idea of that lovely charmer, rather increased than allayed the ferment of my spirits; and the young Paisanne [peasant girl] had no reason to complain of my remembrance" (240). Smollett himself seems unaware that rather than the language of the lover, Roderick's words are those of the boastful little boy.

Reunited with his friend Strap and finding himself in fortunate circumstances, Roderick briefly resurrects the idealized Narcissa as a goal to be attained: "I fell asleep, and my fancy was blessed with the image of my dear Narcissa, who seemed to smile upon my passion, and offer her hand as a reward for all my toils" (254). Once again he sees her as a goddess to be inspired "with a mutual flame" (255). But she recedes quickly as he engages in fortune hunting. He goes after the teasing Melinda, and not until the affair has proved a dismal failure does Narcissa's name reappear: "I was in no danger of dying for love of Melinda; on the contrary, the remembrance of my charming Narcissa, was a constant check upon my conscience, during the whole course of my addresses; and perhaps contributed to the bad success of my scheme, by controuling my raptures, and condemning my design" (296). That comes as news to the reader, who must also wonder what would have happened to Narcissa had Roderick's scheme been successful.

For all Roderick's protestations about Narcissa after the affair with Melinda, it is immediately followed by, "my attention was wholly engrossed in search of another mistress" (297). His attempt to conquer Miss Biddy Gripewell ends disastrously, with no mention now of Narcissa. Decoyed into a secret liaison with what proves to be a seventy-year-old hag whom he had imagined to be "a lady of fortune, in the bloom of youth and beauty" (300), he describes his feelings while anticipating their meeting: "During the interval between the date of her promise, and the hour of appointment, my pride soared beyond all reason and description; I lost all remembrance of the gentle Narcissa" (303). Up until the very moment of the reemergence of Narcissa in his life, Roderick pursues his fortune hunting, willing to seek the hand of the waspish, "sickly and decrepid," but wealthy Miss Snapper and is prepared to sign a bargain with his friend Banter in order to gain access to her (322–23). Roderick's conduct inevitably raises the question that was asked of Samuel Richardson's *Pamela*: In what way is such a character deserving of a virtuous heroine? The only response can come from a patriarchal society willing to indulge a double standard.

For Smollett, of course, Narcissa's importance to the novel comes with the romantic ending that so many critics have deplored as a complete shift from the genre in which the rest of the novel is written. But, despite his objections to romance expressed in his preface, Smollett willingly employs it for the sake of his narrative as is evident in the treatment of Miss Williams, the fallen woman, in the novel. And it is Miss Williams who provides for the reunification of Roderick and Narcissa, which leads to the novel's happy, if unsatisfactory, ending. With Narcissa's return, the tone of the novel and the conduct of the hero change. From that moment on Roderick's eye focuses firmly on the heroine, and the sexual episodes and fortune hunting fade from view, even when the lovers are separated by her brother's crude intervention and by the hero's quest for the means to provide for their future happiness. The very material of the novel plays upon the romance genre's remarkable coincidences, fortuitous meetings, and happy reunions. Not only is Miss Williams resurrected to provide Roderick with easier access to Narcissa and her feelings as she miraculously turns up as the heroine's maid, but Bowling and Roderick's old shipmates reappear to ease his circumstances, and the hero's long-missing and presumably dead father provides a deus ex machina to permit a joyful conclusion.

Whatever the shift in the genre, however much Roderick's character becomes more stable through Narcissa's influence, and whatever her role in bringing the plot to its close, Narcissa herself remains essentially the same. To be sure, Smollett deepens the idealistic character he has established earlier in the novel and even allows some detail of her conduct that lends further support to the idealization. But she is still seen mainly through Roderick's eyes and thus becomes less a character in herself than a figure that has meaning for him. Even after they clearly seem destined for each other, she remains an image of almost unattainable desire for him. With a decline in his fortunes that leads to his incarceration in the Marshalsea, only "the remembrance of the amiable Narcissa" (397) keeps Roderick from utter despair with society; only her image keeps him going.

As he travels to make his fortune and is far removed from her in Buenos Aires, he is sustained by thoughts of her. During his recovery from a fever, having repeatedly spoken her name in his illness, he avows, "the idea of my lovely Narcissa always found itself to every scene of happiness I could imagine" (414).

The first-person point of view encumbers Smollett's ability to penetrate the surface of Narcissa's emotions, and the novelist's own personality proves an obstacle to creating realistic scenes when gentle emotions are involved. His temperament, which serves him so well in satiric accounts of tavern society and which allows him to move naturally even when caricaturing the ludicrous figures of Wagtail, Medlar, and Banter, thwarts him in romantic expression. He relies on clichés for Roderick's description of Narcissa when he meets her at her brother's house: "the divine Narcissa, blushing like Aurora, adorned with all the graces that meekness, innocence and beauty can diffuse!" (343). In such instances Smollett's style is studded by the word "angel" as a descriptive term, his sentences marked with exclamation points to impress the reader with the sincerity of what is obviously insincere emotional expression.

Smollett looks for ways of circumventing having to deal directly with a romantic situation. On Roderick's temporary return to Narcissa during her imprisonment by her brother, the hero says, "O! that I were endowed with the expression of a Raphael, the grace of a Guido, the magic touches of a Titian, that I might represent the fond concern, the chastened rapture, and ingenuous blush that mingled on her beauteous face" (406). Instead of detail, Smollett offers summary during the action and averts having to describe the tenderness of their parting by pleading an inability to do it justice: "because my words [Roderick says] are incapable of doing justice to the affecting circumstance, I am obliged to draw a veil over it" (406). Some of Smollett's weakest writing appears in Roderick's final reunion with Narcissa. In a passage again punctuated with exclamation points, Roderick's declaration of passion apparently embarrasses the author because he has the hero declare: "I am tempted to commit my paper to the flames, and to renounce my pen for ever, because its most ardent and lucky expression so poorly describes the emotions of my soul." Had he done so, the reader would have been spared: "O adorable Narcissa! (cried I) O miracle of beauty, love and truth! I at last fold thee in my arms! I at last call thee mine!" (425).

The clash in Smollett's temperament and the dichotomy of his narrative abilities are revealed in the scene in which, after their long separation, Roderick and Narcissa came upon each other during a ball at Bath. Smollett the satirist cleverly juxtaposes their meeting with one of the more sordid episodes in Roderick's adventures. Having accompanied the deformed and unattractive Miss Snapper to the dance in his attempt to win her fortune through marriage, Roderick confronts the reality of the beautiful image of his heroine. It is a deftly created ironic contrast between the nobility of idealized beauty and a physical ugliness whose sole lure has been material wealth. Smollett knows well enough how to handle the situational irony, but he seems at a loss in the artificial diction—again punctuated by exclamation points—in conveying Roderick's emotions:

the adorable Narcissa! ... Good heaven! what were the thrillings of my soul at that instant! My reflection was overwhelmed with a torrent of agitation! my heart throbbed with surprizing violence! a sudden mist overspread my eyes! my ears were invaded with a dreadful sound! I panted for want of breath, and in short, was for some moments intranced. (337)

Interestingly enough, for the first time since their separation, Roderick the philanderer, so moved by Narcissa, fears that she may now be engaged to another. His response underscores the extent to which Narcissa exists as an object for him rather than as a character in herself. Even at this point, the emotions are Roderick's. The closest we get to Narcissa's feelings is his perception of an "evident confusion" in her response to him as he sees "the roses instantly vanished from her polished cheeks, and [then] returned with a double glow that over-spread her lovely neck, while her enchanting bosom heaved with a strong emotion" (337).

Smollett does make some attempt to get beyond Roderick's presentation of Narcissa in two ways. The first is his use of Mrs. Sagely and Miss Williams as a means both to convey the heroine's emotions and to underline the respectability of her character. When Roderick seeks to meet with Narcissa during her imprisonment by her brother, Mrs. Sagely, who has in other instances provided Roderick with sound advice, acts as an intercessor and offers him information on Narcissa's feelings for him while warning him not to sully her good character. The last point is underscored by Miss Williams, who, while she serves as reassurance of Narcissa's love for Roderick, reminds him, "How favorable soever ... my lady's inclination towards you may be, this you may depend upon, that she will not commit the smallest trespass on decorum, either in disclosing her own, or in receiving a declaration of your passion" (340). Miss Williams, having suffered the tragedy of betrayal by a false lover, wants Roderick to know that Narcissa is an unlikely target for the easy conquest that leads to the downfall of the innocent.

When Smollett goes beyond Roderick's perspective to delineate Narcissa's character, he offers strong support for Miss Williams's observation. For all her blushes and shyness, Narcissa never resorts to the artificialities that mark the coquettishness of women like Melinda, who has earlier led the hero on in order to gratify her own vanity. Nowhere do Narcissa's honesty, purity, and sense of decorum declare themselves more clearly than in her letter to Roderick declaring her feelings. The device, which offers more insight into her emotions than all Roderick's comments, makes the reader wish that Smollett had used it or some equivalent more extensively. It is a nice blend of romance and practical common sense and makes her more of a woman than does the hero's idealized version of her:

To say I look upon you with indifference, would be a piece of dissimulation which, I think, no decorum requires, and no custom can justify. As my heart never felt an impression that my tongue was ashamed to declare, I will not scruple to own myself pleased with your passion, confident of your integrity, and so well convinced of my own discretion, that I should not hesitate in granting you the interview that you desire, were I not over-awed by the prying curiosity of a malicious world, the censure of which might be prejudicial to the reputation of

Your
NARCISSA (352)

The qualities indicated in that letter are borne out everywhere in Narcissa's conduct. When Roderick becomes overly familiar with her, she responds to his "boldness with a severity of countenance" (345). The effect is to cause him to "become as much enamoured of her understanding, as [he] had been before of her beauty." As she continues to quiet his excesses, he can speak only of "her irresistible eloquence" (346). Even at their moment of most heightened emotions, when Roderick can barely "restrain the inordinate sallies of desire," she acts "with her usual dignity of prudence" to turn off his "imagination from the object in view" (425). Her conduct recalls her earlier response to the love poetry that she recognized as being directed to her when he was supposedly a servant in her aunt's household. Even their caresses are "chaste" (354).

Once having declared her feelings for him in her letter, Narcissa behaves consistently to demonstrate her admirable qualities. She displays her sensitivity to his emotions when she innocently arouses his jealousy. She appreciates the precariousness of their relationship as she worries about his true financial status, knowing that her own fortune depends upon her brother's approval of a marriage, thus endangering the prospect of their union. Most significantly, she refuses to heed the gossip about Roderick that filters through to her from the petty denizens of the world around her. Even after he has recounted to her the story of his life, Narcissa, having pledged herself to him, loyally offers her "most endearing protestations of eternal love" (363).

It is easy to see in all this Smollett's concept of feminine perfection; in consequence, Narcissa does not exist as a genuine woman in the novel. Her purpose is to serve the plot and Roderick—as character and man. She is there to bring about the happy conclusion to the narrative and to provide the hero with final bliss and contentment. Roderick puts it well as he admires her in her wedding attire—"her bosom, thro' the veil of gauze that shrouded it, offered a prospect of Elyzium!" (469). She is there to gratify his appetite, and his image to describe the consummation of their love suggests that: "O heav'n and earth! a feast, a thousand times more delicious than my most sanguine hope presaged!" (430). It is especially interesting that even here, where the image is material, the relationship becomes idealized as Roderick describes it—or refrains from doing so: "But let me not profane the chaste mysteries of hymen" (430). *Profane* and *chaste* remove the action from the ordinary world to that of religious romance. It is fitting that the final image of the novel is that of a pregnant Narcissa, now Roderick's—"something to crown *my* felicity" (435, italics added). There is no doubt about the purpose of Smollett's heroine.

Narcissa is the heroine of Smollett's first novel, but as an introduction to his concept of a heroine no character better serves the purpose than Aurelia Darnel in his penultimate novel, *Sir Launcelot Greaves.* Her perfection surpasses that of Narcissa. Smollett's adventures of a modern knight in quest of the hand of a beautiful maiden may be a parcel of absurdities, a work designed to boost the circulation of the *British Magazine* that he conducted with Oliver Goldsmith. Indeed, its very romance between lovers of good estate clearly aimed to gratify the well- established taste for such material among contemporary periodical readers.[19] His least successful novel may overflow with excessive emotion as he burlesques the work of his revered Cervantes. It may pile exaggeration upon exaggeration in its characterization and caricatures. Nevertheless, for all its overblown language and for all its unrealities, it presents a notion of a heroine fundamentally in keeping with the leading ladies in his other novels. Aurelia, certainly not unlike Narcissa and Serafina and, to a lesser extent, Emilia and Lydia, exists simply to advance the story of Smollett's hero, to direct the hero's conduct in such a way as to enhance his virtues and to permit the author to express his satiric interests.

Launcelot's mad journey to rescue Aurelia from a tyrannical uncle who seeks to control her fortune provides a host of circumstances that, whatever their outrageousness, allows Smollett to satirize various social abuses at the same time that he both uses and ridicules the romance genre. Those escapades during which fortune brings Launcelot close to Aurelia serve as further spurs to the knight's quest. The very outset of his journey emanates from the kind of abuse that the law permitted guardians and parents in their control over wards and children—a point more seriously made by Samuel Richardson in *Clarissa*, but also tellingly exploited in Smollett's play on romance.

As Launcelot continues his search for Aurelia, his exploits provide Smollett with the material to expose the absurdities and abuses in local elections, particularly the buying of votes; his journey leads to an inspection of the penal system and presents a picture that foreshadows the arguments for John Howard's calls for reformation later in the century. During Launcelot's incarceration in a madhouse as he proceeds to rescue Aurelia from similar circumstances, Smollett exposes a system that permitted perfectly sane people to be locked up in private sanitariums by those seeking to take advantage of them. For Smollett, himself a medical doctor, the very bizarre treatments advocated for the mentally ill naturally became the targets of satire. If there is none of the satire on the moral frailties of the hero tempted by sex that Smollett dwells on at length with Roderick Random and Peregrine Pickle, it is because Greaves's moral life is of a different order. He is not named Launcelot for no reason—although perhaps that ideal of male chastity is also an object of ridicule. Alone of Smollett's heroines, Aurelia emerges from the novelist's treatment without a hint of sexuality as viewed from Launcelot's desirous eyes. Whatever her charms—and they are ample—they fail to stir in Launcelot that sexual appetite that characterizes the behavior of such heroes as Peregrine and Roderick as their eyes feast upon their brides. Instead, Launcelot, like the rest of the cast of characters in the novel, regards Aurelia as an angelic being—chaste beyond reproach.[20]

Through the relationship between Launcelot and Aurelia and in the character of the heroine herself, Smollett satirizes the genre of romance. The writer has it both ways: he ridicules the very form that he employs for the development of his satiric narrative.[21] Just as his romantic endings and his heroines in *Roderick Random* and *Peregrine Pickle* become instruments for Smollett's overall satiric purposes, the character of Aurelia and Smollett's treatment of his love story in *Greaves* allow him to turn romantic material into a vehicle to convey his satiric intentions. By virtue of Aurelia's very real qualities of attractiveness, Smollett marks the distance from Cervantes's tale of an unattractive Dulcinea whose imaginary beauty signals Don Quixote's madness. Romance itself proves useful in attesting to Launcelot's sanity even as it allows Smollett to poke fun at the genre. To ignore Smollett's play upon the excesses of romantic idealization and to fail to note how the novelist's diction underscores his satiric intentions require blinders that a critic wears to serve some overriding thesis such as a determination to place Smollett within the tradition of sensibility in the novel.[22]

The satire on romances comes together most neatly in the scene of temporary reunion between the lovers that takes place on the road. Aurelia first appears before Launcelot while wearing a mask. In the hero's discovery of her true identity, Smollett deliberately employs an overblown diction, abundant exclamation points, and numerous dashes to convey emotion too overwrought for complete sentences. The heroine blushes, sighs, and faints. Smollett's description of her beauty seems boundless; he quotes from Ariosto's *Orlando Furioso* to stamp her as unparalleled: "Aurelia shone with all the fabled graces of nymph or goddess" (123). The lovers' emotions reflect all the excesses of sentimental romance: "he looked and languished; she flushed and faultered: all was doubt and delirium, fondness and flower." Launcelot finds his voice to thank providence and extoll her beauty: "this fragrant flower of beauty, glittering with the dewdrops of the morning; the sweetest, gentlest, loveliest ornament of human nature" (124). But for all this emotional glory, the action pauses with the serving of tea, an anticlimax recalling the phrase of Smollett's beloved Pope in the *Rape of the Lock*: "Tea was served." And the anticlimax is punctuated by Launcelot's rushing off from this romantic highlight when he receives word that "some rogues were murdering a traveller on the highway" (125). He leaves behind his indescribable jewel to chase after a phantom.

To be sure, the novel everywhere mocks the romance genre. Later in the narrative, when Launcelot discovers Aurelia's presence in the madhouse, he responds in terms dear to the pens of romance writers: "At once he recognized it to be the voice of his adored Aurelia. Heavens! what was the agitation of his soul, when he made the discovery! how did every nerve quiver! how did his heart throb with the most violent emotion!" (190). Without hesitation he gives way to tears. It is a response that the realistic and stoical Smollett might have given to ridicule the tender-hearted hero in the novel of his fellow Scot, Henry Mackenzie, the later fashionable *Man of Feeling*.

The heroine herself—whether in appearance or conduct—belongs to the genre of romance, and yet it is important to note that her characteristics and how she is used are near kin to Smollett's serious treatment of heroines in his other novels. These are women who appear more than mortal—the pedestal seems to have been created with them in mind. Aurelia's wedding dress is "the emblem of purity" and Launcelot greets her as "divine Aurelia" (198). When she tells her cousin, Mrs. Kawdle, that Launcelot "has been my guardian angel," the latter replies, "that as Aurelia esteemed the knight her guardian angel, and he adored her as a demideity, nature seemed to have intended them for each other; for such sublime ideas exalted them both above the sphere of ordinary mortals" (197).

As Smollett describes her, she does, indeed, belong to the sacred beauties of romance, and yet the terms used to capture her divine physical characteristics bear a striking resemblance to those employed for the idealized portraits of Narcissa, Emilia, and Serafina in Smollett's other novels. Almost as though attempting to assure the reader that Aurelia exists in fact rather than in fiction, Smollett allows the major description of her to come from Tom Clarke, the young lawyer and godson of Launcelot, as he recounts to a company at an inn the series of circumstances that has led Launcelot to play the role of a modern Quixote:

Mr. Darnel's niece and ward, the great heiress, whose name is Aurelia, was the
most celebrated beauty of the whole country—if I said the whole kingdom, or
indeed all Europe, perhaps I should but barely do her justice. . . . [Then, quoting
from Nicholas Rowe's play *The Fair Penitent*, he continues,] O! she is all that
painting can express, / Or youthful poets fancy when they love!. . . . At that time
she might be about seventeen, tall and fair, and so exquisitely shaped—you may
talk of your Venus de Medicis, your Dianas, your Nymphs, and Galateas; but if
Praxiteles, and Roubillac, and Wilton, were to lay their heads together, in order
to make a complete pattern of beauty, they would hardly reach her model of
perfection.—As for complexion, poets will talk of blending the lily with the rose,
and bring in a parcel of similes of cowslips, carnations, pinks, and daisies. . . . Miss
Darnel is all amazing beauty, delicacy, and dignity! Then the softness and expression of her fine blue eyes; her pouting lips of coral hue; her neck, that rises like
a tower of polished alabaster between two mounts of snow. (27–28)

The quotation is long because Clarke is long-winded, but it is worth
giving in detail because the physical qualities are not only those of Aurelia
but also of Smollett's other heroines. It is a concept of womanhood: a
perfect beauty accompanied by the best qualities of character, all embodied in the heroine's virtue and chastity. She is not real, nor intended to
be. She is man's ideal of the feminine—a goal that will ultimately settle
the hero's desires. Clarke goes on to make her something more than one
can hope to find in any real woman, "some supernatural being [who] not
only resembles an angel in beauty, but a saint in goodness, and an hermit
in humility; so void of all pride and affectation; so soft, and sweet, and
affable, and humane!" (27–28). Whatever the romantic excesses that Smollett plays with her in his burlesque of the romance genre, the fact remains
that Aurelia's attributes are those of his other heroines and represent his
notions of female perfection.

Even as Smollett goes on in the novel to describe her conduct, it is not
only a play upon romance but an index to his ideas of womanhood employed throughout his fiction. So overpowering is Aurelia that Clarke's
eccentric sailor uncle, Captain Crowe, "was struck with admiration of her
unqualified beauty" (83) when she passes him in disguise in a coach. She
charms others—like Dolly Cowslip, the innkeeper's daughter who ultimately marries Clarke. Seeing Aurelia in distress, Dolly willingly comes
to her aid as a waiting lady and becomes the conduit for information
between her and Launcelot. Aurelia later displays her generosity by amply
rewarding Dolly. Her purity is such that when Launcelot first rescues her
in a carriage accident, she demurely responds to his declaration to her
mother that he would do anything for her preservation, indicating her
feelings only with the flush on her cheeks and the sparkle in her eyes. It
is not she but her mother who informs Launcelot, "Aurelia looks upon
you with the eyes of tender prepossession" (34). Like any good romantic
maiden, she faints away in the fullest expression of emotion. And yet she

is a young woman of good sense as evident in her seeing through the artifice of Lord Sycamore, who is being thrust upon her as a suitor by her wicked uncle. Notice, too, that she is a lady of fortune, an important feature of all Smollett's heroines. Evidently real virtue for Smollett had to be accompanied by good social status and a reliable income.

Still, whatever their qualities, Smollett's women exist to serve his heroes or to enhance the author's satiric purposes. The latter is evident in Smollett's contrasting Aurelia's unaffected conduct and dress with those of ladies of fashion. When Launcelot visits the King's Bench prison, he observes the most grievous example of a woman so addicted to her own extravagant tastes and so concerned with trying to impress others in her social circle that her ludicrous behavior continues even after it has brought her to disgrace. Observing Aurelia's virtues prior to their wedding, Launcelot outlines a mode of living that would have gratified those authors of conduct books and periodicals that ridiculed the conduct of fashionable ladies:

He found her beauty excelled by her good sense, and her virtue superior to both. He found her untainted by the rage for diversion and dissipation; for noise, tumult, gewgaws, glitter, and extravagance. He found her not only raised by understanding and taste far above the amusements of little vulgar minds; but even exalted by uncommon genius and refined reflection, so as to relish the more sublime enjoyments of rational pleasure.... He found her heart incapable of disguise or dissimulation; frank, generous, and open; susceptible of the most tender impressions; glowing with a keen sense of honour, and melting with humanity. (205–6)

Even her wedding dress reflects her rejection of the affectations of the times. Smollett's satiric comparison of Aurelia and ladies of fashion underscores the qualities he expects in a heroine.

But that ideal woman, Smollett repeatedly makes clear, proves her value as she serves the hero. Mr. Fillet, a surgeon and midwife, speaks for Smollett as he describes the function of the chivalric lady to provide animation for a knight, giving him strength to exert his valor. In Launcelot's own words, the value of a woman in chivalric adventures suggests a kind of epitome for the function of Smollett's own heroines:

it is from love that the knight derives all his powers and glory. The bare name of his mistress invigorates his arm: the remembrance of her beauty infuses in his breast the most heroic sentiments of courage, while the idea of her chastity hedges him round like a charm.... A knight without a mistress is a non-entity, or at least a monster in nature, a pilot without compass, a ship without rudder, and must be driven to and fro upon the waves of discomfiture and disgrace. (106)

Like all Smollett's heroines, Aurelia serves that purpose. She functions as the object of the hero's noble quest no less than the ladies of chivalric romance spurred their knights to venture forth to battle the evils of the world.[23] Aurelia provides the basis for a plot that restores the hero's mental health.[24] Through her the changes are effected in the novel, whether symbolic or dramatic, as they influence Launcelot's conduct and, as one critic notes, the very theme of the novel is provided as "Union with Aurelia Darnel reconciles the laws of individual conscience with divine laws embodied in her heavenly perfections, and the individual is properly merged within society."[25] Whatever the romantic exaggerations, then, Smollett's parody in the novel still makes clear the function of his women. Indeed, the very last sentence of *Greaves* proclaims "the birth of a son." What more could a man ask of a woman?

More complex than Aurelia, but no less idealized, Serafina (later disguised as Monimia) plays a more prominent and active part in *Ferdinand Count Fathom*. In his "Dedication" to the novel, Smollett forecasts the role that she, together with her fiancé, Renaldo, will play in his moral fable. It is not a promising pronouncement of the kind of characterization that he will employ. His villainous eponymous antihero, Fathom, is intended to convey such unmitigated vice in a succession of vicious acts that, the novelist declares, he fears that the reader may be "fatigued" by the narrative details. In order to offset the effect, Smollett proposes to contrast Fathom's behavior with figures of virtue, "characters of transcendent worth, conducted through the vicissitudes of fortune, to that goal of happiness, which ever ought to be the response of extraordinary desert" (1–2).

It is a formula for black and white characterization, allowing for no nuance or shading and permitting no degree of depth in either the hero Renaldo or the heroine Serafina. The limitations on the latter prove even more severe since the novelist allows one-third of the novel to elapse before she first appears in the inset story of Don Diego, her father, whose tyrannical conduct regarding her marriage has driven both his wife and daughter from his household. It takes another hundred pages before Serafina, now known as Monimia, reappears in her own person, the betrothed of Renaldo, who, like her, has been reduced to the most straitened circumstances. Although the amount of space allotted to Serafina suggests the author's unwillingness to develop her as a character much beyond her function as a counterpart to Fathom's evil, the two names that he chooses for her indicate, at least, that, whatever the limits of her character development, she will serve to make some points for him beyond that of a foil to Fathom. With Serafina Smollett designates those angelic traits in his heroine that will stand in opposition to Fathom's satanic character. The name Monimia has more artistic subtlety and importance for Smollett's purposes.

In choosing the name Monimia—drawn from Thomas Otway's tragic heroine in the drama *The Orphan*—Smollett indicates that for all his concern for a moral fable, he has not yielded his satiric temperament, here directed against the excesses of romance. *Fathom* is Smollett's most experimental novel. It deliberately mixes genres; the elements of romance serve both its moral and satiric purposes.[26] Borrowing heavily from Otway's play to achieve the stage effects that he so much admires, Smollett seeks to attract the audience taste for drama that merges terror (see the scene at Monimia's "tomb"), tragedy, and sentiment, but, at the same time, by underscoring the details of romantic feeling, provides satiric commentary on romantic genres. Contrasting the misfortunes of Otway's heroine with the happy conclusion of his character in the novel, he simply extends the sentiment in a manner that both serves his purposes for plot and offers a parodic view of sentimental romances. Whatever his own attraction to such emotional theatrical renderings as those found in Otway's work and in the performance of Mrs. Cibber in the role in the play, the commonsensical Smollett could not fail to recognize the ludicrousness of romance that he willingly used for his narrative needs even as he parodied it just as he played upon the concept of the man of feeling in his characterizations of all the good people in his novel, including Serafina.[27]

For both purposes Smollett emphasizes the otherworldly spiritual qualities implied by Serafina's name. When Renaldo describes her as "divine" (298), he repeats a label that others throughout the novel have used to depict her. Hers is a "seraphic voice" (209), and as Renaldo stands before what he believes to be her tomb, he regards her as more a saint than a human being. Her beauty appears beyond compare; her voice, a kind of ethereal music. Clearly she has been sanctified. As she "reemerges" to life from her "tomb," she is indeed seraphic: "those well-known features, seemingly improved with new celestial graces" (323), her divinity compared to that of angels.

Smollett underlines this divinity—her role as angelic opposition to Fathom's deviltry—with a continuous play upon romance that tends to undercut satirically the worst features of the genre. Discovering his beloved to be alive, Renaldo responds:

he ravished a banquet from her glowing lips, that kindled in his heart a flame, which rushed thro' every vein, and glided to his marrow: this was a privilege he had never claimed before, and now permitted as a recompense for all the penance he had suffered; nevertheless, the cheeks of Monimia, who was altogether unaccustomed to such familiarities, underwent a total suffusion. (326)

To be sure, Smollett never in his writing finds appropriate language to relate the emotions of love (the gastronomical metaphors are particularly embarrassing), but here this excessive writing not only underscores the virtuous and virginal purity of his heroine, but in a neatly subtle way exposes romance (including Smollett's) to satire. Renaldo and Serafina had been in close and familiar contact over a long period of time. She had renounced her father's plans for her marriage because of her love for Renaldo. Together they had suffered through the most trying circumstances. And yet at this point close to the novel's end, he had not yet kissed her. Smollett had scoffed at the impossibility of such notions of romance when he recounted Fathom's conquest of Celinda earlier in the novel. There he had ridiculed the idea that two people of opposite sexes could be in close correspondence "without degenerating from the platonic system of sentimental love" (163). The point should not be forgotten here even as Smollett celebrates the celibate relationship of the lovers. Romance is not Smollett's forte, but rather a subject for his skepticism.

Indeed, the novelist's view of the relationship between his hero and heroine reveals itself as clearly in *Fathom* as in the rest of his work, and it is antithetical to the sentiment of romance that he repeatedly satirizes, despite the fact that his idealized notions of heroines belong to the despised genre. Indeed the function of Serafina does not differ from that of Smollett's other heroines, who are designed for his heroes. For all the glories of Serafina, Smollett regards her as Renaldo's "prize" to be shown off to society (364). The author's account of their wedding night, resembling scenes in *Roderick Random* and *Peregrine Pickle*, displays masculine control of these perfect woman, not the sentimental relationships of romance. Smollett's terms depicting the male appetite are embarrassing to the modern reader, but not uncharacteristic of such masculine novelists as, for example, his more accomplished contemporary Henry Fielding. As Renaldo approaches Serafina's bed chamber on their wedding night,

[He] entered the apartment, and like a lion rushing on his prey, approached the nuptial bed, where Serafina, surrounded by all the graces of beauty, softness, sentiment, and truth, lay trembling as a victim at the altar, and strove to hide her blushes from his view. . . . [Smollett then concludes:] Here let me draw the decent veil, that ought to shade the sacred mysteries of Hymen: away from unhallowed scoffers, who profane with idle pleasantry, or immodest hint, these holy rites. (351)

To which drawing of the veil, Damian Grant, recent editor of the novel, says, "amen." Considering the imagery of Smollett's account of the nuptial night, Grant declares, "It is perhaps just as well that Smollett draws 'the decent veil' on these events" (383–84, n. to 351).

Throughout the novel Smollett uses romance in two ways (as he frequently does in his work). The genre serves his purposes for plot and for the confrontation of the opposing forces of good and evil. At the same time, Smollett appears ever mindful of its excesses, whether in narrative or characterization. The figure of Serafina (Monimia) stands central to both purposes. Everything about Serafina's story marks her as the heroine of romances, and if, in its excesses, it mocks the genre, it also permits Smollett to create a moral fable consistent with the plan that he outlines in his "Dedication." Her early conflict with her father portrays the wretched struggle with parental tyranny. Her willingness to give up everything for the seemingly impoverished Renaldo, who has entered her household disguised as a German musician, displays the all-for-love thesis of the romance genre. Their struggle to survive under the most vicious circumstances and the fairy-tale conclusion in which she is restored to her lost parent and married to her prince charming belong to the make-believe world of romance. And throughout it all, Serafina displays all the qualities of an idealized Smollettian heroine in her chastity, dignity, and loyalty.

As Smollett renders his narrative through unlikely coincidences—such as Renaldo's coming together with Don Diego—he cannot have been unaware of his dependence on the genre that his story satirizes. Within the perfect romance tradition, Renaldo receives a letter that Serafina had written at the moment of despair, a time when she says she "will be no more" (301). Its coming to him represents romantic fantasy in the extreme. Yet it sets up for Smollett the means for unmasking the villainous Fathom and ultimately restoring the lovers to each other. Smollett indeed has it both ways: ridiculing the devices of a genre that he depends upon for his narrative structure and closure.

Nowhere does that combined use of romance stand more evident than in Serafina's struggle with Fathom. That, after all, is Smollett's central concern in the novel, the ultimate triumph of good over evil, which makes her idealization essential to his purposes. In the starkest colors of black and white the pair confront each other. Serafina's virtue finds itself pitted against the ugliest depravity that has managed to mask itself behind a cunning and artifice that have given it the form of charm. Fathom, who has tricked Renaldo, his father, and seemingly half the world, works his wiles against the innocent Serafina, leading her to believe that Renaldo has betrayed her while offering her himself as the only available source of safety and security. In no ordinary story could she withstand such pressures—even Richardson's Clarissa, a paragon of virtue, fell before a similar devil named Lovelace. Still, armed with the simple weapons of Smollett's most ideal heroines, Serafina overcomes the satanic attack of Fathom. Love and incredible good fortune, as well as exemplary character, allow her to triumph.

Throughout the conflict with Fathom, Serafina's primary defense is her undying love for Renaldo—the loyalty characteristic of Smollett's idealized heroines. Not even after Fathom has tricked her into believing that the hero has deserted her for another does she relinquish her feelings for him. Unfortunately, Smollett cannot deepen the character of Serafina by getting inside her to explore her emotions firsthand. Most of what the reader is given comes through the perspective of a clearly masculine narrator, and only in her letter to Renaldo does Smollett attempt to go beneath the surface of her character. Even that conveys the clichés of romance: "I will not call you inconstant or unkind. I dare not think you base or dishonourable. [Because you left me for another] I was all at once abandoned to despair, to indigence and distress, to the vile practices of a villain. . . . Let not my wrongs be visited on the head of Renaldo, for whom should be offered up the last fervent prayers of the hapless Monimia" (301). The reader can only ask why any woman feeling so betrayed should respond in this fashion. Permissible for romance or for the idealized notions of noble womanhood, it is hardly convincing.

Unable to convey Serafina's emotions except externally, Smollett relies, as he must, upon action to attempt to reveal her feelings. Unfortunately, these are the stock materials of romance, satisfactory for Smollett's narrative purposes and suggestive of his satire on the genre, but inadequate to display convincing characterization and satisfy the demands of a novel whose major concerns are realism. Smollett is especially severely limited by the allegorical function of Serafina. She must remain a tool for his building a bulwark against Fathom's depraved conduct, and the author finds no means for rendering in the process a credible female character. If Fathom, throughout the novel, is invariably described in terms that label him the "devil incarnate, " a "diabolical fiend," and an "artful serpent,"[28] Serafina represents heaven's opposition to hell's champion. Repeatedly, Fathom describes her as having supernatural powers as she defends herself against him. When she is rescued from his ultimate assault, she naturally finds sanctuary in a church, and God provides the protection of the appropriately named Madame Clement. Not surprisingly, then, when Elinor, whom Fathom has debauched, seeks forgiveness for the repentant Fathom, she turns to Serafina, cast in the role of the Virgin Mary just as Elinor suggests Mary Magdalene. Serafina, indeed, pleads for mercy for her tormentor and sets their conflict as part of a divine design: "Heaven perhaps hath made him the involuntary instrument for bringing our constancy and virtue to the test" (341).

Smollett leaves no doubt about what he intends to convey in the opposition of Fathom and Serafina. To be sure, the deliberately moralizing passage in which he assesses the hideousness of Fathom's conduct may be no more than the shallow apology that Damian Grant has termed it, "when we realize that Monimia's 'death,' which prompts it, is in fact a simple stratagem (modelled on the 'death' of Hermione in *The Winter's Tale*) designed to put Fathom off the scent—and useful to Smollett in another way, since he can again make a sudden transition to another scene" (381, n. to 242). Nevertheless, its message clearly conveys the allegorical role of Serafina in the novel:

Perfidious wretch! thy crimes turn out so atrocious, that I half repent me of having undertaken to record thy memoirs: yet such monsters ought to be exhibited to public view, that mankind may see how fraud is apt to overshoot itself: and that, virtue, though it may suffer for a while, will triumph in the end; so iniquity, though it may prosper for a season, will at last be overtaken by that punishment and disgrace which are its due. (242)

Indeed, contrary to Grant's comment, the passage, rather than falsely misleading the reader, offers a foreshadowing of the narrative's conclusion.

Restricted in Serafina's characterization by what he regards as her primarily allegorical function in the novel, Smollett can find no better means for examining her emotional life than by relying on the extravagant female behavior characteristic in the romance. Some of this indeed bears touches of the author's satiric view of the genre. Surely, when Serafina rebuffs Fathom's attempted rape by thwarting his schemes and those of his confederate Madame la Mer and then shows extraordinary strength by taking a sword to him "to protect her virtue" (237), Smollett intends a thrust at the inadequacies of Richardson's heroine in opposing Lovelace. Still, overall, Smollett's depiction of Serafina's conduct displays the trite portrayals of the romance, a sign perhaps of the failings in his own perception of feminine behavior and his appeal to popular taste.

Whatever the reasons for the characterization, Serafina expresses the traditional sentiments of the idealized romance heroines: a sense of martyrdom, a resignation to dying, and a weak-kneed response to threatening circumstances. Under stress she looks to death to protect her: "she flattered herself with the hope that she should not long survive" (216). Refusing to complain publicly of her plight, she "endeavoured to devour her griefs in silence; she in secret bemoaned her forlorn fate, without ceasing; her tears flowed without intermission" (214). Or, again, "a flood of tears gushed from her enchanting eyes, and she instantly withdrew to her own apartment, where she indulged her sorrow to excess" (216). Despite her refusals to complain, she cannot resist the powers to weep and swoon. Yet, for all that, her beauty is such that even death will not destroy it. At the very height of her determination to die,

Yet her charms, far from melting away with her constitution, seemed to triumph over the decays of nature: her shape and features still retained that harmony for which they had always been distinguished: a mixture of majesty and sweetness diffused itself in her looks, and her feebleness added to that soft and feminine grace which attracts the sympathy, and engages the protection of every humane beholder. (235–36)

Thus it is with Smollett's ideal womanhood: nothing causes it to decay. Only in romance does declining life lend physical beauty and charm to the natural graces of life.

Smollett's addiction to the romance tradition that he repeatedly satirizes in his work inevitably expresses itself in the characters of his heroines. So serviceable in his comic and grotesque characterization, his caricature creates only an air of unbelievability in his idealized romantic females even when he does not intend to burlesque the type. Evidently representing Smollett's own views of perfect womanhood, they escape fictional reality. Used for the sake of his plot development and to bring forth the qualities of his heroes, the true interest of his narratives, or to provide material for his satire, such women as Serafina, Narcissa, and Aurelia have little life of their own and lack genuine emotional content.

Consider, for example, Smollett's general description of Serafina. It is virtually interchangeable with those not only of Narcissa and Aurelia, but of Emilia and Lydia as well. They share the same generally secure social positions and financial security, always with sufficient ties to male interests to keep them dependent. Without exception their beauty is enhanced by customary female accomplishments and reinforced by their qualities of loyalty to the men they love. Their virginity is unassailable—their very lips held sacredly intact for that wonderful moment of commitment to the hero. In the end, they become prizes for their husbands to display and vessels for the perpetuations of their husbands' lineage. Nothing can truly obstruct their transition from idealized maidenhood to perfect matrimony.

Certainly Smollett's detailed description of Serafina's physical beauty and impeccable talents could easily serve as a pattern for the heroines of any of his novels. Even before she has appeared, her father informs the reader of her virtues: "she was mistress of every elegant qualification natural and acquired. Her person was . . . the confessed pattern of beauty. Her voice was enchantingly sweet, and she touched the lute with the most ravishing dexterity" (117). Fathom himself is "struck dumb with admiration" (201) as she enters the room:

her stature was tall; her motion graceful; a knot of artificial flowers restrained the luxuriancy of her fine black hair that flowed in shining ringlets a-down her snowy neck. The contour of her face was oval; her forehead remarkably high; her complexion clean and delicate, tho' not florid; and her eyes were so piercing as to strike the soul of every beholder. (201)

And on and on. Added to that are "her superior understanding, her sentiments of honour, virtue, gratitude, religion, and pride of birth" (202). What more could any man ask of woman?

It would be excessive to note the repeated compliments of Madame Clement and Renaldo's friends to Serafina's qualities and accomplishments. Suffice to repeat that she is Smollett's ideal of womanhood, although his literary talents and his own personality and intentions as an artist prevent him from breathing life into her or allowing the reader to envision her as anything other than a fictional tool to serve Smollett's

purposes, which do not include the creation of women with ordinary emotions and desires. Moreover, intent upon presenting her and Renaldo as
embodiments of virtue in opposition to Fathom's evil, Smollett can hardly
be expected to provide her with the qualities of genuine womanhood.[29]

So enduring, indeed, are her idealized qualities that when Serafina reappears many years later in Smollett's *Humphry Clinker*, she has lost none
of her enchanting, divine attributes. Matt Bramble, the valetudinarian hero
of Smollett's final novel, declares, "the countess is the most amiable
woman I ever beheld." His Yorkshire host praises her handsomeness. If
the two grotesque women, the host's wife and Matt's crabby sister Tabby,
dissent, Smollett makes clear their jealous natures, the "censorious daemon" by which they are taken (168). Seeing her at a ball in Edinburgh,
Matt's nephew Jerry proclaims, "The countess of Melville attracted all
eyes, and the admiration of all present" (224). Time had not diminished
either her beauty or her charm, both being beyond mortal limits. Smollett's own summary repeats the term that he has used for Serafina throughout *Fathom* as Lydia, his ingenuous heroine in *Clinker*, cries out "with
great emotion": she's an angel" (168). So indeed she must be as she again
demonstrates in Smollett's final novel when she offers protection to the
daughter of Fathom and Elinor, who also make an appearance in the
work.

Two of Smollett's heroines—Emilia in *Peregrine Pickle* and Lydia in
Humphry Clinker—have qualities that set them apart from their fictional
sisters in his other novels, and the differences may be traced to literary
causes. Emilia appears to be Smollett's response to Richardson's portrayal
of Clarissa, and Lydia owes a good deal of her character development to
Smollett's use of the epistolary technique in his final novel. Consider the
importance of the formal elements of fiction as they limit Smollett's other
heroines. Narcissa lacks depth because she is seen mainly from the point
of view of a first-person narrator limited by his own emotions and concerns. With Serafina Smollett restricts the possibilities of breathing life into
her character because he chooses to use her as a symbol of virtue in opposition to the consummate evil of his villain. The angelic Aurelia suffers
from an absence of simple human characteristics as she provides an object
for Sir Launcelot's quest for an ideal world to counter the abuses of reality.
Only Lydia comes close to realizing the features of genuine womanhood
exemplified in Emilia, and that is because Smollett has the advantage of
an epistolary technique that permits him to go beneath the superficialities
of her appearance in the eyes of her fellow travelers. The remarkable
achievement, however, is in Emilia; it is most striking because it comes in
a story told by a masculine narrator whose primary concern is with his
hero's progress. Clearly, it is in the playing off of Emilia against Clarissa,
at least as Smollett sees it, that allows him to create believable and admirable female behavior. Although Smollett had a high regard for Rich-

ardson and did not want to offend him in any way, his creation of Emilia suggests a direct rebuttal of Richardson's treatment of his heroine.[30]

Not that Emilia by any means bears no kinship to Smollett's other heroines. Like them she certainly functions to allow the novelist to develop the character of his hero and advance his plot. Clearly she displays some of the characteristic conduct of Smollett's—and more generally the eighteenth-century novel's—notions and expectations of idealized womanhood. At appropriate times she can show her feminine weakness by swooning with the best of heroines. Saved from a fire, she and her cousin Sophy properly faint away. When Peregrine departs for his journey to the Continent, she and Sophy yield to their emotions by bursting into tears. After successfully outwitting the philandering Perry when he attempts to renew their romance, rather than triumphing in her victory, Emilia suffers upon learning of his distress and has "recourse to a smelling bottle" (390). Interestingly enough, Sophy understands the cause while Godfrey, Emilia's brother, with true masculine insensitivity (as Smollett perceives it) has no notion of what disturbs her. Like any good romantic heroine—and she certainly is that regardless of her other characteristics—Emilia responds to the trick played on her by Pipes, Perry's loyal aide, who informs her that Perry has hanged himself because of his despair over their romance, by following the pattern of heroines of popular fiction: she "shrieked aloud, and dropped down senseless upon the floor" (593).

But for all that, Emilia emerges not as a cardboard cutout of a beautiful woman with no other agenda than that of snaring a husband, but as a real person ruled by her principles and determined to live her life on her own terms. Whatever the idealized characteristics of feminine conduct she may share, for example, with the heroine of Smollett's first novel, Emilia is no Narcissa. Smollett, indeed, seems to have deliberately altered the standard features of the stereotypical heroine of contemporary fiction to suit a much darker novel than his first work. Moreover, Emilia's role in the plot and structure of *Peregrine Pickle* proves essential to Smollett's purposes.[31] With greater adeptness than anywhere else in his work, he manages to suggest the innermost emotions and desires of a heroine. He fashions a young woman as tough-minded as the novel in which she appears, and indeed *Peregrine Pickle*, written when Smollett appears to have been most at odds with the world around him, surely is the most tough-minded of his fictions with the exception of *The History and Adventures of an Atom*, one of the nastiest pieces of literature in the century. Emilia herself belongs less to the fictional genre of the mid-eighteenth-century novel than to the earlier Restoration comedies with their heroines in constant verbal battle with rakish heroes whose libidos must be curbed by wit and contrivance if they are ever to be led to the altar.

In appearance and conduct, Emilia would fit easily into a play like William Congreve's *The Way of the World*. Reading about her beauty, it is

not difficult to imagine a Mirabell extolling her merits. She moves about
in her world with the same sense of self, the knowledge of who and what
she is, that recalls Millamant's self-assuredness in the play. Like Millamant
she responds with common sense to the realities of her world; she cannot
be tricked by idle words expressing love that come with no promise of
marriage; she recognizes the significance of money in shaping relationships
with her lover. As Emilia engages in verbal duels with Peregrine, echoes
emerge from the marriage contract bargaining scene between Congreve's
hero and heroine. Finally, like Millamant, Emilia's words and actions and
the narrator's comments on her emotions suggest a sexuality generally
lacking in her female counterparts in Smollett's other novels.

For all of Smollett's inability to capture the necessary characteristics of
witty dialogue, from beginning to end Emilia displays a strong resemblance to Restoration comedy heroines, a type far different from the Clar-
issas of the contemporary novel.[32] The earliest description of her—and it
is important to note that she appears early and plays a role throughout
greater than that of Smollett's other heroines—places her in the milieu of
Restoration stage comedy. No more than sixteen when she first meets
Perry, she exudes all the beauty of the earlier dramatic heroines, and the
description of her suggests their sensuality:

[Perry] was struck with admiration at her beauty. She seemed to be of his own
age, was tall, and tho' slender, exquisitely shaped; her hair was auburn, and in
such plenty, that the barbarity of dress had not been able to prevent it from
shading both sides of her forehead, which was high and polished; the contour of
her face was oval, her nose very little raised into the aquiline form, that contributed to the spirit and dignity of her aspect; her mouth was small, her lips plump,
juicy and delicious, her teeth regular and white as driven snow, her complexion
incredibly delicate and glowing with health, and her full blue eyes beamed forth
vivacity and love: her mein was at the same time commanding and engaging, her
address perfectly genteel, and her whole appearance so captivating, that our young
Adonis looked, and was overcome. (94)

To be sure, although the voice here is that of the narrator, the description comes through Perry's eyes, and thus the sense of her sexuality reveals
his feelings. Nevertheless, what permits him to react as he does suggests
Emilia's own sensuality. For all the conventionality of the language that
describes Emilia's beauty, the words go beyond the superficialities of appearance to indicate the nature of the heroine herself. Still, Smollett does
not diminish the extent of Emilia's beauty—in that she certainly resembles
all his heroines. When she appears later at a theater, the narrator asserts
that "she eclipsed all the female part of the audience, each individual
allowing in her own heart, that the stranger was by far the handsomest
woman there present," and then he ironically concludes, "except herself"

(401). At her wedding Emilia displays the same "dignity of mien and divinity of aspect" that Smollett ascribed to her at the outset (776). So impressive are her beauty and manner that they overcome Peregrine's cynical, curmudgeonly friend, Cadwallader Crabtree. Again, like Smollett's other heroines, the newlywed Emilia beams with the benefits of her marital state so that she stuns every observer, "from the pert templar to the Sovereign himself, who was pleased to bestow encomiums upon the excellence of her beauty" (780).

But, of course, it is not merely her particularly sensuous beauty that makes Emilia a special Smollettian heroine. From that very first meeting with Perry, which overwhelmed him with her physical attractiveness, Emilia comports herself in a manner befitting a Restoration heroine. It is Perry who loses control in their relationship, unable even to dance his best with her. She displays composure and self-assurance. Upon their subsequent meeting, despite her youth, she plays a sexual game of cat-and-mouse with mature dexterity. She coyly leads him on and then holds him at bay. Smollett sets up the game when she appears "in a most inchanting undress, with all the graces of nature playing about her person" (96). Alone with Perry, Emilia allows him to proclaim "his love in the most passionate terms" as he seeks to "be admitted into the number of those admirers whom she permitted to visit and adore her." Still, she does not let him turn her head, and she responds with a mixture of diffidence and encouragement: "She affected to look upon his vows and protestations as the ordinary effects of gallantry." But she does not discourage them. Instead, she suggests that she lives too far away for him to carry on a desired relationship or go through any pains to achieve it. As Smollett puts it, it is a "favourable hint," intended to entice Peregrine, and it succeeds as he promises to solicit her mother's permission to visit her. She does not hide her own inclinations when she gives him the location of her house and suggests "he would be no unwelcome guest." If her appearance at the beginning of the scene "rivetted the chains of his slavery beyond the power of accident to unbind," her seemingly artless manner, hiding her shrewdness, indicates to the reader, if not the hero, who it is that has held sway in the opening of their relationship (96).

If Perry has not always recognized the powerful qualities of Emilia's mind even as they are evident to the reader throughout the novel, by the end he clearly perceives that she is no ordinary woman, apart from the beauty that sets her above others. Desperate to possess her as his wife, Perry sees in her the attributes that so often make Restoration heroines attractive as they play their roles in battling with the heroes of the comedies. In words that set up one of the most charming scenes in the novel, Perry regards with full appreciation "the poignancy of her wit, and the eloquence of her understanding" (761).

Smollett follows with an exposition of these characteristics. To her brother who has arranged for bringing the two lovers together, and without realizing that Perry is hiding in the next room, Emilia speaks in the kind of bantering tone used by Restoration heroines to reveal their sentiments while affecting not to be controlled by their emotions: "Is not this . . . a most provoking scene to a young woman like me, who am doomed to wear the willow, by the strange caprice of my lover? Upon my word, brother, you have done me infinite prejudice, in promoting this jaunt with my obstinate correspondent: who, I suppose is so ravished with this transient glimpse of liberty [since he has not appeared on time], that he will never be persuaded to incur unnecessary confinement for the future." Then, having expressed her anxiety at Perry's absence, she flippantly concludes: "Heigh ho! who would imagine that a sprightly girl, such as I, with ten thousand pounds, should go a begging? I have a good mind to marry the next person that asks me the question, in order to be revenged upon this unyielding humourist. Did the dear fellow discover no inclination to see me, in all the time of his releasement [from debtors' prison]? Well, if ever I can catch the fugitive again, he shall sing in his cage for life" (773). This time Smollett has the words and the rhythm just right for his Restoration mimicry. Congreve's Millamant could not have put it better.

Even the terms on which Emilia accepts Perry's proposal convey the Restoration heroine's wit that combines her anxieties and determination to be in control: "I ought to punish you, for your obstinacy, with the mortification of a twelve-month's trial; but 'tis dangerous to tamper with an admirer of your disposition, and therefore, I think, I must make sure of you while it is in my power" (775).

In order to bring forth Emilia's characteristics, Smollett provides a theme in her relationship with Perry that centers upon the values of money and social position, a commonplace concern in Restoration comedy. Not only the lovers but also the world around them regard status and finances as requisite for a romantic attachment. When Perry first meets Emilia's family, her mother's concern focuses on his economic situation. Regardless of his attractiveness, if his fortune is not sound she will not approve of their relationship. After Perry's attempted rape of Emilia, her mother— not knowing the full extent of his conduct, but aware that he has insulted her daughter's honor—proudly points to Emilia's familial connections and good breeding as she rejects the hero's desired rapprochement with his lover. Commodore Trunnion, Perry's guardian, first regards Emilia as a fortune hunter and warns his ward against her. When he learns of her family history and that she is the daughter of a "brave officer, who had served his country with credit and reputation" (360), Trunnion gives his approval to their marriage. When Perry indicates a change of heart, the commodore worries about the young lady's honor since he believes Perry has made love to her.

But the lovers themselves display the same concern for money and social position, and this provides for the development of plot itself. For all of Perry's "passion for Emilia" upon their very first encounter, his own superior financial condition makes him wary of an attachment. It becomes a "struggle between his interest and his love" (97). Perry later rejects Trunnion's admonitions about his treatment of Emilia, regards the old man's views as unworldly, and believes he can satisfy his passions without marrying her. When he comes into Trunnion's fortune, he has not thought of marriage for his "vanity and pride" turn him to wealthier prizes such as "a rich heiress, or opulent widow" (397). To be sure, he still desires Emilia, but on his own terms. Seeing her at the playhouse and mindful of his superior fortune, he makes no advances to Emilia for he is fearful that "some ladies of fashion . . . would think the worse of him, should they see him make his compliments in public to a person of her figure." But then perhaps they would imagine her "some handsome Abigail, with whom he had an affair of gallantry" and that would enhance his reputation (398).

But the importance of money—and, to some extent, power—in their relationship becomes evident in Emilia's conduct. In their world finances prove significant to both sexes, particularly to people concerned with their own individuality. Emilia, no less than Perry, is cognizant of the importance of being independent of her partner's fortune. When Perry had the money early in the relationship, he felt superior to her. Now, after Emilia has become independently wealthy through her uncle's will, Perry, whose resources have been dissipated, regards himself as unworthy of her. The empowered Emilia can openly express her feelings for him and does so forthrightly:

as the late favourable change in my situation, impowers me to avow my genuine sentiments, without fear of censure, or suspicion of mercenary design, I take this opportunity to assure you, that if I still maintain that place in your heart, which I was vain enough to think I once possessed, I am willing to make the first advance to an accommodation. (759)

Remarkably bold words for an eighteenth-century heroine, they indicate not only that love remains an important element in their romance, but that it hinges for its consummation on financial security. Smollett makes clear the combination of the two as he details Emilia's understanding of Perry's reluctance, because of his pride, to accept her offer before he finds himself in a position of having a fortune to offer to her. The combination of her motives as she makes her advance to Perry clearly emanates from the narrator's description of her feelings for her lover now that she can act with the assuredness born of her good fortune: "her plan . . . which was no other than that of securing her own happiness, in espousing the man upon whom she had fixed her unalterable affection. Confident of his honour, and fully satisfied of the mutual passion with which they were inspired" (761). The modern reader may have difficulty in accepting the word "honour" in relation to Perry, who, after all, has womanized his way through England and Europe and has behaved viciously to the heroine, but Smollett and his audience were more inclined to accept the kind of masculine sensibility underlying the situation. At any rate, Emilia is in love, and, like those Restoration heroines who, to the outrage of critics like the Reverend Jeremy Collier who demanded an end to such dramas, gracefully accepted the "reformed" rakes on the seventeenth-century stage, she finally places the values of her heart above those of her head. Her decision seems less odd when seen in the context of her times that found Richardson's female readers pleading with him to permit the villainous Lovelace to marry Clarissa, whom he had savagely raped.

The play between Emilia's emotions and common sense characterizes her behavior throughout the novel, and her judgment—apart from this major and final decision—invariably controls her feelings. Smollett carefully presents Emilia as an open, unaffected, yet very sensible and sensitive woman, qualities he clearly admired in his heroines. When Perry comes to her home and responds impulsively to her as she opens the door, she takes it in good stride, without affectation. Clearly pleased with his affection and not put off by his forward manner, she reacts by teasing him on "his assurance." When in the course of the day he offers addresses that might seem to go beyond the bounds of propriety on such short acquaintance, although obviously pleased with his emotions, she "carefully avoided the confession of a mutual flame; because she discerned, in the midst of all his tenderness, a levity of pride which she durst not venture to trust with such a declaration" (99).

Twice she employs her feminine wiles to hold him at bay, to keep him off balance, and to indicate her independence—a major virtue in a Restoration heroine. First, she assures herself of Perry's attention at a ball by turning away three of his rivals so that they will be engaged with other young women when Perry arrives to be her partner. She later employs other admirers to arouse his jealousy and to demonstrate that "she had other resources, in case he should flagg in his affection." It is on this second occasion that Emilia shows her abundant common sense. When Perry behaves sullenly because of a berating from Commodore Trunnion, even though aware of his discomfort and need for sympathy, she wisely refrains from yielding to his obvious distress:

she could not give her tongue the liberty of asking the cause of his disorder; for, notwithstanding all the candour of his addresses, he never could obtain from her the declaration of a mutual flame; because, tho' he had hitherto treated her with the utmost reverence of respect, he had never once mentioned the final aim of his passions; and however honourable she supposed it to be,.she had discernment enough to foresee, that vanity or interest co-operating with the levity of youth, might one day deprive her of her lover, and she was too proud to give him any handle of exulting at her expence. (141)

Whatever Emilia's romantic sentiments, Smollett is at pains to separate her from the ordinary heroines of sentimental fiction.

Emilia's ability to parry Peregrine's designs upon her honor, her wit and wisdom, despite her youth, display the most admirable qualities of Restoration comedy heroines. The scene in which Perry's aide Pipes presents a stupidly written replacement of the hero's letter to her has all the comic tones familiar to farce, but Emilia's response to it reveals her tough-mindedness and self-assurance as she perceives it properly as ridiculing her and "the passion he had formerly professed" (105). With determination she resolutely deals with the situation by ousting Perry from her heart, a feat that she can accomplish, the narrator states, "for she enjoyed an easiness of temper that could accommodate itself to the emergencies of her fate; and her vivacity by amusing her imagination, preserved her from the keener sensations of sorrow" (105–6). Her conduct torments Perry as he seeks to regain her good graces. Throughout a chapter (XXIV) in which the mystery of the switched letter finally is clarified, Emilia proves unyielding. When Perry finally gets to her through her cousin, later her sister-in-law, Sophy, he must throw himself before her to get her to yield to his pleas. Still, Emilia reveals her true feelings for him—and what Smollett regards as female passion—when she reacts jealously to Perry's innocent kissing of Sophy's hand in gratitude for her mediation.

To Perry's "vanity and pride," Emilia counters with dignity, self-possession, and shrewdness. When Perry returns after a seventeen-month absence and behaves not like an ardent lover, but rather "a conceited petit maitre," she rebukes his neglectful conduct over that period, not with words, but with a composure far more powerful than an outburst of anger. Smollett's omniscient point of view permits access to her motives: "[she] had summoned all her own pride and resolution to her aid; and by means of a happy disposition, so far overcame her chagrin at his indifference, that she was able to behave in his presence with apparent tranquility and ease." Using all the charms of what Smollett terms her "coquettry," she plays him off against her other male visitors. When he himself puts on airs, although she is "fretted out of all temper," she maintains her dignity and defeats his "libertine" behavior as he affects gallantry. She manages the situation nicely: "she kept her person sacred from his touch, and would not even suffer him to ravish a kiss of her fair hand" (360–62).

In the events surrounding Perry's attempted rape of Emilia, she displays the same strength of character. Indeed, Smollett's determination to portray her as a strong, powerful woman in control during the most difficult circumstances raises serious questions about the verisimilitude of her final acceptance of the hero as the novelist bows to the conventional conclusions of Restoration comedies. Indeed, Smollett yields none of his masculine sensibility as he contrasts Emilia with Richardson's Clarissa since, in effect, he argues that a determined woman can manage to thwart even a rapist—a point of view that puts the onus for the act on the victim rather than on the perpetrator. But, whatever problems it ultimately poses for the writer, his treatment of Emilia marks her as a full-blooded woman rather than the "milliners' dummies" that some critics have discovered indiscriminately in all his heroines.[33] Just prior to Perry's attack on her, Emilia thwarts his advances, showing "prudence and resolution sufficient to contain her tenderness" (402) when he fails to express any honorable intentions. She withholds his most outlandish behavior in her report on his conduct to her uncle, allowing the reader to perceive her innermost feeling for Perry, her desire for him that she is still unwilling to cast aside forever. Without offering her uncle the details that would cause him to break off the connection irrevocably, "she said every thing which she thought would satisfy his care and concern for her welfare" (403).

Finally aroused by Perry's attack on her, Emilia demonstrates her own capability in combatting him. She is unforgiving. Matching wits with him, she uses "prudence and penetration," her "circumspection," to thwart his attempt to abduct her (413). She relentlessly turns away his schemes to renew their relationship. Even at the time of her brother's marriage to Sophy, when Perry is invited as a guest, Emilia refuses to yield. She threatens not to attend the ceremony and agrees only after he promises not to "renew the old topic, nor even speak to her in the stile of a former acquaintance" (587). At the wedding itself she counters Perry's tricks to make her jealous by flirting with another guest, arousing Perry's anger and producing a violent effect on him. Even when Perry's jealousy results in his illness and he beseeches her sister-in-law to intervene, Emilia holds fast. Although she relents to the extent of agreeing to read the letter he has sent to Sophy and asks her brother and his wife to inform Perry that she does not want to be the cause of his despair, Emilia insists that she desires no further correspondence with him. Until the final chapters of the novel, when she can stand on equal terms with him, she remains steadfast in her position.

Throughout their relationship Emilia plays the game of love with all the intensity of a Restoration heroine, and she plays it with the object of bringing her lover to heel. Smollett, through his narrator's observations and descriptions of Emilia's inner life, brings forth, as he does not manage to do with his other heroines, except Lydia, Emilia's emotional life, the human feelings that direct her actions. At the same time, he indicates that her conduct is consistently governed by her common sense. In the conclusion of their very first encounter, the pattern with her lover is set. When Perry is forced to return to school under Trunnion's orders, Smollett describes Emilia's emotional response while displaying her control over her passions. Alert to Perry's announcement of his departure, "she stood in silent expectation of hearing some melancholy tidings.... Though she strove to conceal her sorrow, nature was not to be suppressed; every feature of her countenance saddened in a moment, and it was not without the utmost difficulty that she kept her lovely eyes from overflowing." At Perry's assurance of his return, they are carried away with transports of joy, but by the time of her mother's appearance on the scene, Emilia, like Perry, has sufficient control "to behave with great decency and resignation" (101).

After the incident in which Emilia has been outraged by Pipes's delivery of his rewritten letter from Perry, Emilia accidentally meets the hero, and Smollett provides a good account of her emotional life: her desire for Perry and her self-esteem that protects her from him. Brought together with him, she is as excited as he: "She perceived and partook of his emotion; for their souls, like unisons, vibrated with the same impulse." Still, she restrains herself through "pride and resentment" (120), qualities generally reserved for Smollett's heroes. In their conversation she matches him quip for quip and tone for tone; she flicks her fan at him with dismissive irony for what she regards as his inconstancy. With a fine combination of hope that the letter was indeed spurious and an awareness that she has her lover on the run, she refuses to let him off easily. She guesses that he will make every endeavor to clear up the matter as he does in the subsequent chapter (XXVI). Still, she determines to make him suffer in the power game that they are playing. Using his omniscient point of view, the narrator conveys both the motives and devices leading to her victory: "she had a spice of the coquette in her disposition, and being determined to whet [Perry's] impatience, artfully baffled all his endeavours" (122).

Smollett repeatedly plays off Emilia's strong emotional feelings against her outward demeanor and allows the reader to realize the fullness of her character. When, after their long separation, Perry sees her in the audience at a playhouse and she observes his recognition, she guesses his intentions and "summoned all her fortitude to her aid, and prepared for his reception." Despite her pleasure at his deferential conduct when he addresses her, "she suppressed the emotions of her heart, and answered his compliments with affected ease and unconcern" (398). Smollett's technique of seeing inside her character both reveals her genuine feelings and softens the account of the coolness of her reception. Much the same treatment marks the account of Emilia's behavior at the subsequent meeting of the pair. The novelist makes clear that Emilia's behavior reflects a combination of "hope and fear," the natural emotions of a young virgin unsure of her lover's intentions. Although Emilia's eyes give away her true feelings, her prudence and common sense protect her from yielding to his speeches and she does not deign to respond with any "acknowledgment of a mutual passion, because, in the midst of his vows of eternal constancy and truth, he did not mention one syllable of wedlock" (400–401).

In all this description of Emilia's emotional life, Smollett suggests her underlying sexual feelings. Given the conventions of the respectable novel of his times, it is the best that he could be expected to do in presenting the desires of a heroine. With lesser characters and with fallen women, the novelist had greater access to displaying overtly sexual emotions within limits. A John Cleland in *Fanny Hill*, of course, had no difficulty in dealing overtly with sexuality in his appeal to pornographic interests. For Smollett the strength of such emotions could merely be suggested. He manages it only through a kind of displacement. When, for example, Perry views Emilia at their reconciliation, the narrator states, "her bosom heaved with such bewitching undulation, that the cambrick could not conceal or contain the snowy hemispheres, that rose like a vision of paradise to his view." Emilia's "cheeks [that] glowed with a most delicate suffusion" reveal her inner desires (774). The perspective may be Perry's and the words the narrator's, but the heaving bosom and glowing cheeks are Emilia's—signs of her own sexual desire that give her the full dimensions of womanhood despite the limitations that keep Smollett from going inside her mind at this point.

Yet for all of Smollett's concern for providing Emilia with greater embodiment than any of his other heroines, she remains, like them, essentially less important in herself than as a device for moving along the plot and permitting the development of the hero's character. In all of what has already been said about her, she is seen in terms of her responses to Perry. He goes through his lengthy adventures in company with a vast variety of characters, but she never exists outside his presence or his consciousness. Emilia serves as either a means of directly displaying his best and worst characteristics when she deals with him or acts as a totemic symbol guiding his behavior or indicating his progress and lapses on the path to maturity. Even when she disappears physically she remains either as a beacon to his better self as he thinks of her or as a reminder to the reader as he dismisses her from his thoughts that he has a distance to go to maturity.

Smollett indicates from the outset Emilia's role in the novel. As Perry leaves her for the first time, the novelist sets forth the manner in which she serves as a vehicle for his plot: "Though their mutual passion was by these means suppressed for the present, it was not altogether extinguished, but glowed in secret, though even to themselves unknown, until an occasion which afterwards offered, blew up the latest flame, and love resumed his empire in their hearts" (107). As Perry goes off with Emilia's brother, he callously engages in affairs, particularly taking on without "moderation" young ladies "Among the lower class of people" (165). Despite his great feelings for Emilia, he makes a conquest of Mrs. Hornbeck, cuckolding her husband. In the very next chapter, without any compunction, he sends a "tender billet" to "his dear Emilia, to whom he repeated all his former vows of constancy and love" (204) and then almost immediately attempts to rape a French innkeeper's wife. For all his protestations of love for Emilia, he quickly takes on a mistress on his arrival in Paris. With dispatch he puts aside his thoughts of marrying Emilia to indulge his emotions with other women. Smollett's charitable narrator attributes his conduct to his regretting a decision made through the "rawness and inexperience of youth" (218). A message "from his charming Emilia" remains unanswered, having "arrived at a very unseasonable juncture, when his imagination was engrossed by conquests that more agreeably flattered his ambition" (217).

Through long stretches, Perry dismisses Emilia from his thoughts. He cavalierly turns the Grand Tour into a sexcapade, bedding down wherever possible, chasing after a married Flemish beauty or making a conquest of a nun. Still, upon his return to England after an absence of eighteen months, he easily picks up again "the image of his charming Emily, which other less worthy considerations had depressed" (353). His intentions, however, are considerably less than honorable as he plans to have Emilia without marriage. Here, as in the entire episode of Perry's subsequent attempted rape of Emilia, Smollett indicates a forgiving attitude toward his hero. Ultimately, he regards Perry's behavior as the impetuosity of youth, a part of the natural growing process for a young man in his position. To be sure, Smollett does not condone his conduct, but his words betray a sympathetic consideration of the waywardness of a somewhat spoiled youth:

Sorry am I, that the task I have undertaken, lays me under the responsibility of divulging the degeneracy in the sentiments of our imperious youth, who has now in the heyday of his blood, flushed with the consciousness of his own qualifications, vain of his fortune, and elated on the wings of imaginary expectation. Tho' he was deeply enamoured of miss Gauntlet, he was far from proposing her heart as the ultimate aim of his gallantry, which (he did not doubt) would triumph oe'r the most illustrious females of the land, and at once regale his appetite and ambition. (353)

This comment originates in moralizing and moves without irony to sympathetic understanding.

Like the comments of a modern critic who assesses Emilia's punishment of Peregrine as too harsh in the circumstances and attributes her behavior throughout to her excessive pride, Smollett's judgment clearly represents a very masculine point of view. To see Perry's conduct as a form of misguided youthful effervescence and to find it less heinous than Lovelace's behavior in Richardson's *Clarissa* reveals an insensitivity difficult to excuse.[34] Smollett himself seems deliberately to have expressed his disapproval of Richardson's heroine by contrasting her weakness and gullibility with Emilia's strength in thwarting Perry. But, as noted earlier, that, too, suggests Smollett's male perspective on the incident, mitigating the hero's conduct by implying that a determined woman can find the means of preventing rape.[35] His attitude and his willingness to take Peregrine's actions rather lightly were far too general in the period. For all the shock that the scene creates for a modern audience, Smollett's contemporaries, including female readers, apparently regarded such behavior with a remarkable degree of equanimity.[36]

Smollett's tone on the subject of Perry's amours is consistently as cavalier as his hero's conduct. In the chapter in which Perry, along with Emilia's brother, goes forth to seek further amorous adventures in Bath, Smollett blithely describes it as: *"The two Friends eclipse all their Competitors in Gallantry"* (370). "Gallantry" consists in overwhelming the ladies, despite the fact of Perry's supposed attachment to Emilia and his friend Godfrey's great love for his cousin Sophy. Seeking no "agreeable companion for life," Perry finds little gratification in his conquests, mainly because of his air of superiority, but also, as Smollett reminds the reader, whether Perry realizes it, because "of his attachment to Emily, which was stronger than he himself imagined" (380). Still, it is not an attachment that prevents him from a succession of triumphs in the bedroom. Smollett's tolerance of his hero's conduct remains steadfast, even in the grossly understated wording of the chapter heading for his account of the attempted rape: *"He prevails upon Emilia to accompany him to a Masquerade, makes a treacherous Attempt upon her Affection, and meets with a deserved Repulse"* (404).

Coming just past the midway point in the novel, the scene of Perry's attempted rape marks the nadir in the hero's moral development. It also brings back Emilia as an active character and provides her with the opportunity to display genuinely heroic qualities that set her apart not only from Smollett's other heroines, but from the vast majority of female characters in the eighteenth-century novel. To be sure, Smollett focuses mainly on Perry, but in the novelist's obvious intention to play off his heroine's conduct against that of Richardson's Clarissa, Emilia emerges in the fullness of a strong female character. Although ultimately slightly less malicious, or at least less successful, than Richardson's Lovelace, Perry behaves with equal relentlessness in his endeavor to assail Emilia's virginity. Through cunning, guile, and finally force, Perry presses his attack, and Emilia displays her strength and wisdom in holding him off.

Perry plays the role of predator. Over a period of several nights of entertainment, he builds up her confidence through an assiduous courtship. Having invited Emilia's friend to a masquerade, believing she will decline, he proceeds to keep her away after she has accepted—first attempting unsuccessfully to ply her with medicine to make her ill and then using a letter to her mother to free himself from her encumbrance as a kind of chaperone for Emilia. Because she has never before attended a masquerade, Emilia is in high spirits, an inviting and seemingly accessible target. Perry uses wine and dancing to arouse her. She loses her defense temporarily as he "began to ply her with all the elocution of love." For all her weakness in the situation, however, Emilia maintains the sharp wit of Restoration heroines: "Her eyes began to sparkle with unusual fire and vivacity, a thousand sallies of wit escaped her, and every mask that accosted her, underwent some smarting repartee" (404–5). Heady as she is, she lets her defenses down. Her feelings moved "in favour of the man she loved, [she] abated considerably of her wonted reserve, listened to his protestations with undissembled pleasure, and in the confidence of her satisfaction, even owned him absolute master of her affections." Pretending to take her home, he presses forward with excessive kisses, "which she pardoned as the privilege of intoxication" (406).

Nevertheless, whatever her state of exhilaration and her undeniable feelings for Perry, when he tricks her by not returning her to her uncle's house and tries to cover his action with excuses, she has "too much penetration to be imposed upon by this plausible pretext" (406). Unlike Richardson's Clarissa, Emilia has too much worldly wisdom to be taken in by a designing man. When Perry's advances become more direct and his proposals indecent, Smollett conveys the horror of the assault on her respectability: "Heavens! what were the emotions of the virtuous, the sensible, the delicate, the tender Emilia's heart, when she heard this insolent declaration from the mouth of a man, whom she had honoured with her affection and esteem! It was not simply horror, grief, or indignation that she felt . . . , but the united pangs of all together" (407). Failing to understand the irony of her "hysteric laugh," Perry forces himself on her physically. To this point Smollett has narrated the action, but now he moves to direct discourse to convey the fullness of her emotions and the power of her character. "Sir, I scorn to upbraid you with a repetition of your former vows and protestations." She rips into his "dissimulation" and disdainfully turns him away, "Sir, you are unworthy of my concern or regret. . . . As for your present attempt upon my chastity, I despise your power, as I detest your intention." When she charges him with "impious stratagems to ruin my peace and reputation," her words are those of a displeased goddess addressing an unworthy mortal, but she is also a spirited and angry woman (408). Still, Smollett concludes with the effect on Perry, indicating the novelist's main interest. Without a touch of irony and without questioning whether it should even matter to Emilia, Smollett records Perry's reactions: "While he deeply resented her disdain, he could not help admiring her spirit, and in his heart did homage to her charms" (409). For Smollett, after all, the theme and values are those of his Restoration model; Perry behaves with the rake's customary self-interest, and Emilia will be the virtuous virgin who ultimately yields to him.

Even the aftermath conveys these attitudes. Emilia, with all her propriety, returns his gift of jewels with a note of appropriate disdain: "That I may have no cause to reproach myself with having retained the least memorial of a wretch whom I equally despise and abhor, I take this opportunity of restoring these ineffectual instruments of his infamous design upon the honour of EMILIA" (410). Perry, on the other hand, never fully comprehends the nature of his own conduct. When Emilia's mother rejects his attempts to have her intervene with her daughter, he is "piqued" and attributes it to "her own vanity rather than good sense" (421). Pursuing his own passions in order to get Emilia off his mind, while still "biased by a passion [for Emilia]" (575), he acts throughout with an assuredness that she finally will be his prize if he desires it. Nothing better indicates his— and presumably Smollett's—attitude than the language used to describe Perry's entrance into their bridal bedroom: "the delicious scene, where he found her elegantly dished out, the fairest daughter of chastity and love" (779). Whatever Emilia's qualities as a woman, for Smollett and Perry she remains the inanimate object of a man's desire, a feast to be enjoyed by a male hero so long as she submits to the values of a double standard. Unfortunately, no Restoration heroine ever got more.

No Restoration heroine, but interesting in her own way, Lydia, in *Humphry Clinker*, is a different kind of Smollettian heroine, and her difference relates to her fictional purposes in the novel. Using her for the progress and unity of the work, for the development of his overall theme, for bringing out the fullness of Matt Bramble, his central character but no young hero, and for enlivening his satire, Smollett rounds out Lydia's character in a manner distinctly unlike his generally simple idealization of such a heroine as Aurelia in *Greaves*. Without altogether foregoing those traits that he customarily ascribes to his model females, he nevertheless provides Lydia with a realism beyond his familiar caricatured idealism. Smollett's multiple point of view in the novel's epistolary technique permits him to delve into her weaknesses and strengths by presenting her own letters, comments on her in reports from her fellow travelers, and the contradictory views that emerge from a comparison of the two, a leitmotif that underscores the clash between appearance and reality that is a major epistemological concern in *Humphry Clinker*.[37]

Despite the limited number of Lydia's own letters, they are sufficient to permit Smollett to go well beyond the creation of a flat character. Lydia's letters, numbering eleven, compare with six for her aunt Tabby and ten for Win Jenkins, Tabby's maid—the two other women accompanying Matt on his journey. Still, hers are far more substantial in both length and content. Their literacy contrasts with the malapropisms, misspellings, and ignorance of those of the other women. Where Tabby cannot speak freely of her adventures and feelings to her correspondent, her housekeeper, Mrs. Gwyllim, Lydia can openly discuss her problems with her school chum, Letty, the recipient of nine of her letters. Win, like Lydia, can be outspoken in her correspondence with her fellow servant, Mary Jones, but Smollett's concerns with using her for social, verbal, and sexual satire hardly permit a genuine development of the character through her short notes back home. Through the breadth and depth of Lydia's letters, Smollett presents a romantic young heroine whose journey allows her to display the fullness of her character as she matures in her understanding of the world, although Smollett creates a consistency in her character that provides the necessary verisimilitude. At the same time, Smollett's technique advances his variety of purposes as the young woman comes of age.

Quite naturally the bulk of Lydia's communication concerns her affairs of the heart. It is, after all, as Matt's and her brother Jery's first letters make clear, a major reason for the Brambles' travels that form the narrative adventure of *Humphry Clinker*. Having fallen in love with "Wilson," apparently a strolling player although finally revealed as the son of Matt's old friend, Dennison, and a very worthwhile matrimonial prospect, Lydia has set the entire family in turmoil. To rescue her from a fate worse than death—and, indeed, had Wilson proven to be what Matt and Jery believed, she might well have suffered the fate of Smollett's fallen women—Matt undertakes the trip that comprises the structure of the novel. In her letters Lydia, while giving evidence of greater complexity than the rest of her family recognizes, does serve Smollett's satiric purposes in his attack on the genre of romance, and, in consequence, retains many of the characteristics of the heroines of such fiction.

Still, from the very outset of her correspondence, Lydia demonstrates greater depth than Aurelia, Serafina, or Narcissa. While no Emilia, neither is she a "feather headed girl," a "cardboard heroine," an open-natured innocent unable to dissemble, a weakling ready to yield to the will of her elders, and an insipid creature unworthy of serious attention.[38] Smollett neatly begins with two contrasting epistles from Lydia—one to Mrs. Jermyn, her boarding-school mistress, and the other to her close friend Laetitia (Letty) Willis. In tone, style, and content, the pair of letters together display a more fully developed character than has been suggested by modern critics who have found in the early letters especially a naïve, altogether innocent young woman, one whose sole purpose appears to be to permit Smollett to satirize sentimental romances or develop a comic romance.[39] To be sure, in Lydia's character, Smollett does that, but for his fictional purposes he goes well beyond simple parody.

Lydia's letter to Mrs. Jermyn is a fine mixture of contrition and self-praise. Recognizing the character of the recipient, she proceeds formally and with an appropriate sense of decorum. The prose, clear and orderly, conveys a sense of humility without stooping. Lydia begins proudly enough: "I never harboured a thought that was otherwise than virtuous; and, if God will give me grace, I shall never behave so as to cast a reflection on the care you have taken in my education." That established, she confesses—but barely—that she has "given just cause of offence," but it appears somewhat excusable, this lack of "prudence," because of her inexperience. If, indeed, she ought not to have left herself open to Wilson's advances, perhaps her lapse can be forgiven since it reflected the goodness of her heart and her innocence: "he behaved so modest and respectful, and seemed to be so melancholy and timorous, that I could not find in my heart to do any thing that should make him miserable and desperate." Much to the point, she declares circumlocutorily that her virginity remains intact. There were no "familiarities," "nothing contrary to innocence and honour." In a note of prescience, important as later events turn out, which suggests her intuitive intelligence, she suggests that Wilson will prove to be more than he now appears (9). The letter as a whole displays a political sense that belies the simplicity of a romantically befogged heroine.[40]

To be sure, even in the letter to Mrs. Jermyn, Lydia offers the customary tears of the romantic heroine expressing her "distress." In her own words, she becomes the hurt creature of sentimental fiction, "poor, disconsolate, forlorn." Nevertheless, even these tears seem not altogether artless. If they cannot move a heart so hardened as that of her aunt Tabby, she recognizes their effect on her seemingly irascible uncle Matt: "My uncle, who was so dreadfully passionate in the beginning, has been moved . . . ; and is now all tenderness and compassion" (10). While her comment suggests her own ability to play a role, it also serves—indeed, a major purpose of Lydia in the novel—to indicate that Matt, despite his harsh exterior, hides his kindness behind a tough appearance.

With Letty Lydia disdains role playing. Here Smollett gives full vent to his satire on the romance genre, and in Lydia's breathless writing come forth softly comic echoes of the sounds of sentimental heroines. Her punctuation itself indicates the fullness of Lydia's emotions; her openness contrasts with the formality that marks her letters to Mrs. Jermyn. Her letter to Letty indeed must be secreted out of the family's abode through the good graces of Win, who has become her confidante. For all her contrition in her words to her schoolmistress, she still wants and desires Wilson. "O, my dear Letty!," she laments, "what shall I say about poor Mr. Wilson? I have promised to break off all correspondence, and, if possible, to forget him: but, alas! I begin to perceive that will not be in my power" (10).

In a way, her correspondence with Letty serves as a furtherance of her illicit liaison and reveals a little more of what her relationship with Wilson had been, not quite as innocent as suggested by her note to Mrs. Jermyn. She sends Letty Wilson's picture, to "either keep it safe till better times, or return it to Mr. Wilson himself, who, I suppose, will make it his business to see you at the usual place" (10). So, in a sense, she is maintaining her correspondence with Wilson through Letty and, at the same time, revealing the nature of their earlier relationship. With beautiful duality her sentences capture her emotions, offering her sense of familial duty in conflict with her romantic feelings. If Letty does return the picture to him, Lydia, imagining his response, says:

> You may tell him I have no occasion for a picture, while the original continues engraved on my—But no; I would not have you tell him that neither; because there must be an end of our correspondence—I wish he may forget me, for the sake of his own peace; and yet if he should, he must be barbarous—But 'tis impossible—poor Wilson cannot be false and inconstant. (11)

Even as he enjoys his satire on romance, Smollett here—as he has found it difficult to do with the heroines of his other novels, trapped as they are in picaresque or near-picaresque narratives with their external points of view—manages to express neatly and reasonably the emotions of a young woman rather than those of the idealized fictional heroine.

That Smollett, indeed, seeks to play games with the romance genre becomes apparent when he quickly follows up with Wilson's letter sent to Lydia. Intercepted by Jery, Wilson's note is included in Matt's letter to his correspondent, Dr. Lewis. Here, at least, Wilson proves himself a character as much a part of romance as Lydia is. Written breathlessly, employing exclamation points, expressing appropriate despair that Lydia is being taken away from him, it offers expressions like, "Good God! I never heard your name mentioned without emotion! the most distant prospect of being admitted to your company, filled my whole soul with a kind of pleasing alarm!" Gushing over her "charming eyes," "sweetness of temper and affability," and kindness (15), Wilson, like the heroes of romance, ultimately sinks under the weight of his own sentiment into self-despair: "The sun seems to deny me light—a cloud hangs over me, and there is a dreadful weight upon my spirits" (16). Like the sentiments expressed, the clichéd diction marks the excesses of romance that Smollett parodies.

Noteworthy, however, in even this lover's effusive praise of Lydia, is the absence of any true lauding of her beauty, apart from the comment on her "charming eyes." As will be seen in comments by others, Smollett does not portray Lydia, as he does his idealized heroines and Emilia, as possessing overwhelming physical attractions. Where such models of perfection as Narcissa, Serafina, and Aurelia dazzle not only their suitors, but the world at large, with an attractiveness that sets them apart from the rest of womankind, Lydia, as seen by Wilson, Matt, and Jery, displays no stunning beauty. For his last heroine Smollett appears to be balancing his portrait so that, for all of her attractive qualities, Lydia emerges as a far more believable young eighteenth-century woman.

It is also a sign of Smollett's greater maturity as an artist that he uses a final pair of letters from Lydia to Mrs. Jermyn and Letty to round out the structure of his novel.[41] Occurring as they do near the conclusion of the work, these letters recall the complex character of Lydia that Smollett first presented and, at the same time, suggest the effect of the journey that has exposed her to society. If her letter to Letty reveals again her romantic emotions, fundamental to her character, and that to Mrs. Jermyn her ability to shift poses, to play to the instincts of authority and to suppress her most effusive feelings, the latter also indicates a young woman whose experiences have given her a greater self-possession.

Political shrewdness characterizes Lydia's importuning Mrs. Jermyn to intervene with Letty's mother to permit her daughter to act as maid-of-honor in the wedding with Wilson/Dennison. Behind the controlled style and diction marking the first part of the letter and the seemingly obsequious closing with its "Your most affectionate / humble servant, / and penitent," Lydia's epistle maintains throughout a sense of self-assurance. To be sure, she cleverly expresses her gratitude for Mrs. Jermyn's tutelage. Still, in her very opening sentence, she subtly rebukes Mrs. Jermyn for having ignored her apologetic letter "with which I troubled you in the spring." When she makes her grand announcement of her forthcoming marriage, she carries it off with a triumphal air: "At present, I think it my duty to make you acquainted with the happy issue of that indiscretion by which I incurred your displeasure." Her apparent acknowledgment of the faults in her earlier behavior turns into a quiet boast of the superiority of her judgment when she recounts the outcome of her "indiscretion": "Ah, madam, the slighted Wilson is metamorphosed into George Dennison, only son and heir of a gentleman, whose character is second to none in England, as you may understand upon inquiry." Still describing herself as "your poor Lydia Melford," who suffers from "weak nerves and strong apprehensions," she nevertheless gloats about her gaining as a mother-in-law Mrs. Dennison, "who is the object of universal love and esteem" (336).

But, after all, the letter seeks Mrs. Jermyn's intervention with Letty's mother and that requires another tone as well. In phrases punctuated by exclamation points and appealing to her schoolmistress's emotions, Lydia shifts back into the role of the pleading young pupil: "My dear Mrs. Jermyn! my ever honoured governess! let me conjure you by that fondness which once distinguished your favourite Liddy! by that benevolence of heart which disposes you to promote the happiness of your fellow-creatures in general!" Still, she does not conclude in the same manner. Far more assertively, she assures Mrs. Jermyn of her new trustworthiness: "I will engage to return her [Liddy] safe, and even to accompany her to Gloucester." With a greater sense of assuredness, she reminds her correspondent of her change in status—one achieved despite the qualms of her elders, one that gives evidence of the superiority of her instincts to theirs—and promises that she will "present to you under another name" (337).

With Letty again Lydia requires no poses and needs no game playing. To be sure, when she describes the places she visits, she plays up the excitement to impress her uninitiated friend,[42] but otherwise she speaks her emotions freely and expresses the full sentiments of the romance heroine. The contrast between the two letters—that to Mrs. Jermyn and this to Letty—indicates how well Smollett understood the possibilities of the epistolary novel in revealing character. In her letter to Letty Lydia permits the reader to comprehend her genuine sentiment. It is a reminder of Clarissa's opening up her emotions to her closest correspondent, Anna Howe, in Richardson's novel. For Smollett here, as nowhere else in his novels, the epistolary technique permits a glimpse into a young heroine's trepidations as she stands on the brink of marriage. The difference between Smollett's treatment of Lydia and his other heroines indicates the generic importance in character development and reminds the reader of the difficulties that a novelist like Smollett has in creating a female character to the fullest when the perspective is either that of the heroic male character or a narrator whose focus is on the actions of a male protagonist.

Lydia's letter to Letty bears all the signs of her emotions. Here, again, she reverts to dashes and exclamation points as she describes her feelings about forthcoming events. She marvels at her good fortune and is overwhelmed by it so that she fears it cannot last. Without the guile that she employs with the authority figure of Mrs. Jermyn, she fully recounts her emotions as she begs her friend to "come and do the last offices of maidenhood to your companion":

O Letty!—O gracious heaven! how my heart palpitates, when I tell you that this only son of Mr. Dennison, is that very identical youth who, under the name of Wilson, has made such ravage in my heart!—Yes, my dear friend! Wilson and I are now lodged in the same house, and converse together freely ... and in three weeks or a month, if no unforeseen accident occurs, your friend Lydia Melford, will have changed her name and condition—I say, if *no accident intervenes*, because such a torrent of success makes me tremble! I wish there may not be something treacherous in the sudden reconciliation of fortune—I have no merit—I have no title to such felicity! Far from enjoying the prospect that lies before me, my mind is harassed with a continuous tumult, made up of hopes and wishes, doubts and apprehensions—I can neither eat nor sleep, and my spirits are in perpetual flutter. (335)

Whether Smollett's other heroines harbored the kind of feelings Lydia reveals, the reader cannot easily know. Generic limitations generally stand in the way of exploring their feelings and the only certain connubial bliss belongs to the heroes who pounce upon them with animal delight on their wedding nights.

Between the two sets of letters to Mrs. Jermyn and Letty, much of Lydia's remaining seven concern her clandestine romance in some way.

What they reveal is a combination of her romantic emotions and a sound sense that often expresses itself in a necessity for hiding from others than Letty her genuine feelings. That duality emerges in her early letter from Hot Well that describes her meeting with the disguised Wilson. As she tells Letty, like any good romantic heroine, when she discovers Wilson's identity, "I fainted away"; surreptitiously, however, "our looks were sufficiently expressive." Even as she displays her ability to hide her actions from Matt while confiding in Win, acts that are uncharacteristic of the idealized heroine, she offers full evidence of her romantic sentiments. She falls in love with Hot Well's "solitude, and this is a charming romantic place." Responding to all its natural beauties, she concludes with the lover's pleasure ·as "all night long sweet Philomel poùrs forth his ravishingly delightful song" (26–27). Still, it is no sweet and simple innocent who finds a way for communicating secretively with Letty through Win.

The pattern continues in Lydia's correspondence from Bath and London. Amidst the happiness in Bath, she writes twice to Letty, revealing the underlying sadness that she hides from her journey companions. Having seen two plays there, she recounts for her friend her ruling passion: "I could not help reflecting, with a sign, upon our poor homely representations at Gloucester," an obvious reference to Wilson, who had assumed the role of a player. She indicates the importance of Letty to whom "in confidence" she can reveal her feelings because "You know my heart, and will excuse its weakness" (41), as her elders will not. Only to Letty can she say, as she does in a second letter from Bath, "I am vexed, that neither you nor I have received any further information of a certain person—Sure it can't be wilful neglect!—O my dear Willis! I begin to be visited by strange fancies, and to have some melancholy doubts; which, however, it would be ungenerous to harbour without further inquiry" (58). Despite her assurances to her uncle about the termination of· her relationship, she longs for and looks forward to a resumption of it.

Her London letters are lengthier in their treatment of the topic and offer a sign of the depth of her feelings for Wilson as she has the opportunity to engage in a relationship with another man. When Barton, encouraged by Lady Griskin (her relative), attempts to win her, she makes clear to Letty that she will never yield to another man, although she hides this from her family. Still disturbed that she has not had word of Wilson, and worried that he has deserted her, she vows to Letty, "You know the condition of my poor heart; which, in spite of hard usage—And yet I ought not to complain: nor will I, till further information" (93–94). Clearly these are not the feelings that she conveys to others as she masks her motives from them.[43] Even Jery, always suspicious about her relations with Wilson, fails to comprehend her reasons for rejecting prospective husbands when they are put before her. Somewhat puzzled by her lack of interest in Barton, whom he describes as having "an opulent estate and a great stock of good-nature" (95)—qualifications no young eighteenth-century woman could reasonably ignore—Jery attributes Lydia's response to something uninspiring in Barton's behavior, rather than recognizing that his sister's heart is fully attached to Wilson. For the time being, at least, she successfully carries off her role-playing with her brother.

Lydia's second letter from London on the Barton affair reveals the full complexity of her character. As she relates matters to Letty, she displays not only her romantic nature and fundamental innocence, but also a surprisingly tough-minded realism and an ability to counter the pressures of her elders with linguistic disguises. Speaking freely to her friend, she becomes the romantic heroine in distress. Her intelligence remains evident in a style that, while fully expressing her emotions, nevertheless shows remarkable control. Full of despair, she describes her fears of family pressures even as she vows to remain faithful to her apparently hopeless love for Wilson. She seeks consolation in her religion, but scoffs at the false comforts of what she regards as the hypocrisies of Methodism (Smollett's own prejudice). Taking advantage of her clandestine correspondence with Letty, which she seizes upon "eagerly to disburthen my poor heart, which is oppressed with fear and vexation," she resorts to the language of the sentimental heroine: "O Letty! what a miserable situation it is, to be without a friend to whom one can apply for counsel and consolation in distress!" (134). Signaling her innocence is the fact that throughout all this, Lydia's naivete prevents her from recognizing that her aunt Tabitha believes that Barton's attentions are directed toward her rather than her niece.

Far more indicative of her perceptive abilities and her rather cool handling of the more adult world is her confrontation with Lady Griskin, who intervenes on Barton's behalf. Unlike the male characters who are more easily thrown off the scent by Lydia's resort to stereotypical female fainting and moodiness, Lady Griskin properly guesses that "a girl of my age could not possibly resist so many considerations [as Barton offers], if her heart was not pre-engaged." Although Lady Griskin is only half right since Lydia has already expressed her dissatisfaction with Barton himself in her letter to Letty, she certainly has fixed on the central truth of Lydia's situation: her commitment to Wilson. But when she persists in her questioning and seeks the name of Lydia's lover, Lady Griskin cannot overcome the shrewdness that Lydia has demonstrated in her cautious letters to Mrs. Jermyn. Although Lady Griskin remains unconvinced, Lydia parries her pressure by using her age and inexperience as excuses for her lack of interest in Barton. Buoyed by her confidence in her own sense of constancy as "characteristic of my nature," she turns Lady Griskin aside. It is no simple innocent who informs Letty: "although I had not such command of myself as to conceal the emotion of my heart, I am not such a child as to disclose its secrets to a person who would certainly use them to its prejudice" (134).

As the Barton episode indicates, Smollett—as a result of the advantages of the epistolary technique—manages to get deeper into the feelings of Lydia than he does with any of his other heroines. Only in writing to a close friend would she be likely to reveal the intimacy of a dream, one that she herself fails to fully comprehend and that she avows she has no faith in because "there is nothing so childish as to be moved by those vain illusions." Through the symbolism of its transference of persons and its unveiling of repressed sexual emotions, Lydia's dream captures her genuine feelings about Wilson: "I thought I was in a church, when a certain person, whom you know [Wilson], was on the point of being married to my aunt; that the clergyman was Mr. Barton, and that poor forlorn I stood weeping in a corner, half naked, and without shoes or stockings" (135). With uncharacteristic insight as a novelist, Smollett displays a Richardsonian sensitivity to the conflict between a young woman's desires and the repressive conventions of her society, the problem for both Pamela and Clarissa, Richardson's famous heroines.[44]

In her letters from Glasgow and on the occasion of Wilson's reappearance, Lydia—even as she matures in her point of view—remains for Smollett a romantic heroine whom he can still use to play upon the genre that he employs, as well, for other fictional purposes. The epistolary technique allows him to develop fully Lydia's strongest emotions. As she writes to Letty about the confusion that occurs when a Mr. Gordon is mistaken for Wilson, she has no need to hide her feelings. Tabby cannot describe to Mrs. Gwyllim her adventures in husband hunting because that would be demeaning coming from mistress to housekeeper. Even Win cannot recount her flirtatious behavior with Dutton, for she seeks to maintain an air of superiority to her homebound friend. But Lydia's pouring out of her heart—at least as much as possible from a "respectable" young lady— comes naturally to one familiar with her experiences and sharing her interests and adventures.

Her letter from Glasgow begins with complete openness: "Never did poor prisoner long for deliverance, more than I have longed for an opportunity to disburthen my cares into your friendly bosom; and the occasion [that is, someone to safely deliver her message] which now presents itself, is little less than miraculous" (257–58). Desperate after the mistaken Gordon/Wilson incident because Jery has chastised her, she confesses, "I cannot bear to have my wounds probed severely." Her sentiments have been particularly shaken by Jery's observation that an honorable Wilson would come forward, and as she tries to conceal her feelings she falls into a deep depression. With a full expression of the romantic pathetic fallacy, she identifies her emotions with her natural surroundings: "the country being exceedingly romantic, suits my turn and inclinations." She does not recognize that she is objecting to a double standard when she contrasts her conduct with Jery's as he has moved easily out of a romantic attachment. Instead, she reverts to the fully committed heroine of sentimental romance: "I never admitted but one idea of love, and that has taken such root in my heart, as to be equally proof against all the pulls of discretion, and the frosts of neglect" (258).

Whatever depth he provides for any of his heroines, Smollett never yields his view of woman as essentially made for romance, regardless of her intelligence and maturity. Even at the climax of the novel, when Lydia's ideas of the world have come to closely resemble those of Matt, love is the dominant force in a woman's life, and once more she is a tool for Smollett's play on the romance genre. As she describes her response to a glimpse of the long absent Wilson, she is the weak-kneed romantic heroine always on the brink of fainting away with emotion: "The light forsook my eyes; and I was seized with such a palpitation and trembling, that I could not stand" (308). Shrewd enough to recognize that her brother's interests in his own family pride are as much as in his sister's honor, she moves quickly into a paragraph whose language and style belong to the bewildered sentimental heroine as she fills the spaces with her tears and punctuation disappears in a stream of dashes: "If the terrible suspense continues much longer, I shall have another fit of illness, and then the whole family will be in confusion.—If it was consistent with the wise purposes of Providence, would I were in my grave.—But it is my duty to be resigned" (309).

In letters not directly concerned with her love, Lydia exhibits a nicely balanced view of the young romantic heroine and a woman of good common sense quite aware of the realities of the world. As she speaks, schoolgirl to schoolgirl, to Letty, she fairly gushes with an immature sentiment. Her very salutation to her friend from Bath addresses "My Dearest Companion." She exudes enthusiasm over the exchange of token gifts and vows enduring allegiance as very young girls do: "Love and friendship are, without doubt, charming passions; which absence serves only to heighten and improve. Your kind present of the garnet bracelets, I shall keep as carefully as I preserve my own life; and I beg you will accept, in return, of my heart-housewife, with the tortoise-shell memorandum-book, as a trifling pledge of my unalterable affection" (38–39). From London—in the open excitement of her letter to Letty—she again suggests the innocent romanticism that characterizes their experiences. Attempting to capture the feeling of London, she offers comparisons from the kind of reading that has shaped their romantic imaginations: "All that you read of wealth and grandeur, in the Arabian Night's Entertainment, and the Persian Tales, concerning Bagdad, Diarbekir, Damascus, Ispahan, and Samarkand, is here realized" (92).

For all that, Lydia's letters, revealing her mixed characteristics, also dis-

play sound judgment not often brought to the fore in Smollett's heroines—
although sometimes mentioned in passing in his descriptions of them.
Persuaded to attend a Methodist tabernacle by her aunt Tabby, she does
not succumb to its emotional enticements even in her own troubled state.
Instead she marvels at Tabby and Win's conduct as they "sometimes speak
as if they were really inspired" (135–36). In a far more severe comment
on her aunt's behavior, Lydia generalizes on the female sex. For Smollett
the passage serves two purposes. It offers a satiric comment that expresses
Smollett's general feelings about women and, at the same time, sets Lydia,
as his heroine, apart from the rest. Putting the words in the mouth of a
woman, Smollett gives them particular credence for his audience:

My dear Willis, I am truly ashamed of my own sex—We complain of advantages
which the men take of our youth, inexperience, sensibility, and all that; but I have
seen enough to believe, that our sex in general make it their business to ensnare
the other; and for this purpose, employ arts which are by no means to be justified—
In point of constancy, they certainly have nothing to reproach the male part of
the creation.—My poor aunt, without any regard to her years and imperfections,
has gone to market with her charms in every place where she thought she had the
least chance to dispose of her person, which, however, hangs still heavy on her
hands—I am afraid she has used even religion as a decoy, thought it has not
answered her expectations. (259–60)

Win, too, is included in Lydia's exhortation. But Lydia's views extend
beyond the particular, even as it applies to Tabby's being "employed constantly in spreading nets for the other sex" (308). For Smollett it provides
an opportunity to condemn what he regards as women's predatory nature
in their quest for men, and he tries to make it more effective by presenting
the view through the eyes of his heroine whose comments manage to set
her apart from her sex.

But Smollett's portrait of Lydia, as with those of his other characters in
the novel, obviously is not limited to her own words and letters. Much of
what the reader sees of the heroine comes from her traveling companions,
particularly Jery and Matt. Underlying this contrasting and complementing
by the letter writers, of course, is Smollett's thematic concern for the disparity between appearance and reality. As a result of her situation, Lydia
deliberately hides her deepest emotions from her brother and uncle. Moreover, their perspective, not simply as men but as those whom society has
made "responsible" for her, can never allow them to see the fullness of
her character. Given their relationship to her, it is not surprising that even
her physical description plays no great role in their response to her, and
certainly it is not likely to be the kind of idealized account of the heroine
that comes through when she is presented from a lover's point of view.
At any rate, these factors combine to keep Lydia from appearing to

be a figure of ethereal beauty, an angelic incarnation such as the idealized women in Smollett's earlier novels. Seen from the perspective of Matt and Jery, she is likely to be a poor, vulnerable maiden in need of their paternalistic care and an innocent endangered by the world around her.

Smollett, indeed, seems determined to create a young woman very much a part of the real world. Even as he introduces her critical problem—the romance with Wilson—he does not treat it grandiosely, in terms befitting the tragic situation of a heroine. Although it is clearly the major reason for the Bramble family's journey, Matt, without particulars, deals with it in only part of a sentence in his introductory letter: "A ridiculous incident that happened yesterday to my niece Liddy, has disordered me" (5). Almost as though to demystify the very concept of the heroine, the novelist uses the comic character of Win to first present the details of Lydia's predicament, and her malapropian language denudes the heroine's predicament of all seriousness. Win, who in the course of her letters, as Lydia's confidante, provides a running commentary on the lovesick heroine and the various appearances of Wilson, places the situation in the turmoil of the household—right along with the misfortunes of Tabby's miserable dog, Chowder: "We have been all in a sad taking here at Glostar—Miss Liddy had like to have run away with a player-man, and young master and he would adone themselves a mischief; but the squire applied to the mare, and they were bound over" (7).

This unpropitious introduction of Lydia characterizes the antiheroic treatment that marks the perceptions of her brother Jery and uncle Matt. Neither ever sees her in grand terms. Neither gets beyond a surface impression to the kind of picture presented of her in her own letters. For both men she appears simply as a rather pathetic woman in need of their protection to defend her from her own weaknesses and the dangers of the great world. For all their concern for her and attentiveness to her, Lydia is never more than a decent young woman whose indiscretion with Wilson has placed her in a precarious position that their journey is intended to safeguard her against. To be sure, they have kind words for her, but not a very high regard for her intelligence or excessive praise for her beauty. At no point does she offer the breathtaking attractiveness of Smollett's other heroines. As a result, she emerges as more credible than any of the others, including Emilia.

Jery's physical descriptions of Lydia hardly celebrate a great beauty. Writing to his friend Sir Watkin Phillips in his very first letter, he portrays Lydia as "a fine, tall girl, of seventeen, with an agreeable person; but remarkably simple, and quite ignorant of the world" (8). Later, in his most favorable comments on her, at an assembly in Edinburgh, he does suggest that she presents an attractive figure for others, as he remarks, "nor did my sister Liddy pass unnoticed in the assembly—She is become a toast at Edinburgh, by the name of the Fair Cambrian, and has already been the occasion of much wine-shed" (224). Yet it seems no more than passing notice as it follows upon accolades for the glories of the fabulous Serafina (from Smollett's earlier *Ferdinand Count Fathom*) and her goddaughter, Fathom's daughter, who have accompanied Lydia to the ball. Of course, Jery's description of Lydia is that of a brother, and it is not remarkable that when Letty appears for the wedding, he finds her more attractive than Lydia: "a charming girl, and, in point of disposition, an agreeable contrast to my sister, who is rather too grave and sentimental for my turn of mind.—The other is gay, frank, a little giddy, and always good humoured" (346).

In Jery's eyes Lydia is the frail female, the poor creature in constant need of a man's advice and protection. And, indeed, in part she is as Smollett uses her in his play upon romance, but Jery never perceives that she is more than that. He recounts her weaknesses. After the fire in which Micklewhimmen, her aunt's suitor, makes a fool of himself, "Liddy fainted away" (176). Listening to Lismahago's ghastly tales about life with the Indians "threw my sister Liddy into a swoon" (194). Jery describes her reaction to the appearance at a ball by someone "the express image of that rascal Wilson": "She fainted away" (224). He fears for her mental health following the appearance of a Wilson look-alike: "Liddy is in a peaking way—I'm afraid this unfortunate girl is uneasy in her mind; and the apprehension distracts me" (230). When Matt takes Humphry and the three women to task for attending a Methodist service, Jery notes her "changed countenance," her "great trepidation" at her uncle's reaction and how she begs his forgiveness (137). She is, after all, as Matt puts it, a silly woman. Such beings are in need of a man's protection, and Lydia herself records Jery's coming to her rescue when a group of boat-dockers gets out of hand.

But Jery never does justice to Lydia's stronger characteristics, particularly her acute perception. After the discovery of Humphry's identity as Matt's natural son, a revelation costly to her inheritance, Jery describes, without noting its merit, her generous spirit in accepting her new cousin. He has no way of knowing that his sister has properly assessed a dual motivation in his opposition to her affair with Wilson: but his own admission that his response was as much a concern for "the honour of our family" (332) as for his sister's welfare simply bears out her own judgment that Jery's conduct, while "owing to his regard for my honour," was equally owing to his own "pride" (309).

Lydia certainly is not simply the foolish young girl that her brother believes. What he would never admit is that her intuition and judgment in regard to Wilson, as events demonstrated, were more accurate than his hot-tempered and ill-advised challenges to the young man. Lydia repeatedly asserts that Wilson has qualities belying his appearance as a mere player. Even in her worst moments of despair, she cannot accept Jery's judgments about her lover's motives and the reasons he has not come forth. Without acknowledging his sister's better judgment, he must admit how wrong he has been about Wilson/Dennison. In the end it is Jery confessing that his brother-in-law-to-be towers above him in virtue and is a paragon among men. In a novel playing out a theme of the relationship between appearance and reality, Lydia proves more perceptive about the truth of appearances.

If Jery's views of Lydia tend to make her less heroic than the general run of Smollett's heroines, less a glamorous beauty and more the pathetic young woman dependent upon men's protection, not surprisingly the Lydia emerging through Matt's eyes is equally distant from the idealized heroines of Smollett's fiction. Matt's paternalistic attitude is evident in his approbation of the social organization of the Scottish highlanders. He sees it as "founded on hereditary regard and affection, cherished through a long succession of ages." Expressing his admiration for the chiefs, he finds them receiving obeisance from their underlings "with all the ardour of filial love and veneration; while he, on his part, exerts a paternal authority, commanding, chastising, rewarding, protecting, and maintaining them as his own children" (255).

The passage could not be better designed to explain his relationship with his niece. As he protects her, he demonstrates his finest characteristics. The role she plays exhibits the tenderness underlying his otherwise seemingly gruff exterior. For him Lydia is the innocent female in need of masculine protection. Still, as his response to her objections to marrying Barton indicates, he feels he owes it to his ward, as any good Highlander chief is obliged to think of his followers' best interests, to permit her to make her own choice within the bounds of reason. Clearly, the situation alludes to Richardson's *Clarissa*, and Smollett makes evident his repudiation of the Harlowe family's unreasonable matrimonial demands upon the heroine that bring about the tragedy in the novel. Here, as Jery reports, "[Matt] thought that, in the choice of a husband, a young woman ought not to sacrifice the feelings of her heart for any consideration upon earth—'Liddy is not so desperate (said he) as to worship fortune at such an expence' " (140–41).

For all that, Matt does not regard Lydia as the complex young woman that she is. As he perceives her, indeed, she bears few of the characteristics of the noble heroine, but merely presents a picture of a poor young creature whose gentle and tender nature requires his constant attention. Having abjured a system in which he must bear the burden of caring for the orphaned Jery and Lydia, he quickly shows the other side of his character as he expresses his despair at her "dangerous fit of illness" following her interrupted affair with Wilson. He offers a portrait of her that combines a description of her frailties and accomplishments—those appropriate to an eighteenth-century young lady, but hardly characteristic of the idealized heroine:

> She is a poor good-natured simpleton, as soft as butter, and as easily melted—not that she's a fool—the girl's parts are not despicable, and her education has not been neglected; that is to say, she can write and spell, and speak French, and play upon the harpsichord; then she dances freely, has a good figure, and is very well inclined; but, she's deficient in spirit, and so susceptible—and so tender forsooth!— Truly, she has got a languishing eye, and reads romances. (11–12)

From such a passage and from Jery's description of Lydia, the reader could hardly be prepared for the later comments in the novel by Mr. Dennison as he praises Lydia's beauty when she is about to marry his son: "one of the most lovely creatures I ever beheld" (328). Seeing Lydia through the eyes of a brother and uncle hardly provides a vehicle for emphasizing the kind of physical beauty associated with Smollett's other heroines.

Indeed, whatever the greater complexity in Lydia's character that Smollett manages to convey, it is clear from Matt's letters that the novelist himself simply regards her as significant less as a character than as an instrument for other fictional purposes. Her presence in the work allows Smollett to reveal Matt's true nature, to provide a narrative thread that binds the novel's structure, and to permit a running satire on romance. Indeed, Matt's views focus on the romantic heroine's weaknesses—allowing Smollett to carry on his play on the genre of the sentimental novel and, at the same time, bring forth his own brand of sentimentality in presenting those characteristics of Matt that expose him as the good-natured man in the tradition of Oliver Goldsmith's play and the *Vicar of Wakefield*. As Matt sees her, Lydia is an innocent victim of her inexperience and excessive emotions. He bemoans her having gone to a boarding school, "which, next to a nunnery, is the worst kind of seminary that ever was contrived for young women"; being "so long cooped up [there] . . . she became as inflammable as touch-wood" (12). Displaying his own class-consciousness, Matt objects especially to Wilson, whom he believes to be a strolling player. Still, with obvious sympathy, he contrasts his own kindness with Tabby's behavior as her chastisement has caused her niece to behave as any heroine of sentimental romance: "[she] first swooned away, then dissolving in a flood of tears" (14). He goes on to describe with concern the illness brought on by the trials of her romance.

Matt's tenderness develops throughout his response to Lydia. Surely, there is something autobiographical in Smollett's treatment of the relationship.[45] *Humphry Clinker* was written following the death of his daughter Elizabeth, and Matt's gentleness toward Lydia, coming from the character who most resembles the author, appears to serve as a vehicle for expressing Smollett's deeply personal feelings. Indeed, when Matt perceives Lydia's affection for him after he has been rescued from an accident, he accepts Lydia as a daughter rather than simply a niece.[46] At any rate, Matt's repeated concern for his niece characterizes the softer side of his nature throughout the novel. Writing from Bath, he declares that his willingness to go to London stems from a desire "to give Liddy a glimpse of London. She is one of the best hearted creatures I ever knew, and gains upon my affection every day" (54). When Lydia confesses having secretly met Wilson and promises never again to correspond with him without her uncle's knowledge and approval, Matt easily forgives her and accepts her apology, which is accompanied "with a flood of tears" (144–45). Her tears and fears repeatedly move Matt and bring out his best instincts. Seeing her terrified by his wrath when she has attended Methodist services, he responds by placing the blame on Tabby, finding her aunt "the sole conductress of this machine" (137–38). He truly does not know what goes on inside her, attributing her shaken condition after the appearance of Wilson's look-alike to a cold, but he is clearly upset that "Something uncommon is the matter with that poor child; her colour fades, her appetite fails, and her spirits flag.—She is become mopey and melancholy, and is often found in tears" (235). Not even Jery's accurate judgment in this instance puts Matt on the right track. He regards Lydia as a fragile heroine of sentimental romance, and she fulfills the role. Fearing that her sudden meeting with Wilson as Dennison will try her "delicate nerves," he tries to ease the surprise. He is not wrong about the effect as she greets her lover "trembling in the utmost confusion" (329) as she "blushed, and trembled, and faultered" (330).

Perhaps a comparison of Lydia's and Matt's letters from Bath and London best illustrates the major function that Lydia plays in the novel. In order for her character development to be meaningful as evidence of Matt's ultimately sound judgment, Smollett must make her more substantial than the frivolities of tearfulness and fainting would suggest. He accomplishes that effectively—apart from the insights offered in her own letters—by providing Matt's account of her strength and intelligence in her encounter with the officious and determined Lady Griskin, who attempts to press the case for a marriage with Barton. With evident pleasure, Matt reports Lydia's rebuff: "I beg your ladyship's pardon, (exclaimed Liddy, with great vivacity) I have nothing to expect from such a measure, and I hope my guardians will have too much compassion to barter my peace of mind for any consideration of interest or fortune" (144). Devoid of any foolishness or weakness, her words mark her underlying strength and intelligence whatever her kinship to the sentimental and mindless heroines of romance.

The letters themselves (33–38, 38–42, 45–48, 86–90, 90–95), frequently and justly described as among the novel's chief comic delights, shrewdly play off age against youth and experience against innocence. Where Lydia is awed by the crowds, activities, and fashions, for Matt (and Smollett) these betoken the leveling of society, the indulgence in luxury, and the disappearance of civility. Both Matt and Lydia recognize their responses may well be shaped by age and health. Still, they focus upon what interests them. For Lydia it is the astonishments of architecture she has never seen and sights of unimaginable "splendour and variety" (91). For Matt it is all a kind of decadence worthy of his sermonizing.

Nevertheless, and it is significant for Lydia's later attitudes, even at her highest point of excitement, she hints at feelings that echo his. It is an important point for demonstrating Smollett's concern for verisimilitude in her character and not merely, as some critics have argued, a sign of a sudden maturation in her character at the end of the novel.[47] Although she recovers quickly from the "head-ach and vertigo" (39) that she experiences in Bath, Lydia's ailment confirms Matt's lamentations about the incessant noise there. Despite her finding, as Matt does not, the spa-waters tasteful, she is put off by the "frightful" appearances of the ladies bathing in the hot water (39–40), much as Matt is dismayed by the evidence of illness marking the bathing and drinking water—"those ulcers, floating on the water" (45). For all the delight that she expresses—indeed, even in the manner in which she overexudes—Lydia serves to confirm what the mature Matt finds in the evidence of Bath and London.

In a way those points where Lydia subscribes to Matt's opinions foreshadow her late letter to Letty, when the journey has neared completion. Her summary of her feelings serves to confirm and validate Matt's view of their experience and to suggest that the experience has brought her closer to reality and his attitude toward life. It is no sudden revelation, but a gradual deepening of instincts that were already present. Expressing her tiredness with the "itinerant way of life," the "perpetual succession of objects" (307), she moves comfortably into Matt's evaluation: "Nature never intended me for the busy world—I long for repose and solitude, where I can enjoy that disinterested friendship which is not to be found among crowds, and indulge those pleasing reveries that shun the hurry and tumult of fashionable society—Unexperienced as I am in the commerce of life, I have seen enough to give me a disgust to the generality of those who carry it on—There is such malice, treachery, and dissimulation, even among professed friends and intimate companions, as cannot fail to strike a virtuous mind with horror; and when Vice quits the stage for a moment, her place is immediately occupied by Folly" (308). The words might well be Matt's and confirm, as intended, his view of reality. For those who believe Smollett mellowed in his final novel, they pose a solid rebuff.

Finally, whatever these letters from Bath and London do to demonstrate Lydia's function in developing Matt's character and underscoring Smollett's theme, they also create—along with her letters throughout—a dif-

ferent kind of Smollettian heroine. Smollett's epistolary technique reveals
Lydia's emotions, to get a view that does not simply come from others,
and to permit a genuine assessment of her maturation—none of which can
be said of her sister characters in Smollett's fiction.

It is in Lydia's novel that Smollett most clearly projects the ultimate
fate of his perfect heroines when he establishes his notion of the ideal wife
by providing examples of the good and bad helpmate and by finally indicating what path Lydia herself will follow. Matt Bramble's letters to his
correspondent Dr. Lewis about meeting in his travels with two old college
chums—first Baynard and then Dennison—permit Smollett to express his
ideas on the perfect spouse (the natural progression of the idealized heroine) even at the same time he develops the most significant theme of his
novel.

Smollett first sets forth his negative example in a long inset that offers
an exemplar of the luxury that he believes to be the greatest affliction of
his time. In the person of Baynard's wife, as John Sekora correctly points
out, there is the most complete delineation of "the vain triumphs of luxury," what today might be described as conspicuous consumerism whose
sole purpose is to demonstrate through materialistic greed a sense of superiority to the rest of society. As Sekora puts it, Mrs. Baynard's conduct
"reeks of social perversity."[48]

Bramble's description begins with an account of the lack of taste that
has converted Baynard's estate from an old Cistercian monastery into an
atrocious mixture of the classical and Gothic. It proceeds to a narrative
of the destruction of an essentially good but weak man by a woman of no
talents, but desperate ostentation. Having believed himself to have made
a "prudent marriage," Baynard discovers himself encumbered by a woman
whose demands can only lead to his destruction, and his kindness merely
encourages her worst vices. He imagines that he can change her by moving
from fashionable London society to life in the country. Nothing can control her. In Bramble's words, "her ruling passion was vanity, not that species which arises from self-conceit of superior accomplishments, but that
which is of a bastard and idiot nature, excited by shew and ostentation."

Place does not matter to her. Living in the country, she must outdo her
neighbors with a display of servants, equipage, and furnishings. Demanding a house in London and rebuffing her husband's designs for "a comfortable [and economic] plan of living," not impoverished but reasonable,
she gets her way with tears that Baynard is unable to resist. As a result,
they are "sucked deeper and deeper into the vortex of extravagance and
dissipation, leading what is called a fashionable life in town." A European
journey to save expenses only increases the demands for luxury as she
now must compete with royalty, to "be on the same footing with the
counts, marquises, and cavaliers."

Their household, along with their way of life, is a disaster wrought by her affectation and his inability to withstand her insatiable desires. They are surrounded by "a mob of beings pleased with rattles, baubles, and gew-gaws, so void of sense and distinction, that even the most acute philosophy would find it a very hard task to discover for what wise purpose of providence they were created." Devastating as a wife, Mrs. Baynard is also a failure as a mother. Their son, "a shambling, blear-eyed boy, [is] very rude, forward and impertinent." Despite Baynard's desire to send him to a boarding school, Mrs. Baynard insists on keeping him at home, coddling and protecting him. Nor is she any better as a hostess. Her conduct and hospitality outrage Bramble. "Ungracious indifference," along with affectation, characterizes her social behavior.

For Bramble Mrs. Baynard "was dead to all the genuine sentiments of conjugal affection; insensible of her own honour and interests, and seemingly destitute of common sense and reflection" (285ff.). Having excoriated her behavior in his account of his visit with Baynard, Matt resumes his attack after her death when he is called upon to straighten out Baynard's affairs. He details the extravagance of her addiction to luxury. His list is like an accountant's report of a nightmare of bankruptcy. Ridding the estate of supernumerary servants, selling off her jewels and unnecessary furniture, he provides a convincing picture of the lifestyle that has brought financial ruin to Baynard. What, after all, could be more conclusive than the fact that the "clothes, laces, and linen" that Baynard's wife leaves to her maid are valued at "five hundred pounds, at a moderate computation"! (342).

While the main focus of Bramble's account fixes on the luxury that characterizes Mrs. Baynard's behavior, thus supporting the theme of the novel, it also indicates Smollett's own notion of marital relationships and his expectations of a good wife.[49] To be sure, Mrs. Baynard is an extreme example of the bad wife, but she also suggests the novelist's general fear of a woman's manipulation of her husband. Indeed, Smollett emphasizes his dread of a wife's domination as he presents examples of the manner in which not only Mrs. Baynard, but two of her friends, manipulate the men that they have married:

Mr. Baynard was subjugated by practising upon the tenderness of his nature. Mr. Milksan, being of a timorous disposition, truckled to the insolence of a termagant. Mr. Sowerby, who was of a temper neither to be moved by fits, nor driven by menaces, had the fortune to be fitted with a helpmate, who assailed him with the weapons of irony and satire; sometimes sneering in the way of compliment; sometimes throwing out sarcastic comparisons, implying reproaches upon his want of taste, spirit, and generosity. (294)

Not only for Bramble, but for Smollett, as well, there were more ways than one of a cunning woman turning a man into "a pitiable wretch"

(294). Much better, Matt believes, as he describes the wife of another friend Sir Thomas Bullford, for a man to be fortunate enough to find "a good-natured sensible woman, with whom he lives upon very easy terms" (297).

Such a woman, indeed, is the wife of Dennison, Matt's other college chum and the father of the young man Lydia is to marry. The inset, carried in two letters and balanced by Matt's and then Dennison's comments, neatly serves Smollett in a number of ways. To begin with it offers the kind of balance that characterizes the novel as a whole: seeing the same circumstances from varied points of view. In conveying Smollett's theme of an attack on luxury the Dennison story contrasts with that of Baynard. And, finally, the opposition of the Dennisons' and Baynards' marital relationships relieves Smollett of what his readers might otherwise regard as a sign of his misogyny by offering an example of his idealized notion of woman's role in marriage that would be consistent with the conventional views of his contemporaries.[50]

Although far more limited in its details of Mrs. Dennison herself than in those of Mrs. Baynard—evil being more interesting than good—Smollett's account clearly juxtaposes the characters of the two women and their effects upon their households. Coming as they do after the discussion of Mrs. Baynard, Matt's very first words about Mrs. Dennison make apparent the intended comparison: "He [Dennison] is blessed with a consort, whose disposition is suited to his own in all respects; tender, generous, and benevolent—She, moreover, possesses an uncommon show of understanding, fortitude, and discretion, and is admirably qualified to be his companion, confidant, counsellor, and coadjutrix."

Both the attack on luxury and assertion of the wife's appropriate role in the marriage stand plainly evident in Matt's description of the Dennisons' way of life (320ff.). Dennison, it should be noted, takes the initiative in decision making, but his wife is there to support the measures he decrees. When financial circumstances become difficult in city-living, he, "with the approbation of his wife, immediately determined to quit business, and retire into the country." It is he who disdains the luxury of the fashion and expense of being "upon the footing of a gentleman." Again it is Dennison who rejects urgings by others that "were chiefly founded on the supposition, that he would be obliged to lead a life of extravagance and dissipation, which he and his consort equally detested, despised, and determined to avoid." He is under no pressure from Mrs. Dennison to vie with his neighbors. She apparently has no desire—or at least expresses none—to follow the latest fashions in dress or to yield to the "oppressive imposition of ridiculous modes, invented by ignorance, and adopted by folly."

When the words are Dennison's rather than Matt's (325ff.), the picture remains unchanged of a sensible, undemanding wife who cheerfully fulfills her household and maternal duties. Where the Baynards' domicile has suffered from Mrs. Baynard's demands for "improvements," that of the Dennisons reflects good taste. Dennison notes his wife's accommodation and adjustment to country life despite his fears that she would react otherwise. Instead of seeking out fashionable company, she has found companionship in a congenial, honest, and simple country woman as a neighbor. Dennison expresses his satisfaction with the life they have chosen and declares, to his and presumably Smollett's satisfaction, how his friends might enjoy the same circumstances were it not for "the pride, envy, and ambition of their wives and daughters." Thus, the pitfalls of vanity and luxury reside in the nature and desires of women.

To clinch the importance of a woman's playing her appropriate role in life, Smollett offers the effect of the mother on her offspring. Whereas Mrs. Baynard's son has been spoiled by his affected mother, Mrs. Dennison has reared a noble youth—one certainly worthy to be the husband of Matt's niece. It is not unimportant for the rounding out of Smollett's plot in *Humphry Clinker*. As Jery describes him, young Dennison surely deserves the praise given to him in both Matt's and Dennison's earlier comments:

[He is] one of the most accomplished young fellows in England. His person is at once elegant and manly, and his understanding highly cultivated. Tho' his spirit is lofty, his heart is kind; and his manner so engaging, as to command veneration and love. . . . When I weigh my own character with his, I am ashamed to find myself so light in the balance. (332)

No wonder that a household so in order should provide the place of tutelage for Baynard when his wife's death has set him free to pursue a new life. It is Mrs. Dennison that Smollett's heroines will become after their marriages, for she is the model that Smollett has designed for them to emulate, a carrying on of their perfection. Lydia, in fact, as she informs her friend, is clearly destined to follow her way of life when the adventures of *Humphry Clinker* come to an end.

3

Fallen Women and Women as Victims

Like his heroines Smollett's fallen women generally fit into a pattern of patriarchal stereotyping. By midcentury such characters had become stock figures in art and literature, and in a society with a sexual double standard the victim was frequently further victimized by the artist. William Hogarth's *The Harlot's Progress*, a series of six engravings, presents a good example of how women are largely made responsible for a fate frequently brought on by men's duplicity. Hogarth's innocent young woman falls easy prey to the predatory, sophisticated members of a cynical society. As Hogarth makes clear, however, she contributes significantly to her downfall. Like all women, the cliché goes, she cannot withstand temptation and flattery, an inheritance from Eve. Hogarth—like the satirists of his day, including Samuel Johnson in his "Vanity of Human Wishes"—regards woman as hopelessly vain, an addict of romantic illusions, a body driven by passion rather than governed by reason and common sense. Hogarth's harlot's decline, less intended to convey sympathy than to provide admonition to careless young virgins, is swift and inevitable. She moves from a fashionable bedroom to ugly quarters in a Drury Lane brothel. Poverty leads to Bridewell Prison, and venereal disease terminates in a disgraceful death.

Smollett does not escape the Hogarthian didacticism with its lessons for women. Indeed, the generality of fiction in the period, whether by men or women, made the same point when dealing with seduced maidens.[1] For Smollett, as the many fallen women in *Ferdinand Count Fathom* attest, women's vanity was their primary weakness. For him, too, their emotions once aroused were difficult to curb, and it was the special mark of a heroine that, like Emilia, she could manage that. Women's minds, Smollett clearly believed, were very susceptible to romantic illusions. The excessive emotionalism of a writer like Shaftesbury and an unfettered imagination let loose by romances represented an inescapable threat to their well-being. Who could tell where a fevered brain might guide an emotionally aroused body? Examples abound in Smollett—not only those who yield to temptation, like Celinda or Elinor in *Fathom*, but those who come close and are saved only by an underlying good sense or fortunate circumstances, like Lydia in *Humphry Clinker*. For Smollett women must always be saved from themselves, protected from their own worst instincts. Smollett regards them as the symbols of commodification in his society. He uses them as threats to the social order in their tendencies toward luxury, that debilitating effeminacy that he regarded as endangering his John Bull England.[2] With all their vulnerability, he saw them as particularly open to sexual failings.

Yet for all the stereotyping, Smollett's fallen women present a surprising variety, emerging as with all his female characters from the differences in their functions in the novels, their representations of different social classes, and the kinds of details that he employs to distinguish them from each other. Like a good many of his contemporary female novelists, Smollett obviously also uses their tales to create a realism and salaciousness to appeal to his readers. He employs long insets—like those of Miss Williams in *Roderick Random* and Lady Vane's in *Peregrine Pickle*—as counterparts to and commentaries on the adventures of his heroes. In true masculine fashion, typical of the more general male attitudes of his day, he relates the sexual conquests of his heroes to a demonstration of their manhood. Ever class-conscious, Smollett repeatedly suggests that the sexual morality of women of the lower social orders reflects the values of their class. Contrasting their picaresque conduct with the idealized behavior of his heroines, Smollett adds to the sense of purity demanded of his heroes' brides.

Still, whatever the class of Smollett's fallen women, the reasons for their fall—in the values of a sexual double standard that the novelist applies—result from female weaknesses that it would be unreasonable to expect men to disregard. Smollett is not insensitive as a writer or a person. Certainly he expresses repeatedly in his work and in his personal relationships his detestation of prostitution and his anger with the physical abuse of women.[3] Nevertheless, in his general view of sex Smollett responds with a very masculine assertiveness—indicated, for example, in the conclusions of his novels—of the dominance of his sex. Underlying that response is the eighteenth-century sensibility to the notion of the relationships of sex and power.

The character of the fallen woman or woman as victim does not exist in *Sir Launcelot Greaves* and receives limited treatment, although playing a significant narrative role, in *Humphry Clinker*. The absence of the type is not surprising in *Greaves*. Although corruption and social satire abound in the novel, the pristine character of Smollett's quixotic knight would make the intrusion of sex seem unnatural in the work. To be sure, it is not inconceivable that Greaves's adventures might include an episode in which the hero comes to the rescue of a woman victimized by the sexual code of Smollett's society. Nevertheless, it is understandable that the novelist might conclude that such material might jar the idealized content that marks Launcelot's conduct in his adventures. While the knight battles heroically against such evils in society as the misuse of madhouses and abuses of the law, he never appears to have a sexual thought in his pursuit of the vestal heroine. The closest the novel comes to raising questions of sexuality is in its treatment of the earthy and obviously sensuous maid, Dolly Cowslip, in her romance with the young lawyer, Tom Clarke. But even there, the hints of Dolly's sexual nature are limited—just sufficient to underscore by contrast the angelic purity of Launcelot's Aurelia.

It is more difficult to comprehend Smollett's failure to employ the type in detail in *Humphry Clinker*. Here he could easily have used the example of the fallen woman to delineate the dangers confronting Lydia, the romantic heroine, in her surreptitious engagement with Wilson before he is revealed as a gentleman. Matt could certainly have found a means to point out to his niece the vulnerability of her position by comparing it to an available sample of a fallen woman. Then, too, Smollett could have played off the type against the predatory adventures of Matt's husband-hungry sister, Tabby, as she exposes herself to disaster in her reckless pursuit of matrimony. Surely, Tabby's case might have offered entertaining comic possibilities.

While it is tempting to suggest that the epistolary technique of the novel might have precluded treatment of the topic, the evidence suggests otherwise. Jery, Matt's nephew, should naturally have raised the subject of prostitution in his letters to his young Oxford friend as he describes the variety of scenes in London and Bath. How strange that Jery should not have noticed the street-walkers and prostitutes in the same London that James Boswell explored in regular nightly rounds for easy sexual gratification with the ladies of the night who seem omnipresent in his diary accounts. It is not that Jery is a model of purity—he is hardly Sir Launcelot Greaves—because he informs Watkins, his Oxford chum, that he is willing to pay off an Oxford prostitute who is falsely accusing him of fathering her baby. Although innocent of the charge—while accusing another friend—he cavalierly suggests, like any eighteenth-century gentleman, that the subject can be put to rest through monetary measures: "if the woman should be abandoned enough to swear his bantling to me, I must beg the favour of you to compound with the parish: I shall pay the penalty without repining" (28). When his somewhat unbalanced accuser announces that she is not pregnant, Jery jocularly expresses not relief, but rather disappointment in losing his reputation for potency: "for though my being thought capable of making her a mother, might have given me some credit, the reputation of an intrigue with such a cracked pitcher does me no honour at all" (59). Smollett, like Henry Fielding, looks kindly on the young gallant as seducer so long as his heart is in the right place and he is willing to pay for the offspring.[4]

It is that same masculine double standard that characterizes the one genuine story of the fallen woman in the novel, a tale crucial to its narrative development. It is Matt's discovery that the eponymous Humphry Clinker is his natural son. The revelation rounds out the work and seems to purge Matt's physical-psychological ills. On learning of Humphry's true identity—a child born out of Matt's affair with "Dorothy Twyford... heretofore barkeeper at the Angel at Chippenham" (317–18)—Matt accepts his responsibility as an eighteenth-century gentleman, but true to the type does not grieve excessively over a kind of conduct natural to youth of that class.

To be sure, Matt laments having left the woman and her child to their own devices because of his ignorance of the facts. But that is no more than to say that he would have provided money for them. When he introduces Humphry to Tabby as his son, his words hardly suggest great remorse: "the rogue proves to be a crab of my own planting in the days of hot blood and unrestrained libertinism" (319). There is almost a tone of nostalgia in Matt's remarks as there certainly is in his letter to his old friend Dr. Lewis. Writing to Lewis he describes Dennison, Lydia's future father-in-law, as "our fellow-rake at Oxford." On Humphry as his natural son, his words boastfully pronounce: "It is not without some reason what we Welchmen ascribe such energy to the force of blood." Indeed, for Smollett hot blood was perfectly normal for young gentlemen, but the same fluid in young women extracted a bitter price. Here, there is no great pity for the plight of Dorothy Twyford. The dead woman is dismissed in a single sentence in which Matt regrets that his having changed his name in response to matters concerning his estate has caused his natural son and "thy poor mother" to "have been left to want and misery" (318). Matt's response is the normal expression of a gentleman, almost wistfully recalling his youthful sowing of wild oats and clearly believing that his willingness to accept his offspring, a symbol of his sexual prowess, is sufficient unto the cause. With obvious pride, he boasts to Jery "that betwixt the age of twenty and forty, he had been obliged to provide for nine bastards, sworn to him by women whom he never saw" (28). Pleased, at least by his youthful reputation, he takes pleasure now in his letter to Dr. Lewis in being able to say, "that among all the follies and weaknesses of human nature, I have not yet fallen into that of matrimony" (294). Commenting on Matt's views on sexual love, John Sekora has it just right, that it must be considered for what it brings socially and politically, but is not a "good in itself."[5] That is an eighteenth-century gentleman's judgment.

When all the facts are considered, then, it proves not so remarkable that the novel offers no other examples of the fallen woman. It is understandable that Matt—like Jery—can present a picture of Bath and London without remarking on the thriving trade in prostitution, while he blasts every other aspect of what he regards as the sinfulness and corruption of those places. For his narrative purposes, his leading to the climax of *Humphry Clinker*, Smollett steers clear of the topic until he springs it as a surprise to bring the various strands of his novel to a conclusion.

If the topic is barely touched upon in these two novels, Smollett more than compensates for the absence in his account of his most vicious character, in which the novelist clearly recognizes the relationship between sex and masculine power. Indeed, nowhere in Smollett's novels do fallen women and female victims play a more significant role than in *Ferdinand Count Fathom*, the moral fable that sets the villainous eponymous antihero against the virtuous Melvil family,[6] particularly the flawless Renaldo and his angelic fiancée, Serafina (Monimia). As examples of the "succession of vitious objects" (3)[7] that delineate Fathom's reprehensible character, women repeatedly fall victim to his picaresque guile and deviousness, his ability to discern weaknesses in his targets and to strike almost unerringly at their most vulnerable points.[8] For Smollett they serve not only to mark the degenerate character of his antihero, but to provide for the picaresque plot that enables him to recount the various changes in Fathom's fortunes, and to permit the author to expand the satiric scope of his novel. Female vanity, women's excessive imaginations, their vulnerability to romantic notions provide a large part of the satire in the novel and suggest Smollett's overall view of the sex.

To be sure, men are not immune to Fathom's treacherous charms. Among those whom he dupes are Count Melvil (Renaldo's father), Don Diego (Serafina's father), and Renaldo, but in each circumstance the male character is betrayed as a result of his own virtue. Nowhere are they made to appear as ridiculous as the fashionable ladies of London or the women in the Melvil household. For the former his false charms are such that "no lady, whether widow, wife, or maiden, ever mentioned his name, without some epithet of esteem or affection; such as *the dear Count! the charming Man! the Non-pareil! or the Angel!*" (150). The latter look upon the young Fathom as a model for the honest and unpretentious Renaldo to follow as they "propose young Fathom, as pattern," unaware, as Smollett puts it, of Renaldo's "own superiority in those qualifications which seemed of more real importance than the mere exteriors and forms of life" (19). Clearly, Smollett regards these women of the Melvil household as easily susceptible to the appearances of charm.

Only women of special qualities or protected by particular circumstances can withstand Fathom's assaults, and even they have their vulnerability. Both Serafina and Mademoiselle de Melvil, Renaldo's sister, manage to hold off his attacks. For Smollett it is not unimportant that they have an awareness of their social superiority to Fathom, for the novelist indicates that the predator's easiest victims are more generally members of a lower class. While Serafina, whose particulars have already been discussed in the previous chapter, comes close to being undone in her relationship with Renaldo through Fathom's schemes, she never is capable of willingly succumbing to his advances. The only way for him to have her would be through force and that fails. Her sense of class and her devotion even to what she believes to be an unfaithful Renaldo prove barriers to Fathom's designs. Through several chapters (VI–X) devoted to the villain's pursuit of Renaldo's sister's virtue, Smollett clearly demonstrates how her "appropriate" pride in her family's social position and her solid common sense protect her from Fathom. Although vulnerable to the thievery of Fathom and his household accomplice, she cannot otherwise be taken advantage of by him. That reasonableness that permits her ultimately to enter into a marriage of convenience (apparently approved of by Smollett) serves to defend her from Fathom's attempts to seduce her. Even in her illness the young woman's common sense and social pride enable her to reject his subtle advances.

Less fortunate are a host of other women in the novel. Smollett does not even bother to detail all of Fathom's "conquests." When Fathom ingratiates himself to the vacationers at Bristol through his affectation of medical knowledge, Smollett satirizes the gullibility, particularly of women, misled by the powers of the imagination. Fathom, Smollett tells the reader, "enjoyed free access, egress and regress, with all the families at the well, and no matron scrupled to put her daughter under his care and direction." Rather than recount the particulars of Fathom's triumph over the imaginations of these women, Smollett summarizes his antihero's taking advantage of his opportunities; "though he conducted his amours with such discretion, that during the whole season, no lady's character suffered on his account: yet he was highly fortunate in his addresses; and we may venture to affirm, that the reproach of barrenness was more than once reversed by the vigour of his endeavors" (167–68). Similarly, Smollett employs a kind of shorthand to represent a pattern of Fathom's nefarious behavior and women's susceptibility to it when he recounts, in less than half a paragraph, the villain's hasty departure for England. It was "hastened by the importunities, threatened reproaches of his landlord's daughter, whom he had debauched under promise of marriage, and now left in the fourth month of her pregnancy" (127). Servant girls and landlords' daughters were easy prey to Fathom's false charms and empty promises—unprotected by either social status or the ability to repress romantic emotions. For Fathom these games are less concerned with pleasure than with the exercise of power, an exhibition of his control.

Smollett does detail to great effect for both his narrative development and description of character Fathom's sexual alliances with a variety of women of the lower social orders and invariably the adventures turn on the weaknesses, as he—and Smollett perhaps—perceives them, of the female sex. Fathom's first triumph is with Teresa, four years older than he, a servant in the Melvil household whom he enlists in his scheme to seduce Renaldo's sister in order to force her into marriage. Together they scheme to pillage Mademoiselle de Melvil's possessions, to place the blame on other servants, and to give Fathom greater access to the young woman's confidence. With Teresa there is not a good deal of virtue to overcome. For her, as Boucé notes, Smollett appears to adopt the notions of female sexual criminology from traditional English Puritanism.[9] She "possessed a good stock of cunning and discernment, and was furnished by nature with a very amorous complexion" (27). In itself, that is the greatest danger in a woman for Smollett and his contemporaries. When Smollett speaks of the "coquetries" and artifice she employs to attract Fathom, he goes beyond her description to make a more general comment on women: her playing "upon all those little arts, by which a woman strives to attract the admiration and ensnare the heart of a man she loves" (27). For all of Teresa's toughness, for all of the fact that Fathom perceives that she "was as great a latitudinarian as himself in point of morals and principles" (29), she is no match for the villain. She is, after all, a woman—unequal, without heaven's support, to a man even in terms of cunning and deceit. It is Fathom who knows how to appeal to "her love of pleasure and curiosity" (29). Seeking to bind him to her, the servant girl demands conventional propriety and insists on marriage. Smollett scoffs at her foolishness when Fathom gets her to agree to secret vows: "Surely nothing could be more absurd or preposterous, than the articles of this covenant" (30). After Fathom has left her and she has been briefly successful in continuing to steal from her mistress, Teresa ultimately goes too far, becomes too self-confident, and falls. It is a sorry spectacle of a deceitful servant girl who has been outwitted and used by the picaresque villain for whom she has been a tool and no match.

With the affair with Wilhelmina, a jeweler's daughter, and her stepmother, Smollett elevates his tale of fallen women and female victims on the social scale, this time to play upon the luxury-loving merchant class. Fathom's seductive attacks on the two women in order to bilk the merchant, a device not unusual for the picaresque novelist, underscores Smollett's view of the vanity and jealousy that characterize woman's nature. Entering the household, Fathom assesses the situation in terms that appear to convey Smollett's own sentiments: "he well knew that no road lies so direct and open to a woman's heart, as that of gratifying her passions of vanity and resentment" (45). As Fathom works one woman against the other—appealing to each in turn and using their jealousy to advance his purposes—the results support Smollett's observation.

Smollett links the fortunes of the two women as they fall into Fathom's hands. They share an excess of passion and a resentment of each other.

Their vanity and ignorance accommodate Fathom's purpose. Smollett's treatment of the stepmother, briefer than that of Wilhelmina, nevertheless makes many of the same points. When he says of the older woman, "the reader will not ... be surprised at the rapidity of his conquest over the affections of a lady whose complexion was perfectly amorous, and whose vanity laid her open to all the attempts of adulation" (53), the words might be applied equally to Wilhelmina. Fathom uses the same technique to seduce both women so that they appear ultimately to be begging to be taken by him. When Fathom has triumphed over them, they are linked as examples of how well he has learned his craft "from nature" (61). Still, the older woman is portrayed in more unflattering terms as Smollett dwells upon her "suspicious" nature, "braced by hatred and envy" (64). She continues for some time to be deceived by Fathom because of her vanity" (68), and when Smollett is finally done with her, his term to describe her is a "virago" (70).

The novelist, however, focuses on Wilhelmina. While no Teresa in terms of her criminality, she shares the other woman's passionate nature, that generally feared characteristic in the sex and one expected to be curbed. Smollett leaves no doubt about Wilhelmina's sexual nature. He speaks of her and Fathom's "mutual enjoyment" and recounts her emotions as she admits him to her chamber: she "waited for him with a lover's impatience" (49). Desiring respectability on the same terms Teresa had demanded, she would hold out for marriage, but even before Fathom can employ the same ruse that he had used to deceive Teresa, she yields to his artistry so "that before her passion could obtain a legal gratification, she surrendered to his wish, without any other assurance, than his solemn profession of sincerity and truth" (49). Her open enjoyment of sex runs counter to general eighteenth-century notions about women's emotions.

Like all Smollett's fallen women, Wilhelmina is most vulnerable to flattery. In response to Fathom's glowing tributes, so excessive that the diction resembles the mock-heroic,[10] she reveals a combination of her passionate nature, inexperience, and limited intelligence: "The nymph, whose passions nature had filled to the brim, could not hear such a rhapsody unmoved: being an utter stranger to addresses of this kind, she understood every word of it, in the literal acceptation; she believed implicitly in the truth of the encomiums he had bestowed" (47). When Fathom follows up his verbal assault on her passions and finds her capitulating, his language is ludicrously excessive. Lewis Knapp has noted its approximation to dramatic blank verse, and Smollett's editor finds it altogether unsatisfactory to the context (372, n. to p. 48). However, that was precisely Smollett's point since the satire underscores Wilhelmina's simple-mindedness and lack of sophistication, the fact that she was "unskilled in the ways of man" (48). Indeed, that simple- mindedness is evident in her superstitious nature when she is frightened into believing Fathom is the devil after he emerges from the chimney in which he has hidden in her chamber. How appropriate it is that when Wilhelmina reappears at the end of the novel, she has taken her vows in a convent, the same one that Mademoiselle de Melvil is grateful to have been rescued from after being cast away there by a cruel stepfather. For anyone familiar with Smollett's views of Roman Catholicism as a religion of supernatural nonsense, Wilhelmina's residence proves a commentary on her character.

While Smollett's presentation of Wilhelmina's seduction offers some sympathy for the character, it also indicates his view that the victimized woman—equally apparent in his long inset of Miss Williams' narrative in *Roderick Random*, a sympathetic portrait—plays a role, through her character faults, in her own downfall. The pattern emerges clearly in Smollett's account of the seductions of a clergyman's wife, Celinda, and Elinor in *Fathom*. Within a couple of pages Smollett describes Fathom's undoing of an unnamed clergyman's wife as the antihero plays the role of a doctor. Although Smollett emphasizes Fathom's "delusive arts" and notes that "her mind was enervated by sickness," he also attributes blame to the victim, who "fell a sacrifice to her own security and self-conceit" and an overaroused "imagination" (264). As though that were not enough, he attributes her downfall to her reading, stressing not only her conceit, but the dangers of the kind of romances that were adulterating public taste and morals: unguided "by any person of taste, she had indulged her own fancy without method or propriety" (264–65). Like the bluestocking women whom Smollett distrusted, she relied on her own abilities to shape her reading material to her purposes: "The Spectator taught her to be a critick and philosopher; from plays she learned poetry and wit; and derived her knowledge of life from books of history and adventure." Worst of all, like those bluestocking contemporaries of Smollett, she permitted her hubris to allow her to believe herself ready to compete with men whose company she deliberately sought. For the novelist such conduct suggested that "she despised her own sex" (265). Small wonder that she proves an easy victim for Fathom.

All of the above indicates the satiric thrust of Smollett's treatment. In a few paragraphs he has ridiculed the affectations of a woman attempting to compete in a man's world; he has scoffed at the circle of bluestockings; and he has taken a sharp jab at popular reading tastes, particularly for romances. The conclusion of the lady's sad story allows Smollett to enlarge his satiric field. When the clergyman's wife, torn by her conscience, confesses to her husband, he behaves nobly to her because she appears dreadfully ill and near death. However, when she recovers, his hypocrisy takes over, and he can no longer tolerate a wife "self-convicted of the violation of the matrimonial contract" (266). Forgetting his own commentary on the woman's actions, Smollett snidely ridicules the response of the townspeople of fashion, who insist that because she was unattractive, she must have made the first advances and conclude, "she was always a pert minx, that affected simplicity, and a masculine manner of speaking" (267). For Smollett the final benefit of the episode is its role in pointing his plot toward its conclusion. From this point on, Fathom's fortunes are irretrievably on the descendent and his ultimate decline inescapable.

In Fathom's debauching of Celinda, Smollett plainly concentrates his attack on what he regards as the falsities of romances, but even here the victim is made to share the blame for her disgrace. In some ways Celinda shares the characteristics of Smollett's heroines. Up to the point of Fathom's physical attack, the narrative of their relationship resembles that of sentimental romances.[11] Her father is a country gentleman. She, "a very beautiful young creature" (157), "not only gave marks of uncommon capacity, but as she grew up, became more and more amiable in her person." Still, despite her beauty and accomplishments, she stands in peril. As the bastard daughter of the country gentleman, her position in the household is precarious. Vulnerable in her social position, she displays even greater weaknesses in "a total want of experience" and a "remarkable spirit of credulity and superstitious fear." More to Smollett's point and Fathom's advantage as the villain resolves "to undermine her innocence, that he might banquet his vicious appetite with the spoils of her beauty," she is burdened with an excess of sensibility, passions so overwhelming that "so delicate was the texture of her nerves, that one day, while Fathom entertained the company with a favourite air, she actually swooned with pleasure." For both Fathom and Smollett, "Such sensibility . . . must be diffused through all the passions of her heart" (158).

Using the excesses of her romantic emotions and her preternatural superstitions as points of vulnerability, Fathom overcomes her "purity of sentiment, [an] inviolable attachment to religion and virtue" (159). He employs "dismal stories of omens, portents, prophecies and apparitions" (159). He uses mysterious night music to derange a mind that Smollett declares "credulous enough to believe the most improbable tale of superstition!" (161). Throughout the narrative Smollett strikes at the extremes of fancy, the overwrought imagination that characterizes stories in the romance tradition. When Celinda yields innocently to Fathom as he pretends to protect her in bed from her dreaded fancies, Smollett moralizes with a cynical and satiric comment whose tone is that of Augustan common sense: "Such a commerce between two such persons of a different sex could not possibly be long carried on, without degenerating from the platonic system of sentimental love." (163) In the same manner he comments didactically on the victimized Celinda's situation:

The gradations towards vice are almost imperceptible, and an experienced seducer can strew them with such inticing and agreeable flowers, as will lead the young sinner on insensibly even to the most profligate stages of guilt. All therefore that

can be done by virtue, unassisted by experience, is to avoid every trial with such
a formidable foe, by declining and discouraging the first advances towards a particular correspondence with perfidious man. (163)

Without intending his comment to be ironic, Smollett offers the same
meaningless advice that the sylph provides to Belinda in Pope's *The Rape
of the Lock*: "Most beware of Man." What else is there for woman to
beware of? Little of Smollett's sympathy goes to the victim of Fathom's
perfidy. To be sure, the episode is designed to depict Fathom's reprehensible character. But the woman must bear the blame as she yields to all
the weakest characteristics of her sex. Check your emotions; control your
superstitions; do not put yourself in a situation in which you can be victimized, Smollett airily advises. After all, the key word in Smollett's di-
dactic statement is his depiction of Celinda as a "young sinner." Even in
his description of Celinda's later life—"quite abandoned by decency and
caution" and "every day more and more sensual and degenerate" (165)—
Smollett proves more censorious than understanding and forgiving. Her
ultimate downfall suggests Smollett's demands for her appropriate punishment.[12] The Celinda episode provides him with an opportunity to underscore Fathom's heinous nature and to satirize the exaggerated narratives
of romance, but it also indicates the novelist's failure in comprehending
the nature of a woman's emotions and experiences.

Ultimately, the most important fallen woman in Fathom's nefarious career is Elinor, but the actual tale of her seduction differs little from those
of the others. No more than the other women can she be absolved of
responsibility for her downfall. When she meets Fathom on a coach as a
fellow traveler, Elinor indicates her vulnerability immediately. Smollett's
description, however, again generalizes beyond the particular woman:
"The artful language of his eyes had raised in her breast certain fluttering
emotions, before she knew the value of her conquest [she believes he is
a count]; but now that his rank and condition were discovered, these transports were increased by the idea of vanity and ambition which are mingled
with the first seeds of every female constitution" (139). Spurred on by the
excesses of her imagination—also characteristic of her sex—and undermined by her lack of experience, the simple country girl (straight out of
the *Harlot's Progress*), proceeding to the city where she has no friends,
has no chance against the villain, who, despite her limited charms, "very
honestly marked her chastity for prey to his voluptuous passion" (139).

Smollett does nothing to diminish Fathom's evil—essential to his moral
fable—but Elinor plays a significance role in her own downfall. To be sure,
as the "conquest" follows the customary pattern, the antihero employs his
best devices to deceive her, gain her confidence, and assure her dependence on him. Still, even when she reproves "his advances with all the
marks of anger and disdain," Smollett notes "the passions she had begun

to indulge in his behalf" (140). The terms of her capitulation mark her as a co-conspirator in her own downfall. Passion and ambition lead to her submission—"she loved his person, she was dazzled by his rank" (142). Naive, she permits "freedoms ... out of pure simplicity and good humour, [and] permitted him to take [liberties] with her hand, and even her rosy lips, encouraged him to practise other familiarities upon her fair bosom, which scandalized her virtue" (140). But specially in the terms of her capitulation, Smollett remarks on the female nature that overcomes the "virtuous principles of her education":

all the bulwarks of her chastity were undermined, and she submitted to his desire; not with the reluctance of a vanquished people, but with all the transports of a joyful city, that opens its gates to receive a darling prince, returned from conquest; for by this time, he had artfully concentred and kindled up, all the inflammable ingredients of her constitution. (142)

But Elinor's main function in Smollett's novel is to allow the author to tie together the loose threads in his narrative. Despite his repeated attacks on romance, Smollett here—as in the rest of his work—does not hesitate to use its more ludicrous devices in service of resolving his plots and, indeed, to cater to his audience's taste. Cast aside by Fathom, suffering "the most violent transports of grief amid dismay" (147), Elinor is shunted off to Bedlam's madhouse until Smollett requires her reappearance at the novel's end. As she recounts her story to a forgiving Renaldo and Serafina, Elinor acts as intercessor for a repentant and seemingly mortally ill Fathom. She and her seducer have come together again in debtor's prison. Changed and contrite, Fathom has married her and they have struggled desperately to survive. With all their angelic beneficence, Renaldo and Serafina take the pair under their care and provide a settlement for them to allow them to retire to the country. Far-fetched in the most outlandish tradition of romance, the conclusion nevertheless permits Smollett to bring to a close a moral fable designed to show virtue's ultimate triumph over evil. Elinor, like all Smollett's female characters—fallen women and female victims, comic and grotesque figures, and heroines—serves a fictional purpose that focuses upon the adventures of male heroes.

The point remains true of even the two most extended uses of the fallen woman in Smollett's fiction: the lengthy inset of Miss Williams' tale in *Roderick Random* and the inclusion of the "Memoirs of a Lady of Quality" in *Peregrine Pickle*. Whatever other purposes these stories serve, they function, like all Smollett's female characters, to advance the narratives of his heroes, to draw forth their characters, and to develop the novel's theme. At the same time, the long insets offer good insights into Smollett's basic attitudes toward women, his class-consciousness even in that regard, and his ever-present concern for attracting a reading audience. In themselves the two narratives—one an example of male ventriloquism of the female voice and the other the open expressiveness of a woman's point of view—present an interesting contrast in narrative techniques.

Having first introduced Miss Williams through Roderick's eyes as a deceitful fortune hunter who has betrayed him into proposing marriage, Smollett permits another picture of her before he allows her to recount her story. Roderick's original comments on her in a portion of a paragraph merely present her as a"beautiful creature [who] passed for a rich heiress" (108) before he accidentally discovers her in bed with another man. When he next meets her and generously befriends her in her straitened circumstances, Roderick emphasizes his own emotional response to her. However, Smollett then permits her to speak and her contrition and her apologies to the hero neatly set up the reader's more sympathetic response to her narrative: "Dear Mr. Random, I do not deserve this concern at your hands—I am a vile creature, who had a base design upon your person—suffer me to expiate that and all my other crimes by a miserable death" (115–16).

Still, Smollett's interest in the scene is at least as much with demonstrating the tender side of his hero as it is to evoke sympathy for Miss Williams. Withholding her name until the subsequent chapter and denying her any description except for her woeful condition, Smollett uses the occasion to permit an expression of Roderick's softer sentiments: "Such extremity of distress must have waked the most obdurate heart to sympathy and compassion. What effect then must it have on mine, that was naturally prone to every tender passion?" (116) To be sure, Roderick behaves with becoming sympathy, but that is the point. Smollett's concern here, as throughout the novel, is not with Miss Williams's character, but rather with what her situation has to offer for the development of Roderick's character. Indeed, Roderick's treatment of Miss Williams marks the first significant sign of the benevolent side of his nature.[13]

Still, the episode successfully predisposes the reader in Miss Williams's favor prior to her recounting her history. As Roderick describes her conduct as they mutually tend to each other's needs, all his terms suggest that she is no ordinary prostitute and that her character deserves a better fate. Once more, Roderick emphasizes her beauty, but he reflects as well on her "good sense, and education" and remarks on the care with which she nursed him, giving evidence of her "fidelity and affection" (117).

Miss Williams's narrative bears out ultimately the favorable opinion that Roderick has formed of her character. Its purpose clearly is to advance Smollett's development of Roderick and to underscore his own methods in his storytelling, all of which makes Miss Williams herself seem incidental. In the two-part recounting of her experiences, Smollett employs the bifurcated technique that characterizes the entirety of his novel, a play between the excesses of the romance genre with its exaggerated and fantastic views of the world and the picaresque with its realistic and harsh vision of experience—a contrast between the world of unfettered imagination and the actualities of life.

In his preface to the novel, Smollett condemns romance: he ascribes "its origin to ignorance, vanity and superstition." He deplores its exaggerations and extravagances. Amidst the debauchery imposed by "priest-craft," romance reached an "absurd pitch of credulity" and its works were devoid of "probability" and abounded in the "most monstrous hyperboles" (xliii–xliv). The long chapter of Miss Williams's downfall, her seduction by a vicious "Lothario," exemplifies the dangers of romance to the innocent imagination, the threat to the unfettered excesses of fancy (Ch. XXII).

As Miss Williams tells it, she is the victim of her own imagination nurtured by her addiction to romances and encouraged by her guileless pride. Daughter of a tradesman whose business misfortunes brought about his retreat to his country estate, the remnant of his economic fortunes, she rebels against her strict Presbyterian training and falls prey first to the deistical writings of Shaftesbury,[14] Tindal, and Hobbes and then to the falsities of romance. When she is rescued by a stranger from the assault of a drunken squire, she glorifies her savior, seeing him wholly in terms of the heroes of romance. The diction of her description of his person savors the language of chivalry: "He was about the age of two and twenty, among the tallest of the middle-size; had chestnut coloured hair which he wore tied up in a ribbon; a high-polished for-head, a nose inclining to the acqualine, lively blue eyes, red pouting lips, teeth as white as snow, and a certain openness of countenance" (119). Gallahad could not have been more ideally envisioned by a young heroine whose susceptibility reveals itself in the unconscious sensuousness of the phrase depicting his "red pouting lips."

Describing the effect of her rescuer's conduct and physical presence on her imagination as it had been shaped by her reading, Miss Williams casts it in terms that display her kinship with Charlotte Lennox's heroine in *The Female Quixote*, a young woman whose sensibilities are wrought by her addiction to romances:

All night long my imagination formed a thousand ridiculous expectations: There was so much of knight-errantry in the gentleman's coming to the relief of a damsel in distress, with whom he immediately became enamoured, that all I had read of love and chivalry recurred to my fancy, and I looked upon myself as a princess in some region of romance, who being delivered from the power of a brutal giant or satyr by a generous Oroondates, was bound in gratitude, as well as led by inclination, to yield up my affections to him without reserve. In vain did I endeavor to chastise these foolish conceits by reflexions more reasonable and severe: The amusing images took full possession of my mind, and my dreams represented my hero sighing at my feet, in the language of a despairing lover. (119–20)

No "despairing lover," Lothario, of course, proves a vile seducer. Miss Williams, in the best romance tradition, does not detail the steps in her capitulation, saying that "a recital of the particular steps he pursued to ruin me, would be too tedious and impertinent." However, her reaction to her downfall has all the anguished language of the heroic dramas of Smollett's period, works like Nicholas Rowe's *The Fair Penitent*, to which he obviously was indebted. Not only the diction, but the very exclamation marks that punctuate the overwrought phrases suggest the romance tradition that Smollett found so dangerous to the imaginative reader:[15]

Cursed be the day on which I gave away my innocence and peace, for a momentary gratification which has entailed upon me such misery and horror! cursed be my beauty that first attracted the attention of the seducer! cursed be my education that by refining my sentiments, made my heart the more susceptible! cursed be my good sense that fixed me to one object, and taught me the preference I enjoyed was but my due! Had I been ugly, no body would have tempted me; had I been ignorant, the charms of my person would not have atoned for the coarseness of my conversation; had I been giddy, my vanity would have divided my inclinations, and my ideas would have been so diffused, that I should never have listened to the enchantments of one alone. (120–21)

Like Smollett the fallen woman places the blame for her seduction heavily upon herself.

Throughout the romance portion of Miss Williams's narrative, her character bears strongly on the main story, particularly in the relationship of some of its traits to Roderick's. Like Roderick she falls easy prey to her passions and pride and yields too readily to her emotions. Her story provides a warning to the hero, a foreshadowing of his destiny in a treacherous and perfidious world hostile to those who fail to protect their feelings.[16] The two share physical attractiveness, unworldliness, and an innocent kind of vanity. In the remainder of the chapter, after Lothario has betrayed and abandoned her, Miss Williams displays the same force that motivates Roderick throughout the novel: determination for revenge. Leaving her father's home to confront the now married Lothario, she enters his dwelling and attempts to kill him. Thwarted, she suffers a breakdown, has a miscarriage, and then again falls victim to a ruse by her treacherous lover. Lothario's friend, who desires her, pretends that he will avenge her abuse by murdering her seducer. In her response, Smollett prepares the way for a transition to the picaresque in the second stage of her narrative. Romantic excesses combine with the hard calculation of the picaresque when she declares, "I was transported with delirium of glowing joy; I hugged my companion in my arms, and vowed that if he would make good his promise, my soul and body should be at his disposal" (124). She does yield to him and then falls further into his clutches when he responds to her repentance by producing a letter from Lothario pronouncing his "recovery" from his wounds. As her narrative moves to the picaresque, she becomes first a mistress and then a prostitute, but with the avowal of a kind of feminine Roderick, "as I became every day more and more familiarized to the loss of innocence, [I was] resolved to be revenged on the sex in general, by practising their own arts upon themselves" (127), the code of the picaro.

The remainder of Miss Williams's narrative in the next chapter changes tone and offers the harshly real world of the picaresque that Smollett had forecast in the preface to his novel. Dismissing the excesses and hyperboles of romance, his prefatory comments pronounce his own attachment to the form of *Gil Bias*, but with the modifications necessary for Smollett's artistic purposes. Never a slavish imitator, in his very first novel, he adopts a traditional model while altering its "execution." Most essential for Smollett is to eschew Le Sage's improbabilities and to achieve the "generous indignation, which ought to animate the reader, against the sordid and vicious disposition of the world." It is to that purpose that the continuation of Miss Williams's story functions in itself and in its relationship to Roderick's experiences.

As she continues her narrative, Miss Williams offers a brief but telling portrayal of the life of the eighteenth-century sexual underworld as seen from the perspective of the victimized female. Smollett's depiction may not have the breadth of Defoe's *Moll Flanders*, but because it is described by an educated young woman of quality, in some ways it has a more powerful effect. Never in Miss Williams's tale is there a sense of triumph in her trickery; never is there anything but a tone of anguish over the circumstances that often appear beyond her control. In her attitude toward the male sex—her repeated desire to "avenge myself" (135)—there is the expression of the joylessness of sexuality in prostitution. Smollett here, in some ways, anticipates modern sociological explorations of what can best be described as the "ambiguities of prostitution": "It demands that a woman offer her body but withhold her pleasure, sell her flesh but reserve her emotions, and remain, in the truest sense, impenetrable; it can be seen as her most humiliating subjugation or as her ultimate freedom from male dominance."[17] Not generally able to capture a woman's sentiments, Smollett here, with his seduced maiden, has a sufficiently observant eye for the surface details to be convincing, and in using a female voice of impersonation not remarkably different from that of his fictional hero's manages to get inside his character to explore her emotions.

The picaresque story of this portion of the narrative is in itself not remarkable as a tale. Hogarth's *A Harlot's Progress* had provided the outline not only for Smollett, but for eighteenth-century novelists generally to follow.[18] It is a simple and sad account of decline, but Smollett uses it intelligently, not only to expand the satiric compass of his novel, but to illuminate how the sordid circumstances of existence coarsen the individuals that they affect. In her very first episode after leaving her purported avenger against Lothario, Miss Williams finds a profitable mark in a country judge who pays her a hundred guineas for her sexual favors. Already her language displays a descent in her character as she boasts, "during which [engagement] I behaved in such a manner, as to make him perfectly well-pleased with his purchase" (127). When her narrative is briefly interrupted by a bailiff who mistakenly identifies her with another prostitute, she shows the effects of her way of life on her moral character. Addressing Roderick (to be sure, in a "faultering voice"), she reassures him, "for she knew how to extricate herself from this difficulty very soon, and perhaps gain something by the occasion" (128). Indeed, she does, as she blackmails her accuser and receives sufficient payment to provide for her and Roderick's needs.

The world according to Miss Williams in her picaresque continuation of her narrative is a mirror image of Roderick's. Like him she is fortune's plaything, a tennis ball to be banged from one end of the court to the other; like him she has survival instincts, learning the tricks of her oppressors and turning their games against them; like him she never truly loses her sense of herself even when her decisions and actions have damaged her person. She has Roderick's pride. Her vanity remains intact even when she is relegated to life in a bawdy house: "Having the advantage of a good voice and education over most of my rivals, I exerted my talents to the uttermost, and soon became the favourite with all company" (133). Even as she sells her body, her sense of herself makes it difficult for her to deal with her patrons, "As my spirit was not sufficiently humbled to the will, nor my temper calculated for the conversation of my gallants, it was impossible for me to overcome an aversion I felt for my profession" (130). Still, the line of descent, the power of circumstances, are inescapable in her path downward from mistress to common streetwalker. Duped by a man, she is imprisoned for theft. Abused by other prisoners, she attempts suicide. Even when fate appears to be turning for her, its wheel of fortune quickly spins to catastrophe. A seemingly kindly madam turns against her. When a benefactor appears in the form of a sea-lieutenant, not unlike Roderick's uncle Bowling, he dies at sea.

The significance of Miss Williams's narrative becomes clear in Roderick's response to it. Smollett's female impersonation—his first attempt at it—proves less a concern with her situation than a means for advancing the plot, expanding the scope of his novel, and developing the persona of Roderick in the main narrative. Her adventures permit Roderick and the reader to see aspects of the society in a way not easily discernible through the observations of an outsider. It makes available in Roderick's world another aspect of the sordid and seamy life that Smollett's novel satirizes. Not only does Roderick comment on the relationship of her experiences to his own and regard them as a learning experience, but he responds in such a manner that allows Smollett to assure the reader of his hero's fundamental goodness.

That fundamental goodness, the exposure of Roderick's better nature, is crucial to Smollett's concern for winning sympathy for his hero. As Smollett expresses it in his preface, Roderick is the focus of the author's attempt "to represent modest merit struggling with every difficulty to which a friendless orphan is exposed, from his own want of experience, as well as from the selfishness, envy, malice, and base indifference of mankind." And it has been Smollett's intention to gain from the reader "a favourable pre-possession [that will] engage the ingenuous more warmly in his behalf" (xlv). Roderick's response to Miss Williams advances Smollett's purpose. As Roderick identifies the relationship of their situations, noting their differences as well as likenesses, he is mindful (as apparently Smollett is) of the greater difficulties that existed for the female sex. Her original social status and background were, of course, significant for Smollett, his sympathies for women of quality always greater than his feelings for such common women as Mrs. Hornbeck and the Nymph of the Road in *Peregrine Pickle*.[19] Roderick here deplores the portrait of women reduced to such circumstances as hers and sees the particular tragedy of her decline from comfortable estate. With greater sympathy than might be expected from an eighteenth-century gentleman in his situation, he declares upon the conclusion of her story: "Her condition filled me with sympathy and compassion; I revered her qualifications, looked upon her as unfortunate, not criminal" (138).

When Miss Williams returns to the novel as Roderick's beloved Narcissa's maid, she becomes a conduit to the romance ending that Smollett needs to round out his plot. Her advice to Roderick throughout the concluding portions of his pursuit of Narcissa both advances the plot with some verismilitude and, at the same time, displays her intelligence, fundamental good sense, and general worthiness despite her past. Not only does she provide easier access for Roderick to the heroine in a continuing series of episodes, but she allows Smollett to express Narcissa's feelings for the hero in a way that he otherwise would have found difficult to do considering the idealized treatment of his heroine. Miss Williams's own marriage at the novel's conclusion, to Roderick's loyal friend Strap, lends further to the general romance of the ending. It is important to note that what makes the alliance possible is the fact that Miss Williams was never simply an ordinary prostitute, but rather an unfortunate lady of quality whom fate had condemned to hard times in a fashion paralleling Roderick's own series of buffeting misfortunes. Smollett's own sympathies for her were not shared by contemporary reviewers and have been attacked by modern strait-laced critics. The former either believed, like the salacious novelist John Cleland, that Smollett had masked bawdy material while seemingly deploring such matter, or else, like the reviewer in the *Gentleman's Magazine*, saw the tale simply as an admonitory exemplar— "a warning to one sex and a remonstrance against t'other."[20] For the fussy modern interpreters, Miss Williams's marriage to Strap demonstrates Smollett's lack of taste.[21]

By far the most extensive treatment of the fallen woman in Smollett's fiction, Lady Vane's "Memoirs of a Lady of Quality" in *Peregrine Pickle* runs to some fifty thousand words. No mere inset, like Miss Williams's tale, the narrative at the time of its publication had, and continues to have, almost a life of its own. Whatever Smollett's purpose for including it in his novel, no matter what its justification as a device in the longer plot of Peregrine's adventures, the "Memoirs" has the self- contained qualities of a novella, a story to be read, as it was by Smollett's contemporaries, for itself, regardless of a reader's interest in the remainder of the novel. Writing to her friend, the poet William Shenstone, Lady Henrietta Luxborough surely represented the views of many others when she confessed to having taken Smollett's work from a lending library only because of her interest in the volume containing the memoirs of the notorious Lady Vane. Her comment that the sales of *Peregrine Pickle* depended largely on the scandalous appeal of the "real-life" narrative merely reflects the kind of interest expressed in the novel by Smollett's contemporary readers.[22]

But for a modern audience unconcerned with the roman à clef material that titillated eighteenth-century readers, Lady Vane's confessional arouses speculation about a variety of other topics: Smollett's values and integrity as a novelist, eighteenth-century notions of a woman's sexuality, and the relationship of the fiction itself to literary developments in the period. To understand the first of these concerns requires addressing the authorship of the "Memoirs." Did Lady Vane write it herself? Did she dictate it to Smollett? Was Smollett himself the author? Did he simply revise the manuscript? Was the work the product of another hand? Did Smollett include the work because he was paid to do so and was that his sole connection with it?

From its earliest appearance the "Memoirs" has raised questions about its authorship. Lady Mary Wortley Montagu, praising its style, attributed the work to Smollett. She could not believe Lady Vane capable of the production, but Lady Mary had no way of knowing what Lady Vane could accomplish as a writer.[23] Moreover, Lady Mary's astuteness as a judge of writing style did not prevent her from attributing the authorship of *Roderick Random* to Henry Fielding. Still, not shocked by the morality of the "Memoirs," she insistently asserted Smollett's authorship: "Her style is clear and concise with some strokes of Humour which appear to me so much above her, I can't help being of opinion the whole has been modell'd by the Author of the Book in which it is inserted who is some subaltern admirer of hers."

In the comments of most contemporary readers, Lady Vane's authorship appears as unquestioned as her morality assuredly appeared contemptible. To be sure, John Cleland, reviewing the novel in the *Monthly Review*, found nothing objectionable in either her conduct or willingness to expose it to the public. As Cleland evaluates the work in the context of biographical writing and expresses his approval, he does not so much as suggest that it is by any hand but hers. Cleland's moral judgment, however, must be measured by the fact that he himself had published the scandalous novel *Fanny Hill*.[24] As he saw it, the "Memoirs" "seem to be voluntarily furnished by the Lady Vane herself." Pierre Clement, a French author and friend of Lady Vane, also expressed approval of the work while unquestioningly accepting it as coming from her own pen.[25] His judgment seems far more direct than either Lady Mary's use of "modell'd" and Cleland's "furnished."

Far less charitable in their opinions of Lady Vane's morality but certainly accepting of her authorship, the bulk of contemporary commentary focused on her willingness to make public her outlandish behavior. Behind the public debate about the justification for her response to a bad marriage—a debate energized by the scurrilous Dr. John Hill's competitive publication of *The History of a Woman of Quality: or, The Adventures of Lady Frail* (xvi)—lies a class-consciousness revealing eighteenth-century English attitudes toward women. Even in seventeenth-century France Madame de Lafayette, whose *The Princesse de Clèves* hid high society's infamous conduct behind a fictional mask, had to protect herself with anonymity. But English decorum, whatever the actualities of upper-class sexual behavior in the next century, demanded stricter standards than Lady Vane displayed in her "Memoirs" because flaunting her behavior was beyond the bounds of a lady of her class.

Samuel Richardson, writing to Hester Chapone, makes clear the distinction between what may be expected from ladies of status as compared with women of the lower social orders:

Mrs. Pilkington, Constantia Phillips, Lady V. (who will soon appear, profaning the Word *Love*, and presuming to attempt to clear her *Heart*, and to find gentle Fault only with her *Head*, in the Perpetration of the highest Acts of Infidelity) what a Set of Wretches, wishing to perpetuate their Infamy, have we—to make the Behn's, the Manley's, and the Heywood's look white. From the same injured, disgraced, profaned Sex, let us be favoured with the Antidote to these Womens Poison![26]

For Richardson,[27] Thomas Gray, Horace Walpole, and Lady Luxborough, Lady Vane's scandalous behavior was exhibited not only in her sexual escapades but also in publishing an account of them that places her outside the circle of respectable appearance drawn for ladies of quality

and into the condemned ring of those women writers who gave free expression—or what was regarded as such at the time—to sex. Condemning
her conduct, they had no doubt about her authorship of the "Memoirs."
For Gray Lady Vane used Smollett's novel as "a vehicle." Walpole declared, "My Lady Vane has literally published the Memoirs of her own
life, only suppressing part of her lovers, no part of the success of the others
with her: a degree of profligacy not to be accounted for." Lady Luxborough states it most directly, declaring Lady Vane's responsibility for a
work "published by her *own* order, from her *own* Memoirs, given to the
author for that purpose."[28]

Modern criticism has not been kinder to Lady Vane's reputation, chas-
tizing her for cuckolding her husband and using terms to describe her that
have customarily been applied to the behavior of rakes.[29] But the question
of Lady Vane's real character has been less interesting to twentieth-
century scholars than that of the authorship of the "Memoirs" or, at least,
Smollett's role in its creation. In the most thorough study of the novel—
its composition and its revision—Howard Buck, one of those scholars responsible for resurrecting Smollett's work in the modern period, examined
the available internal and external evidence. Dismissing any claims of
Mackercher's authorship of or connection with the "Memoirs," Buck, on
very insubstantial evidence, suggests some small connection to the original
by Shebbeare, a touching up of the manuscript. He finds more evidence
of Smollett's hand in the revision of 1758, seven years after the first edition. He sees his work in the amplifications and transpositions of material.
Nevertheless, for Buck, Lady Vane's responsibility is everywhere in the
novel. Underestimating her character development in the work, he contrasts it with Smollett's techniques. Buck insists that the "Memoirs" are
not of a piece with the novel"; its style falls far short of Smollett's abilities;
and its moralizing is uncharacteristic of Smollett. According to Buck,
"Smollett had no hand whatever in the Memoirs previous to his revision
of them for the second edition." The very "femininity" of the inset attests
to Lady Vane's authorship.[30]

Whatever the weaknesses of Buck's argument, his conclusion appears
indisputable when the novel's techniques are explored. Suggestions that
Smollett wrote the "Memoirs" from material supplied by Lady Vane,[31]
revised the manuscript from one that she presented to him,[32] or that stylistic evidence indicates that "the final version was done by the same hand
that shaped the rest of the novel"[33] fail to hold up on a careful reading of
the novel. Even at Smollett's best when he describes Emilia's emotions in
the same novel, he fails to capture the feminine emotions truly, particularly as they relate to sexuality. To be sure, the characters of Emilia and
Lady Vane can hardly be compared, but yet the sensitivities of two women
as women could scarcely be more contrasted. Smollett never conceives in
all his fiction of a woman's consciousness of sex; he never reveals an in-

terest in the details of dress and the particulars of place as expressed in the "Memoirs"; he nowhere else recognizes the possibilities of a woman's revulsion to the degradations posed by an unwanted lover.

While still maintaining the possibility that Smollett either wrote the "Memoirs" or worked closely from Lady Vane's account of her experiences, Paul-Gabriel Boucé, more than any other critic, perceives how thoroughly the inset reflects a feminine rather than masculine perspective. Somewhat too cautiously Boucé notes that the "Memoirs" is "full of touches of feminine psychology," a characteristic certainly absent in Smollett's treatment of women's characters in his fiction, except for brief flashes of insight. Boucé's examples go far beyond his rather timid statement in demonstrating Lady Vane's strong hand in recounting her adventures. He cites the scene in which the uninitiated bride openly declares her unwillingness to have sex with her first husband in the naked light of day. When Lady Vane expresses her repulsion at the feeble and clumsy lovemaking of her second husband (Lord Vane), it is indeed, as Boucé notes, without offering sufficient detail, a remarkable account in respectable eighteenth-century fiction, let alone Smollett's novels. Boucé accurately asserts, "Only a woman thinks of dying of grief when her first lover deserts her, but is delighted to learn later that he regrets having left her." Equally to the point is Boucé's summary of the distinction between Smollett's "rudimentary knowledge of the feminine heart" and the "subtleties of amorous machiavellism in [Lady Vane's] anticipating the rupture with an adored lover for fear that he should be the first to make the break."[34]

Boucé does not go far enough. In her descriptions of sexual emotions and her perception of details and places, Lady Vane offers in the "Memoirs" views that no male novelist of the period, least of all Smollett, ever presents. Her repulsion with Lord Vane's lovemaking, alluded to by Boucé, has no parallel in the works of Richardson, Defoe, Fielding, or Smollett. Her sexual awareness in the scene is impelled by her recollection of the satisfaction that she felt in bed with her first husband:

I could not help being affected with this pusilanimous behavior [of Lord Vane]; I remembered Lord W _____ m, while I surveyed the object before me, and made such a comparison as filled me with horror and disgust: nay, to such a degree did my aversion to this phantom prevail, that I began to sweat with anguish at the thought of being subjected to his pleasure: and when, after a long hesitation, he ventured to approach me, I trembled as if I had been exposed to the embraces of a rattlesnake. Nor did the efforts of his love diminish this antipathy; his attempts were like the pawings of an imp, sent from hell to teize and torment some guilty wretch, such as are exhibited in some dramatic performance, which I never see acted, without remembering my wedding-night. By such shadowy, unsubstantial, vexatious behaviour, was I tantalized, and robb'd of my repose. (451)

Lady Vane's sexual passion and her expression of it in the "Memoirs" stand apart from any description in the conventional novels of the period and clearly reflect a woman's emotions rather than a man's view of them. When she enters upon her first "indiscretion" with Mr. S _____ , after her marriage to Vane, she does not hide her motives. She has held out for ten months against her lover's desires, but now, "I could not see the affliction of a man I loved, when I knew it was in my power to remove it." Whatever her momentary qualms, they are overcome by her sexual pleasure: "My heart now flutters at the remembrance of the dear, tho' fatal indiscretion; yet I reflect without remorse, and ever remember it with pleasure" (456). Even well after the affair and its subsequent heartbreak, she uses the same words, "to this day I remember it with pleasure," and remarks on the "tender passions" that dominate it and motivate her actions. As she puts it, "I was *all for love, or the world well lost*. And were the same opportunity to offer, I would act the same conduct over again" (457). Long afterward, when their affair resumes, Lady Vane's language reflects the fullness of her sexuality, the excitement that marks her emotions characterized by a "heart [that] vibrate[s]," indicating her "passions" and "raptures" (488–89).

No less than the amorous sentiments voiced in the "Memoirs," the eyes that record particulars of places and dress clearly belong to a woman, certainly not to Smollett. In language and detail the observations reflect a sensitivity not noticeable in Smollett's writing. As she repairs with a companion to the Bois de Boulogne, Lady Vane describes her surroundings with diction revealing her sex:

after having amused ourselves among the groves, embarked in his grace's equipage, which was extremely elegant, being a calash drawn by six fine long-tailed grays, adorned with ribbons in the French taste . . . we were conducted to a little inchanted, or at least inchanting palace. . . . The lower apartment, appropriated to me, was furnished with yellow and silver, the bed surrounded with looking-glasses, and the door opened into a garden, laid out in a cradle-walk, and intervening parterres of roses and other flowers. Above stairs my female companions lodged, in a chamber furnished with chintz. (459–60)

Similarly, Lady Vane's attention to dress distinguishes her work from that of the male novelist in whose novel her "Memoirs" appears. Even as she embarks on her meeting with Lord W _____ m for their elopement and she fears her appearance may betray her to some person she knows, she gives a concrete description of the details of the manner in which she has dressed in her haste to set forth:

I had put on the very cloaths which I had pulled off over night, so that my dress was altogether odd and peculiar; my shoes were very fine, and over a large hoop

I wore a pink satin quilted petticoat trimmed with silver, which was partly covered by a white dimity night-gown, a full quarter of a yard too short: my handkerchief and apron were hurried on without pinning; my night-cap could not contain my hair, which hung about my ears in great disorder. (439)

It is almost as though Lady Vane had stopped before a mirror to record her disheveled appearance. Smollett, in dealing with a woman, would scarcely have noticed such details.

The essence of Lady Vane's style differs dramatically from Smollett's. As David Daiches points out, the "sentimental elegance" of her narrative resembles the style John Cleland used in his *Memoirs of a Woman of Pleasure*, a far less successful attempt to capture a feminine sensibility.[35] A single comparison between her tale and that of Miss Williams in *Roderick Random* displays the distinction between her feminine sensitivity and Smollett's female impersonation in the earlier novel. Miss Williams is reticent about just those points that Lady Vane elaborates. Compare Miss Williams's refusal to narrate "The particular steps [my Lothario] used to ruin me" (*RR*, 120) with Lady Vane's delight in examining such matters in detail because they are important to her. Smollett, a male ventriloquist, rejects the notes that would make Miss Williams's narrative plaintive at this point of her apology for her life, while Lady Vane fully understands why the details are not, as Smollett voices it, "too tedious and impertinent," but explicatory of the emotions that led her to adultery. Reading Miss Williams's sad tale, Smollett's audience could hardly distinguish it from that of the male narrator, Roderick, whose misfortunes and motivations frequently parallel hers. In his study of Smollett's style, Damian Grant demonstrates how Miss Williams's description of a prostitute's life epitomizes Smollett's general technique as it uses "physical form as a figuring forth of moral reality." Grant notes the manner in which Smollett "urge[s] his prose to a climax of irresistible statement" so that Miss Williams's account "concludes with a merciless simplification of the prostitute's progress"[36] (see *RR*, 137). Nothing in the "Memoirs" resembles this as Lady Vane piles emotion upon emotion without discrimination or climax.

For all that, in a real sense, Lady Vane's "Memoirs" as an essential part of *Peregrine Pickle* is Smollett's responsibility. Even if he did no more than include it, he certainly recognized what it was that he was doing with it to enhance his theme, plot, and hero's characterization. He saw in it the opportunity to extend the social scope of his novel, a means of underscoring his moral intentions, a device for authenticating the reality of his fictional hero by including his adventures with an account of those of a real person.[37] For Smollett her narrative served handily as a comment on Perry's character, his blindness to his own weaknesses.[38] Fully aware of the interesting aspects of her character, Smollett also knew that its combination of picaresque and romance elements and its appeal to prurient interests in gossip would arouse reader interest. Had Smollett been paid to include the work in his novel, his many enemies would have noted the fact with delight.[39] Whatever Smollett's sympathies for Lady Vane and his indebtedness to her for past favors,[40] he would not have permitted the "Memoirs" to intrude upon his fiction unless he found it compatible with his various literary purposes. In Lady Vane's "Memoirs" Smollett found a convenient vehicle for expressing his own views of eighteenth-century life, perhaps even for exploring among high society the weaknesses, the luxury, that he deplored. As W. Austen Flanders observes, Smollett's novels—from *Roderick Random* through *Humphry Clinker*—reveal his interest in "self-revelation" and Lady Vane's "Memoirs," an "autobiographical narrative, in its subject matter and its episodic form, another version of picaresque," held forth great appeal,[41] even as it satisfied the needs of his novel.

For Smollett the picaresque and adaptations of it held a fascination and attraction throughout his career. In Lady Vane's "Memoirs" the narrative structure, social revelations, and arts of survival of the traditional picaresque combine with the elements of the romance novel and its concentration on the life of the sentimental heroine. A summary of its plot reveals a picara determined to get by through all the wiles of her femininity, while the guiding principles of her actions are repeatedly expressed in terms of the distressed heroine who is both the victim and champion of romantic love.

Lady Vane begins with those details of her background that always appealed to Smollett's social sympathies for heroines from good families: well-educated and well-bred. Even at the age of thirteen, however, she exhibits those weaknesses characteristic of Smollett's heroes, particularly Peregrine Pickle, of vanity and ambition. Praise sets her head awhirl as she becomes, on her first and subsequent trips to Bath, the object of a Scottish nobleman's interest, finds herself besieged by proposals, and receives special notice at court. She reveals her openness to romance in her relations with the handsome Lord W[illiam] H[amilton], second son of a duke. Always accessible to flattery, she is overwhelmed by Lord William's attentions and, after small protests about social decorum, yields to clandestine meetings. Despite parental objections, including her father's carrying her off, they finally elope.

Despite straitened financial circumstances, their life together approaches the idyllic. The memoirist exalts in their sexual satisfaction. If her mother and uncle remain unforgiving of their actions, it is, she explains, because of their unfamiliarity with the sentiments of love, the key to her most satisfactory experiences. The couple, aided financially by the queen, survive in their happiness. Only Lord William's jealousy, unwarranted she assures the reader, poses difficulties. When she suffers a miscarriage, her disconsolate husband falls ill, and she attributes it to the anguish he has experienced because of his mistaken view of her conduct. All this, including the manner of his death, belongs to the romance genre.

With her widowhood, the author's experiences turn from the pattern of romance to the picaresque. Pursued by various suitors, but particularly Lord Vane, she manages for a time to thwart efforts to marry her off. Finally, however, she yields to family pressures concerned with her security and consents to marry Lord Vane, who desires her even though she makes plain that she does not love him. While acknowledging his liberality in caring for her needs, she detests him, especially for his ineptitude as a lover. Almost immediately she becomes involved with a series of men, settling finally on S[hirley] when he arouses her jealousy by feigning interest in another woman. Shirley ultimately gets her to yield sexually when he appeals to her sympathy during his illness. Disgusted with Lord Vane's impotency, she runs off to Bath and the Continent with Shirley and has a baby who dies. What follows provides the major motif of her adventures: She runs and Vane pursues her.

As she repeatedly does through the years, Lady Vane returns to her husband for the security of his money, but insists on terms to prevent any intimacy with him. Inevitably, her stays with Lord Vane prove unsatisfactory and she makes her escapes. When Shirley ends their affair, she takes up with the earl of B[erkeley], although she feels no strong romantic attachment to him despite his kindness. Indeed, men invariably show their generosity to her, and her own good nature is evident in the devotion to her displayed by her friends and servants. Men—including Vane—challenge each other to duels because of her. When the Berkeley relationship ends, she demonstrates her survivability by returning once more to Vane, who has come into a fortune. As usual, though, she stipulates the conditions, and their reunion fails.

As lovers vie for her and she moves into other relationships, her financial condition remains precarious. Although she insists that she will not exchange sexual favors for money, she somehow manages to get financial protection from men—the means by which becoming increasingly vague in her narrative. And then, of course, as a last resort, Lord Vane, who never ceases his schemes to bring her home, can finally be depended upon. When the affair with Berkeley ends and a return to Shirley proves unsatisfactory, she takes to the road like any good picaro and finds the means to survive. From a trio of officers in Brussels, she fixes upon one, but Vane finds her again and abducts her. When she escapes and returns to the Continent, she seeks the queen's protection—only one of several times that she turns to the authorities for help, always seeming to know the right places to find it. Ill and in dire circumstances when neither Berkeley, Shirley, nor her father will aid her, she still manages to find a young gentleman who provides her with money and gets her to France from Brussels. Her former lover comes to her rescue when her illness worsens, and she successfully returns to England.

Still insisting that she refuses to sell her love for comfort, Lady Vane nevertheless accepts help from a man fearful of committing himself to a woman because he believes it will give her control over him. Indeed, it is interesting to note throughout her story how sex and power are related themes. During a series of pursuits by Vane and escapes from him, she gains support from a variety of friends, including men. But once more she returns to her husband, only to quarrel with him over financial matters, and ultimately his jealousy forces her to leave him. Vane pursues her, but she employs all her picaresque guile to evade him. With him following her tracks, she takes to the road once more, and in a moment of extreme distress finds protection from a French nobleman. Again, in a time of need, men's money and interest allow her to survive. Still, men do let her down, for like any picaro, she discovers that she is fortune's plaything. A young Englishman, who provides the money for her return to England from Italy and stirs her emotions to the point that she vies with a younger woman for his favors, proves to be engaged. Angry to learn that he has cheated on her, she demands a monetary settlement. Although she despises herself for having sought the money, she willingly takes £1000 from him later. Money, indeed, figures as much in her account as it does in Defoe's *Roxana*, but the details are more vague, almost as though she dismisses the subject even while counting the sum. In the end, she must return to Vane for the security that she insists she disdains, although she does once more demand her own terms.

Like any picaresque, Lady Vane's "Memoirs" could continue without end, each episode seeming only another thrown into the whole. Yet the accrual of incidents permits the same vast panoramic scope characteristic of the adventures of Smollett's own heroes. It allows for commentary on customs and manners in English and continental society in major cities and on country estates. It leads naturally—intentionally or otherwise—to satiric criticism of conduct and mores. Lady Vane's "Memoirs" performs the same function as the journey motif that marks the movements of Roderick Random, Peregrine Pickle, or the group of travelers in *Humphry Clinker*. Focused as assuredly on Lady Vane and her experience as she is driven in pursuit of romance and true love as Smollett's adventurers are motivated in their movements by the desire for revenge or the drive of ambition, Lady Vane's "Memoirs" fits neatly into Smollett's definition in *Ferdinand Count Fathom* of a novel:

A Novel is a large diffused picture, comprehending the characters of life, disposed in different groupes, and exhibited in various attitudes, for the purposes of a unified plan, and general occurrence, to which every individual figure is subservient. But this plan cannot be executed with propriety, probability or success, without a principal personage to attract the attention, unite the incidents, unwind the clue of the labyrinth, and at last close the scene by virtue of his own importance. (2–3)

Lady Vane certainly is a "principal personage," and if "subservient" appears a strange word to describe her role in the "Memoirs," it is at least as appropriate for her as it is for Roderick and Peregrine. The background for all three characters exists to demonstrate their survival capabilities in a hostile world.

If Smollett found in Lady Vane's use of the picaresque, material not only appealing to his own taste but the tried and true formulas that he believed assured him of an audience addicted to rogue tales, criminal biographies, and female scandalous autobiographical writings,[42] he must surely have recognized the romance appeal in her character that would engage the increasing interest in the sentimental heroines in fiction. Modern critics have not hesitated to identify the chief character of the "Memoirs" with the developing taste for tenderness and sensibility evolving in the fiction of the period.[43] The very pattern of the "Memoirs" follows a formula common to a kind of sentimental romance, one in which a woman turns to amorous adventures as a result of a man's advantage over female innocence: coming from a happy family life into the world of men, she yields to a first lover who proves to be her ideal throughout the narrative; as a result of her father's objections, she is forced to flee, and her idyllic marriage is followed by disaster; her subsequent bad marriage then leads to a series of adulterous affairs.[44]

Everywhere in her "Memoirs' Lady Vane's passions and language reveal the sentiments—not to say sentimental expressions—characteristic of the excessive romanticism in the heroines of the romances. From the very outset she is a creature controlled by the emotions of love and willing to die for them. When her first husband must separate briefly from her, she is distraught. She requires his sister's assurance of his faithfulness: "I could not even spare one complacent look to any other woman, but expected the undivided homage of his love. Had I been disappointed in this expectation, I should (though a wife) have rebelled or died" (446). Like any rejected heroine of sentimental romance, she responds to Lord Shirley's termination of their affair, not with an outburst of tears, but with conduct both "delirious and desperate." Her behavior convinces "every body present [that] I would have died under the violent agitation," and until the tears break through, she and her observers are convinced that she "must have infallibly perished in the first extasy of my grief" (469ff.).

Love, she repeatedly declares, takes precedence over all other emotions. While the reader may question the means by which Lady Vane manages to survive, she herself insists on the priority she places on love in any relationship. In her most desperate circumstances, she assures the reader that she rejects offers involving love that would benefit her: "could I have prevailed upon myself to profit by the advances [of the men pursuing her] that were made, I might have managed my opportunities, so as to have set fortune at defiance for the future. But I was none of those oeconomists, who can sacrifice their hearts to interested considerations" (504). She demands "a man capable of contracting and inspiring a marital attachment." Whatever the reader may think about her adulterous affairs, Lady Vane unflinchingly declares: "where I did not really love, I could never profess that passion: that sort of dissimulation is a slavery that no honest nature will undergo" (519).

Capable from the outset of using diction taken directly from the romances, as when she speaks of Lord William's appearing "before me like an angel" (437), Lady Vane becomes increasingly the purveyor of sentiment as the "Memoirs" continues. By the end, particularly in her attachment to the young Englishman who has rescued her on the Continent, she has no other vocabulary than that of the romances. She finds in her lover "a delicate sensibility" indicative of the "tenderness and sentiment that render the heart susceptible of the most refined love" (527). Her own heart is "naturally adapted for the melting passion" (528). "Sensibility" marks the focus of any relationship (530), and when, under distress, she makes the difficult channel crossing it can only be in the name of love. Only italics can serve to express the depths of her emotions:

Love made up for all deficiencies to me, who think nothing else worth the living for!—Had I been blessed with a partner for life, who could have loved sincerely, and inspired me with a mutual flame, I would have asked no more of fate. Interest and ambition have no share in my composition; love which is pleasure, or pleasure which is love, makes up the whole. A heart so disposed cannot be devoid of other good qualities; it must be subject to the impressions of humanity and benevolence, and enemy to nothing but itself. (532)

Whether modern readers, any more than her contemporaries, will be willing to accept Lady Vane as one of those "virtue in distress" heroines of sentimental fiction matters less than the fact that Smollett recognized that her story contained all the material that made the genre popular. Always willing to exploit the popularity of existing forms to gain an audience for his work, Smollett surely included the "Memoirs" with a knowing eye on the interests of the reading public.[45]

Indeed, as a professional writer ever-conscious of the market demands—an author who afterwards would fashion a style in his *Critical Review* that would create a serious challenge to the well-established *Monthly Review* and who could recognize in David Hume's *History of England* the kind of work with enough general interest to encourage him to offer a historical work of his own—Smollett clearly perceived the sort of interest inherent in Lady Vane's "Memoirs." Her relations with her husband had been the scandalous talk of the town well before Smollett included her own account in his novel. The novelist surely understood the value it would provide in arousing public curiosity concerning *Peregrine Pickle* itself. Just as he realized that his attacks on David Garrick, Lord Chesterfield, Lord Lyttelton, and a host of others—all of which satisfied his personal antagonism—would invite general gossip about his second novel, he knew that Lady Vane's story would offer material for talk not only in literary but also in social circles. Any reports on sexual misconduct would excite prurient interests, but details of the behavior of a woman well known in society would bring on the activities of pamphleteers, print-makers, and contributors to items in periodicals. Smollett was well enough aware of the importance of contemporary events in creating public atten-tion to include an account of the tribulations of his friend and fellow Scot, Daniel MacKercher, in the same novel as the "Memoirs," appealing to a similar public curiosity about current events.[46]

Smollett grasped the situation accurately. It would have been expecting too much to have looked for genuine understanding of a woman in Lady Vane's position. Her very unconventionality leads to a tale in which she her-self, whatever her feelings of innocence, feels compelled to account for be-havior that she believes natural at the same time that she recognizes that she is defying the standards of her society.[47] Society enjoyed letting her know how it felt. Even before *Peregrine Pickle* had appeared, Dr. John Hill, tak-ing advantage of public interest, brought forth his scalding *The History of a Woman of Quality: or, the Adventures of Lady Frail*, which provided for a debate among readers and Grub Street writers. Pamphleteers took sides on Lady Vane's character, but she was overwhelmingly condemned for con-duct unbecoming a lady in both her marital relations and her published ac-count of them. Periodicals continued to cater to the public taste for scandal right through the end of the year the "Memoirs" appeared. What most aroused excitement, however, was identifying and commenting upon the characters of Lady Vane's lovers. For example, Lady Mary Montagu con-tradicted the author's favorable assessment of Shirley's physical attractive-ness, while Horace Walpole saw Lady Vane's testimonial to Shirley's lovemaking as turning him into a hero. It did not matter that the "Memoirs" never spelled out the names of her characters. Everybody apparently knew who they were. Sir Robert Walpole's mistress, Maria Skerrett, was easily identifiable. Lady Vane's attack on "H __ d __ n, governor, counseller, and steward" to her husband (481), brought forth a defense of Holdman in *A Letter to the Right Honourable the Lady V____ss V*. Horace Walpole eas-ily recognized Sir Thomas Aston, and he delighted enough in the account of Lord Vane's impotence to play upon the information in a pamphlet. The game was inexhaustible, and Smollett had clearly perceived the in-terest it would bring to his novel.

Yet whatever commercial reasons impelled Smollett to include the "Memoirs" in his work, he was a sufficiently serious novelist to attempt to use the inset to further the purposes of *Peregrine Pickle*. No less than the tale of Miss Williams enables Smollett to enhance the characterization, plot, and theme in *Roderick Random*, Lady Vane's "Memoirs" works to the same effect on those elements in *Peregrine Pickle*. Like Miss Williams, Lady Vane serves the purpose of the novel's hero. Rather than the theme of her "Memoirs" standing in ironic contrast to Perry's adventures, as one critic suggests,[48] her experiences provide an essential ingredient for the novel's thematic structure. Boucé's observation that the "Memoirs" offers a warning to Peregrine about the danger of following the passions instead of depending upon "moral good sense" is well taken.[49] Her very life was as much excoriated for her extravagance as its immorality,[50] reflecting the obvious failures of the hero's behavior.

It is in Perry's relations to the heroine, Emilia, however, that Lady Vane's "Memoirs" serves its primary purpose in Smollett's narrative. Smollett positions the inset so that it provides a bridge between the hero's disastrous attempt to force himself physically upon Emilia and his decision to try to regain her trust in him. Smollett sets Perry's frame of mind prior to the inclusion of the "Memoirs." He has followed his attack on Emilia with a mad chase in pursuit of her that leads to a breakdown: "In this humiliation of his spirits, he reflected with shame and remorse upon his treachery to the fair, the innocent Emilia" (419). Although he has not thoroughly learned his lesson—as his response to a letter from Emilia's mother indicates—when the episode is followed by Lady Vane's "Memoirs," the effect upon his conduct is telling.

Perry could not fail to perceive in Lady Vane's story what Lady Mary Wortley Montagu regarded as a text that should be used as a warning to young women against gallantry.[51] Although Lady Mary apparently ascribes the gallantry to Lady Vane, Perry obviously recognizes the effects of his own gallantry on Emilia's innocence. In Lady Vane's description of the attractive gallant able to overcome every virtuous female while refusing to yield his freedom to marriage, Perry would have had to be blind not to see what he has been doing to Emilia. Smollett makes clear Perry's high regard for Lady Vane, expressed in verse and acknowledged in his appreciation for her "uncommon charity" (538). When she responds to Perry's misfortunes and he notes their parallel positions in society's views of their conduct, he looks upon her with admiration. She rejects his verses as being designed for her and guesses the true object of his devotion: "I must be so free as to tell you, it is now high time for you to contract that unbounded spirit of gallantry, which you have indulged so long, into a sincere attachment for the fair Emilia, who, by all accounts, deserves the whole of your attention and regard" (676). As she returns Perry to his true course of love and sets his spirit soaring, Lady Vane indicates how Smollett has skillfully integrated her "Memoirs" into his main narrative. Her inset is no intrusion in the novel and her adventures no contrast with those of Peregrine,[52] but, like the episode of Miss Williams and Smollett's general use of female characters, a device to further the development of his hero's character and advance the plot of his novel.

Whatever Smollett's purposes in including the "Memoirs" in his novel, the modern reader finds interests in Lady Vane's story that go beyond its fictional character. These have to do with the situation of women in eighteenth-century England and, for the student of Smollett's writing, the male author's own rather surprising attitude toward the position of women and their vulnerability in his society.

To be sure, Lady Vane would appear to be something of a special case as she deliberately exhibits her conduct to a community unlikely to forgive her. Indeed, the frankness of her confessional reveals a desperate attempt to overcome society's objections through self-justification. She puts her argument plainly at the outset:

By the circumstances of the story which I am going to relate, you will be convinced of my candour, while you are informed of my indiscretion; and be enabled, I hope, to perceive, that however my head may have erred, my heart hath always been uncorrupted, and that I have been unhappy, *because I loved, and was a woman.* (432–33)

In order to gain her audience's confidence, Lady Vane openly confesses her "vanity" (433, 459, 480). While she does verbal contortions, at times bordering on hypocrisy, to account for her conduct—arguing her "inexperience" (452, 495), insisting that her marriage was only "nominal" (454), or noting her "integrity" (490) when she returns everything to Vane and Berkeley—she attempts to balance her defense with a host of examples demonstrating her benevolence, altruism, and kindness. Coming to the aid of a distressed widow, she simply obeys "the dictates of her humanity" (431).When she loses all her possessions to a highwayman, she not only behaves courageously, but turns her attention to the other woman in her coach. Were she the scoundrel the polite world considers her, why would servants, friends, and even acquaintances come to her aid and comfort? When her maid helps her escape from Vane, the memoirist notes, "like all the women I ever had [she] remained unshaken in her fidelity" (499). She puts off an attempt by Vane to recapture her because "Being universally beloved in the neighbourhood, and respected by my lord's servants, I passed among them untouched" (515). In London, in the countryside, whether among country folk or at court, or even on the Continent, Lady Vane never lacks friends.

More than any point in her argument to convince her readers of her purity of spirit, if not conduct, however, Lady Vane uses an appeal to an understanding of the dominance of love and emotion in human behavior. As she listens to Lord Williams's "transports," how can she be expected to respond "without emotion" or fail to answer them "in sundry favourable glances" (435)? Trying to explain the romantic stirring in her heart, she addresses herself "to those that feel" (435). She cannot control that most natural of all emotions because "love (where he reigns in full empire) is altogether irresistible, surmounts every difficulty, and swallows up all other considerations" (440). Money, Lady Vane tells her romantic readers whom she wants to take into her confidence, must be "despised" by any with "an unbounded benevolence of heart." She demeans mere "sensuality" for she most values "sentiment and imagination" (521). To appreciate the unusualness of her arguments, if not her conduct, it is only necessary to compare them with the behavior of Lady Mary Wortley Montagu, her rather daring contemporary. Aware of her father's objections to her affair with her suitor, Lady Mary, for all her romantic fervor, never lost sight of the financial considerations involved in her situation.[53] Their world, after all, valued money and security above all else regardless of the changes from arranged to affectionate marriages that were occurring.

Smollett must have been moved by Lady Vane's story. If her circumstances were unusual, particularly her self-exposure of her conduct, he nevertheless indicates a sympathy to them similar to that he displayed in his own treatment of Miss Williams in *Roderick Random* and Elinor in *Fathom*. Had Smollett felt anything but admiration for Lady Vane and her remarkable ability to stand up to the worst rebuffs and rebound from severe misfortune,[54] he gives no indication of it as his narrator records her listeners' response to her story. Perry's adulatory poem to the lady apparently echoes the novelist's own sentiments.[55] Not only does Perry express "astonishment at the variety of adventure she had undergone, which was such as he thought sufficient to destroy the most hardy and robust constitution" (538), but another of the auditors attests to the number of favorable accomplishments that she has omitted from her account, acts of generosity that she demonstrates shortly afterwards in her attempts to rescue the hero from his imprisonment.

Of course, the narrative that Perry and apparently Smollett were responding to centered upon the cruel circumstances attendant upon an unhappily married woman in the eighteenth century. For women in Lady Vane's position, depending upon a husband was inescapable. He controlled the money and property, right down to the clothing she wore. Under the law, as an eighteenth-century text on the subject states, "By marriage the very being or legal existence of a woman is suspended."[56] Divorce, easily available to the husband, was highly problematical for the wife. Conduct becoming to him in sexual relationships—signs of his gallantry and masculinity—became heinous behavior on the part of a woman. No wonder that Lady Vane remains insistent that the world does not know the truth of her actions and is 'little ... qualified to judge of private affairs" (456,512–13). Nor is it remarkable that Lady Vane persistently returns to financial matters in her discussion. From Defoe to Jane Austen, novels concerning women stressed the urgency of money matters in their lives. While a recent study of the subject argues that women in novels seemingly have more practical understanding of financial matters than most critics of eighteenth-century fiction accord them,[57] married women, like Lady Vane, at odds with their husbands, had not the luxury of acting upon their knowledge.

Lady Vane's "Memoirs" is a tale of entrapment, her story of victimization by society not all that uncommon for young women of her status. Pressured into marriage by her family—all the change to affectionate interests in marriage did not remove such pressures—she describes Lord Vane "as the last man earth whom I would chuse to wed" (449). She terms the wedding *"the fatal day"* (450). She is contemptuous of his person and behavior. Vane is "the little gentleman" or ironically "My little hero" (450, 520). To ward off his attacks, she declares, requires no more than "a bodkin or a tinder box" (517). Nor does she restrict the view of him to her own eyes; seemingly, the world shares it. Given the opportunity to view Lord Vane in action, Dr. S. and his wife, formerly taken in by him, see his truly despicable character. Lady Vane enlarges on the occasion: "This hath been the case with a great many people, who had but a superficial knowledge of his disposition; but, in the course of their acquaintance, they have never failed to discern and acknowledge their mistake" (509). Evidently the real world shared her opinion. Reflecting a general public assessment, the first Earl of Egmont declared: "He is a very silly young man, half mad, half fool" (796, n. to p. 467). Whatever Smollett's limitations in delving into the feelings of his female characters, his sensitivity sufficiently enabled him to be sympathetic to a woman he admired who was being persecuted, as he saw it, by the social system and an ignominious husband.

4

Comic and Grotesque

Smollett appears most comfortable in his comic and grotesque female characterizations. Taking a type character and emphasizing an essential feature was, after all, fundamental to his literary technique. Like Samuel Johnson's Imlac, he displayed no concern for "numbering the streaks of the tulip." Types rather than individuals commanded his attention.[1] Idealized heroines and conventional fallen women in some ways were simply caricatures, types whose standard features were underscored in his treatment, whatever the differentiations his talent achieved in their creations. Where such portraits of idealized women, however, had the deficiency of generally lacking the vitality essential to giving them a necessary sense of reality, the devices of caricature, natural to Smollett, splendidly served his satiric and humorous purposes. He managed through insistent exaggeration of their appearances and conduct to suggest that not only did they represent a class of people, but, because of the focus on a limited number of characteristics, he conveys the impression that these, indeed, represent the totality of their characters.

Smollett clearly perceived his technique in relation to those of the artists and cartoonists of the day. Like his indebtedness to the visual effects of drama, that to painting is evident in his most important critical comment on his work, the preface to *Ferdinand Count Fathom*. "A Novel," he says, "is a large diffused picture, comprehending the characters of life, disposed in different groupes, and exhibited in various attitudes, for the purposes of an uniform plan, and general occurrence, to which every individual figure is subservient" (2). Smollett's ties to the cartoonists of his time are well documented. His thought processes have been described as conceiving episodes and people in painterly terms, and he clearly viewed himself as "a caricaturist in words."[2] William Hogarth especially provided Smollett with a model, and the artist's convincing caricatures helped enhance the novelist's creation of his grotesque and comic figures throughout his work.[3] At times when Smollett decides to forego detailed accounts in his characterization, he goes so far as to resort to an allusion to the painter-engraver's renderings.[4]

Smollett's interest in grotesque and comic stereotypes accorded equally as well with the omnipresent influence of drama on his novels. The form of characterization had its origins for Smollett in the humours characters amply represented in the Elizabethan and Jacobean plays that the novelist so admired. His own audience, familiar with dramatic representations of various professions, nationalities, and types, readily accepted them as "natural" or "realistic."[5] Obsessive behavior in such stereotypes as "spinsters," sexually available women of the "lower social orders," and dominating wives was commonplace on theater stages. For Smollett, it proved a kind of shorthand to characterization, but his literary ability invested it with greater credibility, interest, and humor than any such other creations at the time. If, as the century progressed, such characterization moved from the stereotypical to the unique, Smollett himself bears responsibility for that.[6]

For Smollett, such characters, however interesting in themselves, never exist apart from the novels they appear in. Never do they stand apart simply to be admired as comic creations.[7] The novelist uses both the grotesque and comic as comments on his society, pieces in the broad satiric canvases that he paints for his readers. They function always in connection with the activities of Smollett's heroes. Even in their appearance, their misshaped noses, low foreheads, and "inflamed" eyes, they offer comic contrasts with Smollett's heroines' attractive features, women whose bodies and faces reflect their superior spiritual qualities.[8] Charles Dickens, an ardent admirer of Smollett, not only found pleasure in his predecessor's caricatures and comic figures, but understood the manner in which Smollett employed them for the enhancement of his novels as a whole.[9] For the modern reader such figures when they portray women have the additional interest of suggesting the novelist's characteristic attitudes toward the sex: his antiromantic views, his class biases, and his general assessment of their interests and understanding.

Like Dickens's novels, Smollett's are peopled with caricatures that provide a real sense of his view of society's truly grotesque and comic nature. Minor characters, they provide the atmosphere for the Smollettian world and allow him a vast sweep of social commentary. As much as his concern for evoking the very odors of eighteenth-century England, they mark immediately the fact that the reader is in Smollett's fictional world and nowhere else. Sometimes their humor is without fun, sometimes it is a mixture that balances laughter and anger, and most frequently its very energy in characterization as a technique expresses Smollett's pure joy in the creation itself.

The world of *Ferdinand Count Fathom* is hardly a realistic one. Yet Smollett's insistent caricature of the grotesque mother of the villain creates a hideous spectacle that convinces beyond reality itself. At the same time, he manages in *Fathom* a different kind of realism in the far more gentle comic portrait of a Parisian bawd, whose credibility for his readers lay in her being modeled on the infamous Mother Douglas. The pair indicate Smollett's ability to provide variety even in his grotesque characterization and suggest how the characters themselves function to offer more than background for his novel as they add to its characterization, satire, and other aspects of the fiction.

Smollett's savage depiction of Fathom's mother has a clearly pronounced purpose. It provides a natural lineage for the amoral, cynical, and brutal behavior that characterizes Fathom's pattern of dissimulation, artifice, and opportunism that marks his conduct throughout a series of wanton and destructive adventures in the novel. His deceit and hypocrisy, Smollett informs the reader, "seemed to have been inherited from his mother's womb" (20). When Fathom artfully employs his wiles to make a conquest of both a young woman (Wilhelmina) and her stepmother, Smollett declares, "In this manner did the crafty Fathom turn to account those ingratiating qualifications he inherited from nature" (61). Even in the manner of her death, as she throws aside caution in order to search for further gains as she pillages a battlefield, Smollett indicates the source of her villainous son's inheritance that will lead to his doom. Foreshadowing Fathom's ultimate fall, the novelist describes the conduct bred from his mother's blood: "We have already recorded divers instances in his conduct, to prove that there was an intemperance in his blood, which often interfered with his caution: and although he had found means to render this heat sometimes subservient to his interest; yet, in all probability, Heaven mingled the ingredient in his constitution, on purpose to counteract his consummate craft, defeat the villany of his intention, and, at last, expose him to the justice of the law, and the contempt of his fellow creatures" (201).

Although Fathom's mother behaves no less despicably than her son, Smollett plays upon the eighteenth-century expectations born of idealized womanhood to make her actions seem even more grotesque. It is a grotesqueness conveyed without physical description—even to the point of encoding her facelessness with the anonymity of keeping her nameless. She is Sin, Satan's daughter, but Smollet mocks her by ironically placing her in the company of ancient heroines like Semiramis, Tomyris, Zenobia, and Thalestris. When she dies while pillaging the dead on a battlefield, Smollett ironically concludes, "Thus ended the mortal pilgrimage of this modern amazon; who, in point of courage, was not inferior to . . . any boasted heroine of ancient times" (16).

Smollett's ironic tone consistently underscores the horrid nature of this camp-follower who preys upon the misfortunes of the living and dead soldiers. Her favors are available to all those who are willing to pay. When peace breaks out, she prays for war. Ah, what a blessing if "Europe might speedily be involved in a general war, so that she might have some chance of reinjoying the pleasures and emoluments of a Flanders campaign" (11). Stalking the battlefield after the fighting has ceased, she slays the injured Muhammadans to make a "comfortable booty of the spoils of the slain" (12).

It is with the distortions of idealized motherhood that Smollett ironically depicts her actions—a technique that he had already put to use in Perry's mother in *Peregrine Pickle*. When Fathom's mother caters to the troops "of the renowned Marlborough's command," the imagery is that of maternal care and nurturing, nursing them with the mother's milk of gin, offering them "the milk of human kindness, which flowed plentifully among her fellow-creatures; and to every son of Mars who cultivated her favour, she liberally dispensed her smiles, in order to sweeten the toils and dangers of the field" (7). For her own son, since her "occupations ... would not conveniently permit her to suckle [him] at her own breast" and the "charge of nursing a child [was too great to] be left to the next goat or she-wolf," she gave him with kindness a beverage, gin, "more energic than the milk of goat, or wolf, or woman" (9).

Through her cunning and pride, like any "good" mother, she provides for her son's fortune—at the same time serving Smollett's future development of his plot. Coming upon Count Melvil, wounded in battle, she acts providently in determining that there may be greater reward in saving his life than in killing him for immediate gain. For the first time in his treatment of her, Smollett lets the reader hear her voice, the *charming* tones of consummate evil: "If ... I can find means of conveying him to his tent, alive, he cannot but in conscience acknowledge my humanity with some considerable recompense; and should he chance to survive his wounds, I have every thing to expect from his gratitude and power" (12). Since Melvil does survive and believes her act one of benevolence, his gratitude provides for Fathom's and the plot's future development. In constructing this malevolent and grotesque figure of Fathom's mother, Smollett thus creates the means for his novel's narrative development and satirizes the eighteenth-century notions of idealized motherhood.

If Smollett obviously detests the character of Fathom's mother and marks his view in his use of the grotesque, another character in the same novel, a Parisian madam, demonstrates that there are grotesque figures in Smollett's fiction who, despite his savage description of them, do not seem to greatly offend him. Modeling her upon Mother Douglas, the notorious Covent Garden bawd (374, n.1 to p. 94). Smollett displays his delight in obvious Swiftian imitation. The cameo portrait, while recalling Swift's sordid depictions of the decayed prostitute, still has some suggestions of Smollett's admiration for her toughness and determination:

[The company was] received by the venerable priestess, a personage turned of seventy, who seemed to exercise the functions of her calling, in despight of the most cruel ravages of time: for age had bent her into the form of a Turkish bow: her head was agitated by the palsy, like the leaf of the poplar-tree, her hair fell down in scanty parcels, as white as the driven snow: her face was not simply wrinkled, but ploughed into innumerable furrows: her jaws could not boast of one remaining tooth; one eye distilled a large quantity of rheum, by virtue of the fiery edge that surrounded it, the other was altogether extinguished, and she had lost her nose in the course of her ministration. . . . Yet there was something meritorious in her appearance, as it denoted an indefatigable minister to the pleasure of mankind; and as it formed an agreeable contrast with the beauty and youth of the fair damsels that wantoned in her train. It resembled those discords in music, which properly disposed, contribute to the harmony of the whole piece: or those horrible giants who in the world of romance, used to guard the gates of the castle in which the inchanted damsel was confined. (93)

For all the ugliness of its details, Smollett's caricature revels more in his creative energy than it suggests any malice. Always alert to possibilities of parody, the writer who applied "as white as the driven snow," a cliché used for heroines by romantic novelists (and sometimes applied by Smollett himself), to the weather-beaten hag must have enjoyed himself with the wordplay. He is obviously in his account not without admiration for the madam's sense of self and her unwillingness to be dominated by others. He uses his grotesque figure to suggest parody of romantic excesses. And he employs it successfully to satirize the hypocrisies of the Catholic religion, as he sees it, when he contrasts the madam with the abbé who has brought the company of men to her quarters and who participates in a ritual of confessionals for her ladies before they perform their duties in her service.

Smollett delights in his ability to vary his techniques in his comic caricature, berating a type figure like Mrs. Gobble in *Sir Launcelot Greaves* without requiring physical description or showing the totality of Miss Snapper in *Roderick Random* in his own and her language, matching her conduct and appearance to his satiric purposes.

In Justice Gobble's wife Smollett economically expands the satiric scope of his novel. Without benefit of physical description of the ignorant, affected, and arrogant character, Smollett caricatures Mrs. Gobble through an account of her conduct and a transcription of her dialogue. He mocks the jargon of the legal profession, ridicules the abuses of the judicial system, and scorns the manipulative and overbearing kind of female that the novelist finds reprehensible and threatening throughout his work.

Even before Mrs. Gobble appears on the scene, Smollett pillories her through the voices of his characters. Greaves, the temporarily incarcerated quixotic knight, learns from one of his fellow prisoners that the justice's wife mirrors her husband's ugly image: "his wife domineered with a more ridiculous, though less pernicious usurpation, among the females of the place: that, in a word, she was the subject of continual mirth, and he the object of universal detestation" (87). Lest the reader imagine that she is truly less detestable than her husband, less dangerous in her abuse of the legal system, Smollett quickly provides an example of what her arrogance and authority means to the ordinary people falling into the hands of abusive legal authorities. As a result of her "pique" because of what she believes to have been an upstaging of her by an innocent young woman at a country assembly, she brings down the wrath of her husband's power to devastate an entire family (90).

Mrs. Gobble's own words reinforce the testimony of others and permit Smollett to enlarge his attack on legal jargon, a satiric target throughout the novel even when it is employed by young Tom Clarke, the hero's godson and an otherwise admirable character. Smollett had become particularly sensitive to legal double-talk after his own problems with the law in his libel trial. Mrs. Gobble's ignorance only underscores the absurdities in the jargon. When Greaves challenges her husband's judicial conduct, she chokes and fumes and blusters:

Sirrah! sirrah! (cried she) do you dares to insult a worshipful magistrate on the bench?—Can you deny that you are a vagram, and a dilatory sort of person? Hasn't the man with a satchel [the scoundrel Ferret who has turned Launcelot over to the law to secure his own release] made an affidavy of it? If I was my husband, I'd lay you fast by the heels for your resumption, and ferk you with a primineery ['writ against one charged with introducing a foreign power into the land'] into the bargain. (94)

But she is not her husband. When he becomes aware of Launcelot's identity and fears retribution, she refuses to back down and only makes matters worse, first by discovering her dual standard of justice—one for the wealthy and another for the poor—and then by taking umbrage at what she regards as the hero's lack of respect for her. She berates her husband for not defending her and then threatens the knight: "I have noblemen to stand by me, with their privilegs and beroguetifs" (96).

While the entire episode with Mrs. Gobble covers only a few pages in the narrative, it is a good example of Smollett's use of a minor female grotesque character to express his distaste for affectation, something that particularly outrages him in the conduct of women. In the same novel, presenting two female characters in King's Bench Prison, Smollett displays the utmost sympathy in his treatment of a distressed female and his utter contempt for what he regards as the excessive affectation and vanity of the sex (168ff.). To be sure, the novelist is anything but gentle in his satire of similar characteristics in his male figures; however, female affectation for Smollett—as it was for most eighteenth-century commentators on the behavior of the sex—proved most provoking.

One of Smollett's more effective uses of the grotesque comes in another narrative vignette, this time in *Roderick Random*. His creation of Miss Snapper as the object of his hero's fortune hunting just prior to the reappearance of the heroine after an extended absence from the adventure, clearly intends a commentary on the depths to which the hero has sunk. It prepares for the turn of events that will ultimately shift the narrative mode of the novel from picaresque to romance. In the contrast between the deformed figure of Miss Snapper and the image of perfection in Roderick's adored Narcissa, the reader is lifted from harsh reality to the wonderland of romantic paradise.

In Roderick's description of events, he eagerly pursues Miss Snapper's fortune regardless of her physical deformity and her wicked tongue. Encouraged by the prospect of her £20,000, he is not dissuaded by his friend Banter's portrait of her as "sickly and decrepid," a "little deformed urchin ... with ... virulence and volubility of tongue" (322–23). The reader, along with Roderick, hears her "shrill female voice" even before Roderick has had the opportunity to view her figure in the dark recesses of a coach. As she takes on a braggart in her company with venomous wit, there is no question about who has won the verbal duel (323–24). As Roderick remarks on a later occasion, however, for one who would have to live with her, it was an "unruly tongue" truly to be "dreaded" and with the prospect of "the horrors of an eternal clack!" (331). Still, whatever his discomfort, Roderick repeatedly recalls her fortune.

With the prospect of her money before him, the hero seeks to put the best light on the sorry picture of Miss Snapper that he offers his reader:

I had the good fortune to find my mistress not quite so deformed nor disagreeable as she had been represented to me.—Her head, indeed, bore some resemblance to a hatchet, the edge being represented by her face; but she had a certain delicacy in her complexion, and a great deal of vivacity in her eyes, which were very large and black; and though the protuberance of her breast, when considered alone, seemed to drag her forwards, it was easy to perceive an equivalent on her back which balanced the other, and kept her body in equilibrio. (326–27)

Whatever the rationalization that convinces Roderick that at £20,000 she is worthwhile as a wife, he cannot ignore what he sees when he goes forth from the coach: "[She] had got more twists from nature, than I had before observed, being bent sideways into the figure of an S, so that her progression very much resembled that of a crab" (331). Smollett does not intend the reader to look sympathetically on Roderick as he observes the audience at a dance at Bath looking upon his companion with "contemptuous smiles" and then concludes that while his pride sees her "as unworthy of his notice," his interest perceives her "as the object of my whole attention" (333, 335). Instead, as the reappearance of Narcissa at this point indicates, Roderick remains unworthy of her nobility and will have further struggles before the romance ending of the novel.

In herself, for all the physical caricature and her inappropriateness as a wife for Roderick with the prospect of her sharp tongue verbally lashing him for a lifetime, Miss Snapper is not altogether grotesque. Although, as with most of his grotesques, Smollett conveys the fullness of her character through her appearance, conduct, and name for his comic purposes,[10] he finds one of her features obviously appealing. He clearly admires her wit, not only in the exchange in the coach, but also when she turns the tables on Beau Nash, the celebrated master of ceremonies at Bath, who attempts to ridicule her with a vicious jest. For all Miss Snapper's absurd pride, she displays an intelligence and sensitivity that the novelist uses to make Roderick's treatment of her appear especially cruel and a sign of his still absent maturity as he prepares once more to woo Narcissa. No fool, Miss Snapper recognizes at once when Roderick looks upon Narcissa what his feelings for her are. As Roderick states, "having a turn, for observation," she sees through his attempts to camouflage his emotions. Smollett thus balances the excesses of his caricature in the figure of Miss Snapper, whose purpose is not only to entertain his audience's taste for the grotesque but also to set up a shift in his narrative and to underscore the defects in his hero's still unfulfilled character.

As the character of Miss Snapper, like that of Mrs. Gobble, indicates, with remarkable brevity Smollett often manages to portray comic female characters in little more than thumbnail-sketches or cameo scenes that permit him to comment on a variety of things, such as the sexuality of the lower classes, the social attitudes of his contemporaries, the abuses in his society, and the conduct of the heroes in his own novels. Never of great significance in themselves, such figures provide the breadth of Smollett's satire and offer deeper insight into his major characters. Brief, but interesting, is his use of the "Nymph of the Road" episode in *Peregrine Pickle*, which displays the author's characteristic attitude toward women of the lower social orders—their attractive sexuality and their easy availability.

The brief sketch has enjoyed continuing popularity largely because of its close resemblance to George Bernard Shaw's expanded version of the narrative in *Pygmalion*. Despite Shaw's denial of having read Smollett's novel and ultimate differences between the two authors' regard for their characters, even a simple summary of Smollett's short tale suggests Shaw's indebtedness.[11]

Meeting the sixteen-year-old nymph on the road, Peregrine, Smollett's hero, finds her appealing enough, despite her bedraggled condition, to buy her from her mother. Without quite knowing what he intends to do with her, Perry returns her to his home under the care of Pipes, his friend and servant. When Pipes, against Perry's admonitions, attempts to seduce her, she vehemently rejects him, noting that she belongs to his master. Like Shaw's Eliza, the nymph battles furiously but unsuccessfully against being bathed and dressed respectably. Perry schemes to educate her in the manners of his own social class and to pass her off as a lady—indicating at least Perry's, and perhaps Smollett's, notions of what it takes to make a lady. Foreshadowing the final outcome of his plan, his major problem is in overcoming her "inveterate habit of swearing" (599), an example of which she has amply demonstrated when rebuffing Pipe's advances. Still, Perry enjoys initial success as he tries her out in a small group of country squires. Recognizing the need to limit her talk, he plies her with the conversational gambits of polite society, instructing her in the personalities and material of the theater, and teaching her the card playing that dominates the interests of the ladies of his acquaintance. Having branched out in his own neighborhood, particularly among his female circle, Perry takes on the more difficult venue of London. He completes the nymph's education by employing his valet de chambre to instruct her in those accomplishments that Smollett and his contemporaries believed to be the chief employments of women: dancing and conversing in French. She performs her role splendidly until one of the fine ladies cheats at cards, and the nymph bursts forth in the Billingsgate language and vulgar gestures that Smollett clearly regarded as natural to her class. Done with his experiment, Perry has no more use for her, but since she is his property, he resents his valet de chambre's elopement with her. Finally, however, displaying his largesse, Perry forgives the couple and helps them purchase a coffeehouse.

For Smollett the story is a vehicle for expanding his satire, the character merely a prop to advance his exploration of the vices and follies of his society. Like Shaw he attacks social pretentiousness and upper-class superficialities. Smollett himself obviously considers women social adornments, involved largely in frivolous and meaningless activities. All that is required for their success lies in their ability to speak well, to dance well, to converse about fashionable topics, and to sprinkle their talk with some French phrases. The nymph's attractiveness sufficiently captivates her audiences until she offends the rules of social decorum.

Unlike Shaw Smollett indicates no interest in her character apart from its satiric and comic possibilities and these are associated mainly with Smollett's class-consciousness. Throughout she is "the nymph," a nameless creature who exists for his hero's benefit and playful purposes, another of Perry's games. The narrator never hints about the morality of Perry's purchasing her, and when the hero is done with her, before her elopement, "he had performed his frolick, and begun to be tired of his acquisition"

(602). Existing as she does for Perry's purposes, the nymph is reified, an object to be seen solely from the outside. She has "agreeable features, enlivened with the complexion of health and chearfulness"; a "hedge-inamorata" and "a buxom wench" suggest her erotic nature (596–97). Looking upon her when she has been made to appear respectable, Perry is "extremely well pleased with his purchase" (599). Expressing what clearly are opinions shared with Perry, the narrator—while underscoring the social satire of the fictional construction—describes not a person, but the molding of an instrument designed for an attack on fashionable society: having been instructed with phrases from Otway, Shakespeare, and Pope and taught a few tunes from opera, the nymph "By means of this cultivation . . . became a proficient in the polite graces of the age; she, with great facility, comprehended the game of whist, tho cribbidge was her favourite game" (600). Using her for satire on the manners and affectations of the upper classes, Perry and apparently Smollett remain blind to the satiric possibilities inherent in the treatment of and attitude toward the girl herself.

Only when Smollett permits the reader to hear the nymph's voice does she at all come alive as a person, and then the novelist reveals his own attitudes toward her social class. Without suggesting the outrageousness of Pipes's attempted assault upon her, Smollett focuses instead on the language of her response. Comic though it is, the nymph's language reflects what can be expected from the earthy lower-class woman, according to Smollett. When Pipes calls her a bitch, she retaliates with all the vituperation of a tough Covent Garden wench:

Bitch! (exclaimed this modern Dulcinea, incensed at the opprobrious term) such a bitch as your mother, you dog. D __ n ye, I've a good mind to box your jaws instead of your compiss. I'll let you know as how I am meat for your master, you saucy blackguard. You are worse than a dog, you old flinty- faced, flea-bitten scrub: a dog wears his own coat, but you wear your master's. (597)

With mock delicacy Smollett spares his reader the full details of her harangue and merely summarizes: "such a flow of eloquence [she offered] as would have intitled her to a considerable share of reputation, even among the nymphs of Billingsgate" (598).

Smollett's class-consciousness expresses itself most clearly toward the conclusion of his novel when the hero again meets his valet de chambre and learns the disastrous aftermath of his marriage. Reverting to type, suggesting the fundamental character of her class (thus ironically betraying the purpose of Smollett's satire that suggested that only superficial manners separated social groups), the nymph, having fallen in love with an Italian fiddler pretending to be a French count, has betrayed her husband. She has robbed him of all his cash and run off with her lover.

There is, after all, a difference between Smollett's treatment of his nymph and Shaw's Eliza. While Smollett fails in his complete portrait of his character to support his view that the distinction between classes lies in "the form of an education, which the meanest capacity can acquire without much study or application" (599), Shaw's Eliza demonstrates the playwright's contention that the difference between a lady and a flower girl is in the way she is treated. For all his satire on the upper classes, Smollett, with all the aspirations of an eighteenth-century gentleman, discloses the social prejudice that underlies his treatment of women. Smollett's heroines are never flower girls but women of independent wealth and established social status. His treatment of the nymph serves to comment on the failures of his hierarchy to function in its appropriate or proper fashion.[12] Smollett's satiric concern in the episode focuses on the false values that dominate an upper class unable to distinguish reality from appearance.[13] He has no intention of deriding the class distinctions themselves. For the conditions of the laboring poor evident in the situation that permits Perry's purchase, Smollett displays no more than comic interest.[14]

Another example in *Peregrine Pickle* of Smollett's class prejudices in his treatment of women appears in his comic characterization of Mrs. Hornbeck, whose very name suggests her accessibility to the hero's sexual desires. Although used primarily to indicate Peregrine's unfaithfulness to the heroine, Emilia, and his need for reform before he is worthy of her, Mrs. Hornbeck provides Smollett with yet another opportunity to depict the erotic nature of women in her social class. Married to the respectable Mr. Hornbeck, a man of means, she clearly has not escaped her social origins, and these, the novelist makes evident, are apparent despite the artifice of dress and affected manners.

As soon as Perry meets her, he recognizes the availability of the former oyster wench: he begins by "squeezing her hand and darting a most insidious glance at the same time. This abrupt behaviour he practised on the presumption, that a lady of her breeding was not to be addressed with tedious forms that must be observed in one's advances to a person of birth and genteel education; and in all probability his calculation was just" as demonstrated by her responses (199). Whatever question there may be that the observation is simply Perry's is negated by the outcome of his design and the vulgarity with which she encourages him.

Only in her ability to gain her desired sexual ends does Smollett allow her a modicum of intelligence, and then it is better described as cunning. With easy means she discovers ways to come up with a contrivance to fool her cuckolded husband. As Smollett notes, broadening his comments to include the female sex, "Women are naturally fruitful of expedients in cases of such emergency" (203). Watched over closely by her jealous husband and put under the protection of a duenna, she manages to bamboozle the old woman when Perry surprises them in their coach. Without hesitation she immediately identifies him as her brother-in-law. For all of her contrivances, however, she has no way of holding on to Perry whose sole interest has been in his sexual conquest. Accepting the British ambassador's request that he return her to her husband, Perry willingly gives her up since he finds no great loss of the conquest "after it was for some time possessed" (222).

Smollett, like Perry, finds Mrs. Hornbeck an easy target. His interest in her as a humorous character permits him a few laughs at her social class. As he does generally with such types, he ridicules her through his use of an epistolary device. Writing to Perry to arrange an assignation, Mrs. Hornbeck foreshadows Win Jenkins's abuse of the language in *Humphry Clinker*:

Coind Sur,
Heaving the playsure of meating with you at the ofspital of anvilheads, I take this lubertea of latin you know, that I lotch at the *hottail de May cong dangle rouy Doghouseten*, with two postis at the gait, naytheir of um vary hole, ware I shall be at the windore, if in kais you will be so good as to pass that way at sicks a cloak in the heavening, when Mr. Hornbeck goes to the *Calfhay de Contea*. Prey for the loaf of Geesus keep this from the nolegs of my hussban, ells he will make me leed a hell upon urth.
Being all from, deer Sur,

Your most umbell sarvan wile
DEBORAH HORNBECK (219)

Particularly, but not exclusively, in its opening sentence—with *Heaving*, *playsure*, and *meating*—her coinages reveal, as do those of Win, the underlying eroticism that Smollett attributes to her class.

For Perry, and clearly for Smollett himself, women like Mrs. Hornbeck are sexual objects for men's amusement. While the affair with her is easily dismissed as an example of Perry's gallantry, the only suggestion of immorality in the adulterous relationship attaches to Mrs. Hornbeck. Smollett finds play in the notion of Perry's revenge on her husband; he achieves his humor by caricaturing contemporary notions about a woman's fidelity to her husband. The novelist's treatment, bent on comedy, ignores any serious questions about his hero's morality for the sake of evoking laughter.[15] If the incident serves to demonstrate Perry's need for correction before he can properly obtain Emilia's hand,[16] it is at the expense of playing upon the very sexuality of a woman who, after all, remains in Perry's mind and Smollett's view an oyster wench. For Smollett the Mrs. Hornbecks of his society represent the playthings of socially superior men.

In his far more general comedic portrait and use of Dolly Cowslip in *Sir Launcelot Greaves*, Smollett again suggests the distinction that he draws among women of differing social classes. Dolly's credentials as an innkeeper's daughter are certified to by her country-girl's confusion about language and her abuse of it in writing. From the outset Smollett marks her origins when she mistakes Tom Clarke's legal discussion of an entail to be a signal that he intends to make a sexual advance upon her. With her dialect—not always consistent in the novel[17]—Smollett appeals to his London audience's sense of social superiority. Throughout the work her dialect, in fact, sets her up, despite her conduct, as something less than a heroic figure. When Dolly writes to Launcelot to assure him of his beloved Aurelia's safety and to promise him that she will keep him informed of her whereabouts after the heroine's abduction by her wicked uncle, the servant girl's epistolary style is, like Mrs. Hornbeck's, a foreshadowing, though less sophisticated version, of Win Jenkins's in *Humphry Clinker*:

The man [Aurelia's uncle's footman] as gi'en me leave to lat yaw knaw my dear leady is going to Loondon with her unkle squaire Darnel.—Be not conzarned, honoured sir, vor I'se teake it on mine laife, to let yaw knaw wheare we be zettled, if zo be I can vind wheare you loadge in Loondon.—The man zays yaw may put it in the pooblic prints.—I houp the bareheir will be honest enuff to deliver this scrowl; and that your honour will pardon

Your umbil servant to command
DOROTHY COWSLIP (130)

Dolly's postscript reveals, as her earlier misinterpretation of Clarke's remark on the entail, her healthy sexual nature. Whereas Smollett's perfect heroines suppress any sexual feelings, his characters of the lower social orders always manifest their physical desires and earthiness in both language and conduct. Whether they are virtuous or openly sexual, Smollett's servant girls and innkeeper's daughters and chamber maids and kitchen help declare their human feelings without the restraints that generally restrict his heroines to stereotypically romantic expressions of blushing and swooning. Dolly juxtaposes her regards to Clarke, whom she obviously has an interest in, with a comment on Squire Darnel's man, describing the latter as "very civil vor sartain," but hastening to add, "but I'ave no thoughts on him I'll assure yaw.—Marry hap, worse ware nat have a better chap, as the zaying goes." It is a clear expression of Dolly's emotions toward Clarke.

Smollett has displayed those emotions clearly enough in all Dolly's relations with Clarke at the same time that he has indicated her sexual attractiveness. When Clarke, during a moment of terror at the inn, has become overly familiar with her, she rebuffs him, but although she "eyed him with a sullen regard, indicating displeasure," Smollett tells the reader it was not a look of "indifference" (9). She is surely not a young woman whose sexuality is hidden behind a veil of idealization. Squire Darnel's footman, whom she certainly knows how to use, is taken by her and is at the end disconsolate to discover—with "a heavy heart"—the "connexion between his dear Dolly, and Mr. Clarke the lawyer" (201). Clarke himself cannot restrain his feelings for her and attempts to enter her chamber, "resolved to renew his practices on the heart of Dolly" (57). Indeed when his godfather, Launcelot, sends him to London along with Dolly, the knight warns him to adhere to proper behavior.

To be sure, Dolly is no romantic heroine above the fray, passively waiting for a hero to carry her off. She does not hesitate to indicate her feelings for Clarke when the young man's eccentric uncle, Captain Crowe, roughly handles the lawyer for whom she "had conceived a sneaking kindness." She comes to Clarke's rescue in a manner difficult to imagine of Aurelia, the heroine: "She twisted her hand in Crowe's neckcloth without ceremony, crying, 'Sha't then, I tell thee, old codger.—Who kears a vig vor thy foolish tantrums?' " (29–30). Without compunction she clearly leads on Squire Darnel's footman in her service to both Launcelot and Aurelia, well aware of her feminine attractions.

Still, if no heroine, Dolly appears real woman to whom the reader, as well as Launcelot, is drawn. She may be no Aurelia in beauty either, as even Clarke avers, but, like a good country girl, she "has got a very good complexion:—indeed, she's the very picture of health and innocence" (27). Smollett needs her for his plot and must make her attractive if both Aurelia and Launcelot are to trust her. She becomes Launcelot's conduit for information about Aurelia, allowing the knight to pursue his maiden. She serves as Aurelia's faithful maid, a waiting woman to share her moments of misery and terror, a dependable confidante. Launcelot recognizes Dolly's sexual attractiveness when she has clearly made a conquest of Squire Darnel's footman. The knight knows, too, that Clarke longs for her, and he proposes their marriage. If Dolly is to be an attendant to Aurelia, she must have admirable qualities, and Launcelot describes them. He praises her "simplicitly" and "goodness of heart" and is "struck with her features" (124). As Launcelot tells her, "you can boast of virtue, fidelity, and friendship" (208). If these are qualities important in a serving class, they are, after all, not insignificant or unattractive in any person. Smollett may treat Dolly as he does, in all her earthiness, because he finds these characteristics identifiable with the lower social order of women, but the reader will find characters like Dolly closer to the realities of womanhood itself than the stylized heroines of his novels.

If Dolly presents a good example of Smollett's simple comic characterization, his portrait of Narcissa's aunt in *Roderick Random* demonstrates his ability to join comic and grotesque in a single character. While limited in the extent of its treatment, Smollett's portrayal of his heroine's aunt effectively illustrates not only his ability as a caricaturist, but the manner in which he employs minor figures—here a female grotesque—to expand his novel's satiric scope, advance his narrative, and develop his hero's qualities. Narcissa's aunt caricatures an already stereotypical learned lady in eighteenth-century fiction and drama. But through her Smollett forwards his plot in which the idealized heroine serves as a guide throughout the hero's most abysmal adventures and provides the material for the novel's romantic ending. At the same time, Roderick Random's relationship with his heroine's aunt permits Smollett to display a fundamental weakness in his hero that accounts for his difficulties along the road to the contrived happy conclusion.

Whatever the reader may feel about the unfairness of Smollett's treatment of the character and its misogynic expression, the development of Narcissa's aunt offers a small masterpiece of the novelist's technique as a caricaturist. Smollett borrows a device from the dramatists that allows him to get beyond the limitations of the first-person point of view of his narrative. Before Roderick meets Narcissa's aunt, she is introduced to the reader through Mrs. Sagely's description of her to the hero, whom she has rescued from desperate circumstances and whom she is now introducing into the lady's service. Like Fainall and Mirabell in Congreve's *The Way of the World* whose conversation foreshadows the behavior of Witwoud and Petulant, Mrs. Sagely details the conduct to be expected from Narcissa's aunt. Terming the lady "a maiden of forty years not so remarkable for her beauty as her learning and taste," Mrs. Sagely labels her "a perfect female *virtuosi*, and so eager after the pursuit of knowledge, that she neglects her person even to a degree of sluttishness." Although Smollett's readers needed no further clues to the character than the term *virtuosa*, Mrs. Sagely spells out its significance: a woman unlikely to get a husband; so "abstracted as it were from the world" and unmindful of reality as to be immune from the "customs of the world" even to the extent that she "never sleeps or eats as other people do." At the same time, by noting Narcissa's aunt's professing "the principles of Rosicrucius," Mrs. Sagely is informing Roderick and Smollett's readers of the woman's sexual oddity (216–17).

Like Petulant and Witwoud in Congreve's play, Narcissa's aunt acts out in detail the behavior predicted for her. As she does so, Smollett adds another dimension to his sweeping satire of contemporary life, ridiculing the aberrations of the "learned lady" who has forgotten the proper role of women in society and in the process has lost touch with reality. Her scholarship is bizarre, absent of true learning, as fragmentary in character as the various unfinished tragedies that clutter her workshop. She has lost all sense of her own sex: her poetry "most extraordinary in a female poet [lacks] the least mention made of love" (221). So much has her sexual identity been lost that when Roderick is called for by her, he finds her "stalking about the room in her shift and under-petticoat only" (218). Her preoccupation with scholarship has affected her mind so that she often fancies herself as a piece of furniture or an animal, and, as a vicious cat, attacks those who confront her and can be calmed only by the soothing music of her niece. In the wildness of her imagination, "she [had] prophesied the general conflagration was at hand, and nothing would be able to quench it, but her water, which therefore she kept so long that her life was in danger." She has to be tricked into filling "tubs and vessels" to put out the "fire" that she thought threatened her home (221).

But it is in Smollett's description of Narcissa's aunt that his caricature most savagely satirizes the "learned lady" in a way that certainly should have outraged the bluestockings of his day, those same women engrossed by Richardson's fiction. On Roderick's first meeting with her, he describes her in gross detail:

She sat in her study, with one foot on the ground, and the other upon a high stool at some distance from her seat; her sandy locks hung down in a disorder I cannot call beautiful from her head, which was deprived of its coif, for the benefit of scratching with one hand, while she held the stump of a pen in the other.—Her fore-head was high and wrinkled, her eyes large, gray, and prominent; her nose long, sharp and aquiline; her mouth of vast capacity; her visage meagre and freckled, and her chin peeked like a shoemaker's paring-knife: Her upper-lip contained a large quantity of plain Spanish [snuff], which by continual falling, had embroidered her neck that was not naturally very white, and the breast of her gown, that flowed loose about her with a negligence truly poetic, discovering linen that was very fine and to all appearance, never *washed but in Castalian streams* [near Mt. Parnassus]. Around her lay heaps of books, globes, quadrants, telescopes, and other learned apparatus: Her snuff box stood at her right hand, at her left lay her handkerchief sufficiently used, and a convenience to spit in appeared on one side of her chair. (217–18)

Here, surely was a lady who could be expected to "spit in her snuff-box and [who] wiped her nose with her cap which lay on the table, instead of a handkerchief."

It is a carefully detailed, if caustic, portrait, and both Frank McCombie and John Sena have shown how Smollett's visual description and narrative derived from medical accounts of hysteria—that ailment peculiarly ascribed to women. Although Sena mistakenly believes that Smollett's readers would be familiar with such material and thus sympathetic to the character of Narcissa's aunt, he finally recognizes Smollett's central point and what lies behind his satire of the learned lady: a "warning ... of the perils of female virtuosity. She who would aspire to genius must forfeit all hope of emotional equanimity, moderation in behavior, and mental tranquility."[18]

Sena is more charitable than Smollett's sensibility deserves. The character of Narcissa's aunt derives not from a medical diagnosis, but from a satirist's contempt for such female aspirations. For the novelist so corrupting do the learned lady's pursuits become that when, "seized with a whim," Narcissa's aunt selects "the school-master of the parish for her lord and husband." The result proves disastrous (340). A woman's pre-occupation with scholarship, according to Smollett, makes her unfit for the normal role of womanhood. Nor was Smollett alone in his contemptuous appraisal of the learned lady, although his portrait is particularly vitriolic.[19] If from classical times the type stood as an easy target for men unsettled by female displays of scholarship, for Smollett's contemporaries such women were particularly onerous. Even those men who believed in the female right to education and accepted their literary endeavors demanded that women should still pursue the common duties ascribed to their sex, that they should know how to make a pudding whatever their talents in translating Epictetus.[20] The perceptive Lady Mary Wortley Montagu, rec-ognizing the unreasoning prejudice of the male population, warned her daughter to hide her learning for fear of her being ridiculed.[21]

At the same time, Smollett employs the character as a comment on his hero and a useful device to advance the plot of his novel. From Mrs. Sagely's first comments on Narcissa's genuine concern for her aunt to Rod-erick's own observation of her treatment of her eccentric relative—con-duct unlike Narcissa's brother's, which is motivated solely by his aunt's fortune—the heroine emerges as an ideal worthy of the hero's aspirations. To achieve his goal Roderick will ultimately have to win the aunt's ap-proval. Smollett makes clear the difficulty in the first words that Roderick hears from her lips—a line from one of her tragedies: "Nor dare th'im-mortal Gods my rage oppose" (218). Although he ultimately triumphs, it will be no easy task. Smollett, in describing Roderick's relationship with the aunt, underscores the serious flaw in his hero's character: his vanity. Pretending to be uneducated during his service to her, Roderick still can-not contain himself when his impetuous nature leads him to reveal his knowledge in triumphant fashion. Moreover, when Narcissa's aunt parades her literary talents before him for his approval, Roderick, again through vanity and in an attempt to impress Narcissa, offers some examples of his own love poems. Such conduct jeopardizes his position in the household and was hardly designed to please the lady. These are perhaps small points, but it is clear that minor characters, whatever their intrinsic inter-est, are used by Smollett to serve the purposes of his fiction as a whole. His treatment of female characters—whether idealized heroines or gro-tesque satires—are intended to function within the novels for some larger purposes, and this, in fact, must affect the way in which they are treated.

Still, Narcissa's aunt, like the other comic and grotesques already dis-cussed, is a minor character, given only brief treatment. Smollett's major achievement in his use of such types comes in the more extensive devel-opment of pairs of characters in *Peregrine Pickle* (Grizzle Pickle and Per-egrine's mother) and *Humphry Clinker* (Tabitha Bramble and Win Jenkins). Here are Smollett's powers at their fullest, devastating in their commentary, able to balance the ugly grotesque against the simply comic, and using everything in his arsenal to satirize the foibles, affectations, and hypocrisies of his society through the portrayal of four female characters, as different as they are alike. Perry's mother has none of the softer qualities of Grizzle Pickle; Tabby has none of the open charm of Win Jenkins. And yet they share some fundamental flaws—signs of fatal deficiencies in one and symbols simply of weaknesses in the other. They are flaws grotesque in one and comic in the other.

In *Peregrine Pickle* Smollett offers two clearly grotesque characters: Grizzle Pickle, the aunt of Peregrine, the hero, and later the wife of his benefactor, the bizarre Commodore Trunnion; and Perry's vicious and unnatural mother. Both women play significant roles in the development of the novel's plot and contribute, as in all women in Smollett's fiction, to a fuller understanding of his male protagonist. Yet the pairing of the two grotesques displays Smollett's recognition of the various possibilities inherent in the literary technique of caricature. By setting up the two as contrasting grotesques, he demonstrates that this type of characterization in one instance can serve comic purposes, allow for satire that creates humor and can be leavened by sympathetic touches, while in the other instance it can allow for an all out attack on the dark side of human nature and undermine commonplace and conventional beliefs about such a thing as the nurturing kindness of motherhood. Grizzle emerges as a comic figure, sympathetic for all her flaws and larger than the stereotypical portrait of the old maid. Perry's mother, as Smollett puts it, is a monster, her conduct a rebuttal to the eighteenth-century concept that maternity breeds tenderness along with childbirth.

From her first appearance in the opening pages of *Peregrine Pickle*, Grizzle puts forth a dazzling display of the grotesque qualities attributed to the typical old maid so popular in the fiction and drama of Smollett's time. In his customary fashion, Smollett foreshadows her eccentric behavior with a description of her bizarre appearance.[22] With biting irony that does not hint of later development in her character, however, he describes her defects of conduct and her physical unattractiveness that, despite her fortune, have kept her a virgin at the age of thirty:

These [financial] qualifications, one would think, might have been the means of abridging the term of her celibacy, as she never expressed any aversion for wedlock; but, it seems, she was too delicate in her choice, to find a mate to her inclination in the city [an observation shortly to be belied by her marriage to the eccentric and equally unattractive Commodore Trunnion]; tho' the charms of her person were not altogether enchanting, nor her manner over and above agreeable. Exclusive of a very wan (not to call it sallow) complexion, which perhaps was the effect of her virginity and mortification, she had a cast in her eyes that was not at all engaging, and such an extent of mouth, as no art or affectation could contract into any proportionable dimension: then her piety was rather peevish than resigned, and did not in the least diminish a certain stateliness in her demeanour and conversation, that delighted in communicating the importance and honour of her family, which, by the bye, was not to be traced two generations back, by all the power of heraldry or tradition. (2–3)

Smollett picks up on the "family pride" of Grizzle to poke fun at her ignorance as well as her pretentiousness. She makes a bad choice of a bride—ultimately Perry's mother—for her brother as a result of her concern for continuing their heritage. Then, when her sister-in-law sends her in quest of a pineapple, maliciously feigning a craving to antagonize her, Grizzle goes on a three-day search because she again is driven by her familial pride and is worried about the well-being of the offspring.

But most of Grizzle's ludicrous behavior centers upon caricature of an old maid's craving for a man. In most ways she foreshadows Smollett's depiction of Tabitha Bramble in *Humphry Clinker*, although ultimately Smollett portrays Grizzle as a more attractive character. Like Tabitha she desperately attempts every means available to her to ensnare a husband. At her brother's wedding, she "summoned her whole exertion to play off the artillery of her charms, upon the single gentlemen who were invited to the entertainment" (16). She pathetically affects airs and manners uncommon to her. Her hospitality and affability have no limits. Conscious of her purpose, she alters her manner of speech and plays the role of the coy and demure maiden. Ludicrously, "conscious of the extraordinary capacity of her mouth, she would not venture to hazard a laugh, modelled her lips into an enchanting simper, which played upon her countenance all day long" (16). Grizzle foolishly attempts to use her unattractive eyes to advantage, falsely pretending to modesty, and lies about her age. When she accompanies her playing on the harpsichord with singing, Smollett slyly notes that her voice was "not the most melodious in the world" (17). All of course is to no avail as Smollett describes the effect on Trunnion, the retired seaman whose sole familiarity with women is his experience with whores at the docks.

For all the comedy in this grotesque portraiture, Smollett manages to suggest the frustration and even a kind of pathos in the circumstances that drive Grizzle. In the process, for all her oddity, she comes across as a more sympathetic character than Tabitha Bramble, although both women have to settle for men as grotesque as they are. Smollett sets forth, not without some feeling, her circumstances after her brother's wedding:

Mrs. Grizzle, who finding her importance in the family greatly diminished, her attractions neglected by all the male-sex in the neighborhood, and the withering hand of time hang threatening over her head, began to feel the horror of eternal virginity, and in a sort of desperation, resolved at any rate to rescue herself from that reproachful and uncomfortable situation. (20)

Smollett underscores Grizzle's grotesqueness by her willingness, indeed her determination, to settle for the peculiar old sailor who has dismissed her advances by drinking "despair to old maids" (20). Her tenacity, no vice after all, permits Smollett to carry on his humor while Peregrine barely exists in the novel, a kind of parody of customary genealogical openings of a good many novels of the period. Indeed, parody obviously marks the scenes in which Grizzle, with the help of his old shipmates who play a prank on him, manages to inveigle Trunnion into proposing to her. When the old sea-dog is tricked into believing that Grizzle is dying after he has rejected her, he brings himself to offer marriage. In a neat parody of traditional romances, Grizzle becomes a "despairing shepherdess" and he her "swain"; as she "reclined in a state of strange expectation, he seized her hand and pressed it to his lips; but this piece of gallantry he performed in such a reluctant, uncouth, indignant manner, that the nymph had need of all her resolution to endure the compliment without shrinking." Despite Trunnion's expostulations about being led to his fate, the old maid looks forward to the termination of her celibacy (34–35).

Smollett uses her marriage and its aftermath to continue his parody of romance. In one of the great comic scenes of eighteenth-century fiction, he describes Trunnion's journey to the altar. Insistent on remaining a sailor in his way of life on shore, Trunnion has established a home that has all the accoutrements of a vessel. Now, he sets forth for his marriage embarked on a horse and equipped with sails as he is attended with his compatriots outfitted in naval regalia. As he proceeds to the ceremony in a manner befitting an old seaman whose ship is tacking with the wind, the horses get out of hand and end in a disastrous gallop that threatens to put an end to the marital plans. As though to emphasize Grizzle's desperation by demonstrating the ludicrousness of the object of her affection, Smollett describes his outlandish appearance as an almost frustrated bridegroom:

He had put on in honour of his nuptials his best coat of blue broad cloth, cut by a taylor of Ramsgate, and trimmed with five dozen of brass buttons, large and small; his breeches were of the same piece, fastened at the knees with large bunches of tape; his waistcoat was of red plush lapelled with green velvet, and garnished with vellum holes; his boots bore an intimate resemblance both in colour and shape to a pair of leather buckets; his shoulder was graced with a broad buff belt, from whence depended a huge hanger with a hilt like that of a backsword; and on each side of his pummel appeared a rusty pistol rammed in a case covered with bear-skin. The loss of his tye-periwig and laced hat, which were curiosities of the kind, did not at all contribute to the improvement of the picture, but on the contrary, by exhibiting his bald pate, and the natural extension of his lanthorn jaw, added to the peculiarity and extravagance of the whole. (38–39)

Like Tabitha and Lismahago's marriage in *Humphry Clinker*, that of Grizzle and her odd bridgegroom shouts out its parody of traditional romance. Indeed, Grizzle's response on learning of Trunnion's accident on his way to the wedding caricatures the conduct of Smollett's romantic heroines: "As soon as she understood the dangers to which her future husband was exposed, she fainted in the arms of her sister-in-law" (41–42). Still, Grizzle remains tenacious in her determination not to let him escape.

Grizzle's tenacity and Smollett's play on idyllic romanticism carry on through the odd couple's married life. Again, Smollett's treatment of the grotesque is put to comic and parodic purpose. Spending her first night with Trunnion in his "garrison," Grizzle discovers that her wedding bed is a hammock, which, of course, falls in the course of their initial marital activities. Showing the strength of her character, the bride takes over in no-nonsense fashion: "In less than two hours, the whole oeconomy of the garrison [their home] was turned topsy-turvey" (44). Despite Trunnion's physical protests, workmen re-do the garrison, and Grizzle takes charge of her husband and his loyal shipmates, Pipes and Hatchway. Within "less than three months [Trunnion] became a thorough-paced husband" (47).

Still, Smollett does not relent in his undermining of the expectations of romance as he details the married life of his two grotesque characters. Behind his comedy the novelist creates a sense of the futility and desperation that characterize Grizzle's life. She experiences a false pregnancy and takes advantage of it and Trunnion in every way. Playing upon her husband's pride, she makes inordinate demands and behaves extravagantly. Yet Smollett evokes sympathy for her when, after experiencing three false deliveries, she becomes despondent and tyrannizes her household, with the exception of Hatchway for whom she has special feelings and finds consoling. Smollett's comedy, even if it continues in comments on what surely is some of Grizzle's religious hypocrisy (not unlike Tabitha's), yields to touches of sadness as she withdraws from society for three months and resorts to the brandy bottle. It is not comedy that marks the observation that Grizzle "could not bear the sight of a child [after her misfortune] and trembled whenever the conversation happened to turn upon a christening" (51). Her emotions make more remarkable—or perhaps more understandable—her feelings for Peregrine that ultimately make Grizzle a more sympathetic character than Tabitha Bramble.

Grizzle's treatment of Perry is a saving grace in the portrait of her grotesque character. Scholars have noted that for all the stereotypical treatment of Grizzle somehow the caricature emerges sympathetically as the story develops.[23] In fact, her relationship to Perry and Smollett's use of her in opposition to the conduct of Perry's mother soften her character even in the early portions of the novel. When she sets forth in search of pineapples at her pregnant sister-in-law's request, Smollett uses the episode in part for its comic effect since, for all her pretensions of medical learning, she knows nothing of current theories that regarded the fruit as harmful to pregnant women. Still, her concerns are genuine.[24] To be sure, her behavior is motivated by her family pride as she performs Herculean labors in order to gratify Perry's mother's unreasonable demands. She is concerned with the Pickle heritage. No matter that her sister-in-law has deliberately set her on the quest in order to make her appear foolish! Grizzle's tenaciousness and loyalty are admirable characteristics. Even more to the point is Grizzle's tenderness once Perry is born. When Perry's mother cruelly goes through a regimen of thrusting the child into cold water, "the tender-hearted Mrs. Grizzle . . . opposed it with all her eloquence, shedding abundance of tears over the sacrifice when it was made" (28).

Grizzle's tenderness grows along with the boy. Impressed by his handsomeness, she overcomes the bitterness of the feelings that accompanied her own false pregnancy. Despite the cruel pranks that Perry plays on her, Grizzle becomes fonder of him, showing her feelings as he goes off to school, warming to him in the face of his mother's unnatural treatment. Smollett notes that in her treatment of the youth, "she seemed to have exchanged the disposition of a tygress, for that of a gentle kid" (153). Despite the novelist's mocking tones as Grizzle lectures Perry on how to behave on the Grand Tour, he leaves no doubt about her sincere concern for her nephew, "presenting him with her own picture set in gold, and an hundred guineas from her privy purse, [as she] embraced him affectionately, and wished him all manner of happiness and prosperity" (178). When Perry returns home after a long absence abroad, Smollett again snickers at Grizzle's provincial parochialism, but clearly displays her humanity that goes beyond caricature as she thanks God for "his happy return from a land of impiety and vice, in which she hoped his morals had not been corrupted, nor his principles of religion altered or impaired" (355). In the face of Perry's conduct abroad, her hopes may appear ludicrous, but her sentiments are genuine.

To be sure, Smollett never yields in his caricature of Grizzle, taking it all the way to her deathbed. As she suffers through her fatal illness, Hatchway, married to Grizzle after Trunnion's demise, writes to Perry about the doctor's treatment of her ailment. The old lady, he reports, has been drained of "six gallons of water. [Then, Hatchway alludes to her taste for brandy]: For my own part, I wonder how the devil it came there; for you know as how it [water] was a liquor she never took in" (583). Still, Smollett tempers his caricature as he describes her charity to the poor. Even more indicative of the fact that Grizzle has come to be less a caricature than a figure to be sympathized with is Perry's response to the news of her illness.

Without hesitation, he vainly rushes to be at her beside. His conduct displays not only the growth in the hero's character, but the attractive aspects that Smollett has lent to the grotesque figure that Grizzle presented in his playing upon the stereotypical old maid. In his development of Grizzle as a surrogate mother to Perry and also to his sister Julia, who had been exiled from her parents' home because of her defense of her brother, Smollett manages to lend breadth to his caricature even as he has employed it for the purpose of plot and as a device for both satirizing eighteenth-century conceptions of motherhood and conveying a sense of his hero's maturation.

Unlike Smollett's treatment of Grizzle Pickle, his grotesque portrait of Peregrine's mother offers no human features in its limning. In words that appear modeled on William Hogarth's engravings, Smollett's caricature delineates the ugliness of evil that lies deep within the soul of the character. Whereas his portrayal of Grizzle focuses mainly on the eccentric antics of an unmarried woman desperately desiring a man and the behavior of a domineering female determined to control the territory of her household, his account of Perry's mother goes well beyond the superficialities of grotesque conduct that has a comic aspect. With an obvious determination to make his readers squirm and to be revolted by her base behavior, Smollett relentlessly describes her unnatural treatment of her first-born, the monstrosity of her actions that an eighteenth-century audience could assess only as uncivilized and barbaric. From beginning to end Perry's mother responds to her son in a fashion outside the expected norms of a civilized society.

So horrendous is Mrs. Pickle's character that critics have been largely at a loss to deal with it. Smollett's early biographer dismisses her as improbable in her fiendishness. As a proper Victorian he found it difficult to conceive of a mother whose conduct so repugnantly repudiated the high ideals of motherhood. Both Howard Buck and Lewis Knapp, outstanding students of Smollett's work, ignore Perry's mother, either baffled by the creation or viewing her behavior as so gross that decency forbade comment. At least focusing on her role in the novel and seeking a rational explanation for her conduct, Ronald Paulson sees in Perry's mother's actions an attempt to dominate her son as she does her husband.[25] While true, the observation hardly does justice to the extent of the mother's malicious and unnatural treatment of her son.

In what is by far the fullest assessment of Mrs. Pickle's character, R. G. Collins presents a badly flawed argument that her behavior emanates from the fact that Perry is her illegitimate son, conceived prior to her desperate marriage to Gamaliel Pickle. Collins, mindful of Smollett's ongoing rivalry with Henry Fielding, sees the novelist as imitating *Tom Jones* as retaliation for what he regarded as Fielding's plagiarism of his earlier novel, *Roderick Random*. To bolster his argument, Collins points to the resemblance between Peregrine's treatment and that of Samuel Johnson's friend, the poet Richard Savage, whose purported "mother," the countess of Macclesfield, denied that he was her son. Collins also notes the parallels between the Savage story and the "Annesley Case," a contemporary cause celebre of an "unacknowledged claimant" whose story Smollett included as an inset in *Peregrine Pickle.*

Nothing in Collins's evidence holds up to examination. If Savage's experience provided a source for Smollett's episode when Perry's mother denies he is her son, her conduct is made even more monstrous for even if Perry were illegitimate, her maternity as all the world knows is undeniable. But Collins has offered nothing that suggests Perry's illegitimacy. His mother's marriage to Gamaliel presents great financial security, and she knows in advance that her husband will be easily manipulable. She has no cause to believe that were Perry indeed illegitimate, Gamaliel would ever discover it to her embarrassment, and, given his character, she would have no difficulty were he to learn the truth. Collins ignores the incident when Perry is an infant and his mother, for an instant, displays some tenderness toward him, but he thwarts her affection (52), showing the natural antagonism between them. When young Perry rejects the harsh pedagogy of a teacher intended to impose discipline on him, how does anyone conclude that he is illegitimate after his mother attributes his conduct to paternal inheritance: "His mother was extremely mortified at these symptoms of stupidity, which she considered as an inheritance derived from the spirit of his father, and consequently insurmountable by all the efforts of human care" (53). Surely the remark refers to Gamaliel Pickle, whom she despises, and to no mysterious father. But, in an attempt to clinch his argument, Collins insists that Perry resembles neither his mother, father, nor younger brother. Even were he illegitimate, why would Perry not resemble anyone in his family? There is no question—even as Collins puts it—that he *is* Mrs. Pickle's son, and certainly, as Paulson has pointed out, Perry has inherited part of his character from her.[26] There would be no reason for him to bear no resemblance to his brother, Gam, and Collins conveniently does not note the existence of Perry's sister Julia, whose good nature reflects the side of Perry's character that separates him from his mother and balances his maternal inheritance of the need to dominate and the cruelty that goes along with it as evident in his mean practical jokes.

Perry's mother is what she is to allow Smollett to pursue his fictional purposes. Her attitude toward her son permits Smollett to get him into the Trunnion household as she turns her back on him. The novelist's finest humor emerges in the description of the various eccentrics in his surroundings. Given his relationship to the Trunnions, Perry takes off easily on the series of adventures that constitute the picaresque plot of the novel. With the indulgence of surrogate parents, he has the means to enjoy without restrictions the travels that ultimately lead to his maturation. In order to soften the hardness of his hero's character, Smollett produces two scenes in which Perry demonstrates the fundamental kindness of his nature as he responds to the deaths of his aunt Grizzle and her husband, the commodore. At the same time, because of the peculiarities of the couple, Smollett evades sentimentality by including humor in his scenes—something that would have been odd in a response to the death of a natural and normal parent. Sentiment, indeed, becomes one of Smollett's targets in his creation of Mrs. Pickle. The novelist relished the molding of a thoroughly evil character as his later relentless portrait of the antihero Ferdinand Count Fathom indicates. He delighted especially in shaking the conventional notions of motherhood as his depiction of Fathom's mother attests to. Here, with Perry's mother, he fully indulges his taste for ugly grotesque as he attacks one of the mid-eighteenth-century shibboleths of sentiment: the myth of an inevitable nurturing, tender, and devoted motherhood.

Feminist critics have abundantly demonstrated that by the time of publication of *Peregrine Pickle* a cult of motherhood was well established in England. Moreover, it had become a "centrally important sentimental trope of late eighteenth-century English literature."[27] Its presentation in the sentimental novels of the period had enormous emotional power in arousing the feelings of the reading public.[28] At the same time, as examples from Locke, Mandeville, and Johnson indicate, English theory rejected the concept of maternal instinct and attributed nurturing behavior to the civilized processes of education, reason, and a code of duty. Such civilized conduct was to be expected from English women and was the mark of conduct that separated them from savages capable of infanticide and cannibalism of their young.[29]

For Smollett, then, the creation of Mrs. Pickle worked in two ways. On the one hand, it permitted him to satirize what he undoubtedly regarded as one of the abuses promulgated by a form of fiction that, although he might use it to further the popularity of his novels, he detested. Sentimental romances were repeatedly the targets of his attack from *Roderick Random* through *Humphry Clinker*. On the other hand, Mrs. Pickle's treatment of Peregrine plainly marked her as something other than the conventional mother of mid-eighteenth-century England, a monster whose conduct placed her outside the pale of civilized society and its expectations. Her cruelty and unnatural behavior serve to set the novel on its course, to send the hero on his adventures that lead to maturation as he finds support in the kindness of the Trunnion household and ultimately conquers those aspects of his character inherited from the horrors of his maternal heritage.

For mother figures, in general, however, Smollett's novels reveal a personal view in accord with that which attributed the nurturing qualities to the civilizing processes of society rather than merely the ties of birth. To

further his narrative purposes and perhaps as a reflection of his own feelings of separation from a mother whom he obviously loved and respected,[30] he creates heroes and heroines whose loss of their mothers in
childhood leaves a gap in their emotional lives that has to be filled by the
kindness and concern of women who play the role of surrogate mother.
Mrs. Sagely protects and nourishes Roderick Random in his time of need
and offers advice that leads to the culmination of his romance with Narcissa. Serafina in *Fathom* depends on Madame Clement's wisdom and loyalty to save her from the villain and to produce the final liaison with her
lover Renaldo. It is Aurelia's natural mother in *Sir Launcelot Greaves*
whose shrewdness and tender-heartedness lead ultimately to the marriage
of the hero and heroine. With no other mature woman to turn to as model
and paragon of virtue, Lydia in *Humphry Clinker* depends on her schoolmistress Mrs. Jermyn from whom she seeks respect and approval. Even in
Peregrine Pickle the hero, rejected by his natural mother, finds a surrogate
in his aunt Grizzle who, for all her oddities, grows into the role of a caring
and concerned "parent."

Indeed, even within *Peregrine Pickle* Smollett offers a counterpart to
Perry's mother in the figure of the heroine Emilia's mother. She is everything that the ideal of motherhood calls for. After Perry has attempted to
rape Emilia, he repents and attempts to regain her favor by appealing to
her mother. Without knowing the full extent of Perry's heinous behavior,
Mrs. Gauntlet responds in a letter that is a model of appropriate maternal
decorum. It displays the full extent of motherly protection, a sense of
dignity, an expression of wisdom and shrewdness—all of the common
sense that characterizes her daughter's own conduct:

I have received the favour of yours, and am glad, for your own sake, that you
have attained a due sense and conviction of your unkind and unchristian behaviour
to poor Emy. I thank God, none of my children were ever so insulted before. Give
me leave to tell you, Sir, my daughter was no upstart, without friends or education,
but a young lady as well bred, and better born, than most private gentlewomen in
the kingdom; and therefore, though you had no esteem for her person, you ought
to have paid some regard to her family, which (no disparagement to you, Sir) is
more honourable than your own. As for the proposal, Miss Gauntlet will not hear
of it, being, that she thinks her honour will not allow her to listen to any terms of
reconciliation; and she is not yet so destitute, as to embrace an offer to which she
has the least objection. (421)

Against such a background of the ideal of maternal care, Mrs. Pickle's
wickedness and unnatural behavior may readily be judged. Smollett in-
cludes the ideal not because he simply accepts the cult of motherhood,
but precisely because he dislikes what he regards as nonsensical evasions
of reality and wants to show that Perry's mother is as much a part of the

world as are those maternal examples of kindness and nurturing. He holds up the grotesque Mrs. Pickle, as he did Fathom's mother, as an example of the foolishness of mistaking the Mrs. Gauntlets and Mrs. Sagelys as the whole picture of women's natural goodness.

Smollett does not restrict the nastiness of Mrs. Pickle's character to her treatment of Perry. Scheming, mean-spirited, and cruel, she is, as Collins notes, not a "practical joker," but rather "a mean trickster."[31] Her only expression of love is for Perry's younger brother, Gam, deformed in body and spirit—an extension of her own evil self. Perry's father is a plaything in her hands. Despite the doltish letter that he uses to propose to her, she accepts because of his attractive fortune. On her wedding night Mrs. Pickle enjoys Grizzle's foolish behavior, recognizing that it provides her with further means for ousting her sister-in-law from the position that she holds in managing the household. Mrs. Pickles does not delay in taking charge, dropping all pretense at "deference, not to say submission" and parading what she regards as her superior "pedigree" to that of the Pickles (18). She dictates to Gamaliel, controls his friendships, takes over the purse-strings. Time and again she thwarts any attempt for him to better his relationships with his son. Foolish as he is, Gamaliel recognizes her corrupt nature, and, though he can do nothing positive to counter it, he finds a negative means of combatting her by deliberately delaying the making of his will. Smollett's narrator makes clear that Gamaliel's actions—or lack of them—result from his fear for his life once he has yielded to her pressures for a testament.

Even greater venom characterizes Mrs. Pickle's treatment of her sister-in-law Grizzle and her daughter Julia. Apart from the several episodes in which she wickedly drives Grizzle from power in her household, the most revealing scenes are those in which she contrives to send Grizzle off in quest of pineapples to gratify what she pretends to be her craving in pregnancy. Recognizing Grizzle's concern for family pride as it relates to the coming Pickle heir, Perry's mother artfully compels her to set off on a search requiring feats similar to the trials of Hercules. To be sure the events bring forth some of the finest examples of Smollett's humor—for Smollett, as usual, never loses sight of his fictional purpose—but the episode also underscores the cruelty that characterizes Perry's mother.

Hatred between the women increases as Grizzle's nurturing of Perry contrasts with his mother's treatment of him. Willing enough to permit Grizzle to care for the infant when she finds it convenient, Mrs. Pickle ultimately ousts her from responsibility—not out of love for her child, but rather through spite. The pair quarrel over Mrs. Pickle's prescription for giving the baby's "blood free scope to circulate" by plunging him "headlong every morning in a tub-full of cold water." It does not matter that Smollett himself regarded such use of water as medically effective or that in this instance the child thrived. Smollett uses the episode to contrast the two women, to show Grizzle's caring nature as compared to the glee with which her sister-in-law performed the action "with her own hands": "The operation seemed so barbarous to the tender-hearted Mrs. Grizzle, that she not only opposed it with all her eloquence, shedding abundance of tears over the sacrifice when it was made; but took horse immediately, and departed for the habitation of an eminent country physician, whom she consulted" (28). In describing the increasing hatred between the two women—centered about their feelings for Peregrine—Smollett's narrator assesses their merits as he notes the "unnatural behaviour" of Perry's mother (109). Enforcing his view of Mrs. Pickle's mean-spiritedness, he summarizes his observations of her conduct when she chooses to ignore Grizzle on the death of Trunnion, her husband: "nor was his [Perry's] mother humane enough to visit her sister-in-law in her distress" (394). Instead, she uses the occasion to reinforce Gamaliel's estrangement from their son.

Mrs. Pickle's conduct toward her daughter Julia virtually rivals that of her behavior toward Perry in its unnaturalness. Despite her mother's teaching and threats, Julia develops an affection for the brother she does not know. When brother and sister meet, Mrs. Pickle responds with an emotional outburst that Smollett describes as "unnatural aversion" (170). Perry intervenes to keep his mother away from his sister, and Mrs. Pickle's reaction bears out the description: "Her eyes gleamed with all the rage of indignation, which choaked up her utterance, and seemed to convulse her whole frame; she twisted her left hand in his hair, and with the other buffeted him about the face, till the blood gushed from his nostrils and mouth" (171). As for her daughter, who knows that her mother will blacken her reputation in the neighborhood, Mrs. Pickle bars her from her home and "renounced her as unworthy of her affection and regard" (172). For Smollett's narrator Perry's mother can be described only as a "she-dragon" (173).

Mrs. Pickle's fury with Julia because of the young woman's sympathy for her brother marks the onset of a set of incidents designed to emphasize her unnatural behavior. Upon Julia's marriage, Perry's mother must be kept away out of fear for the havoc she will cause. Mrs. Pickle and her husband's conduct is characterized as "unnatural barbarity" (358). She herself certainly deserves the characterization as she prevents her weak-willed husband from reconciling with his daughter. Lest the reader believe that Perry's mother's behavior is restricted to her family, the narrator notes that the justice of the peace, whom she calls upon to prevent the marriage, was "no stranger to the malevolence of the mother" (358). Smollett effectively contrasts her treatment of Julia with Grizzle's generosity to the young woman. In opposing Julia and Grizzle's behavior to that of Perry's mother, Smollett gives emphasis to Mrs. Pickle's unnatural conduct. In place of the expected maternal emotions of Mrs. Pickle, the reader is presented with the surrogate motherhood of Grizzle to both of Mrs. Pickle's offspring, and Julia's sympathetic response to her brother plainly substitutes for what should have been his mother's reactions. As Perry returns to England after his tour of the Continent, it is Julia who demonstrates the kind of feelings that were the ideals of motherhood expected at the time: "her heart began to throb with violence; and running out in the hurry and perturbation of her hope, she was so much overwhelmed at sight of her brother, that she actually fainted in his arms" (355).

Mrs. Pickle's monstrous behavior is most evident in her treatment of Perry. Without explanation it begins prior to his birth with the incident of her demands for pineapples, which, as George Rousseau has pointed out,[32] medical theory regarded as "a powerful stimulant to abortion." Whether, as Rousseau argues, Smollett's readers, but not Mrs. Pickle, would recognize the significance of her choice, the fact remains that it foreshadows the entirety of their relationship. From infancy on, Perry's mother displays unrelenting antagonism toward him. She pushes him off to school when he is four years old; sends him further away when he is six; and responds to Trunnion's reports on his good progress with "indifference and want of faith" in his account (56). After not seeing him for four years, she lacks all interest in him or, as the narrator puts it, she "was perfectly weaned of that infirmity known by the name of maternal fondness" (62). Smollett's comment clearly intends to remind the reader of the soporific nonsense promulgated in sentimental romances about the innate characteristics of motherhood.

Mrs. Pickle's antipathy toward her son and Smollett's linking it to his attack on popular notions in romances continue after she has relinquished all claims to Perry and allowed Commodore Trunnion to take over his life. When she confronts him on his return to Trunnion, "her countenance changed, she eyed him with tokens of affliction and surprize, and bursting into tears, exclaimed her child was dead." She labels Perry an imposter. Smollett's narrator, conveying the novelist's message about the falsities of romantic notions of maternal love and caring, declares, "This unaccountable passion ... had no other foundation than caprice and whim" (64). Like modern psychoanalytic theory, the remark makes mother hate as natural as mother love or at least as likely. Smollett carries on his argument even after Perry's mother has given up her claim that he is not her son, for "she still continued to abhor him, as if she really believed him to be such." Irate even when she is questioned about him, she behaves, according to the narrator, "like a most rancorous stepmother," behavior labeled as "unnatural caprice" (78–79).

Right into Perry's adulthood his mother's rage continues, and Smollett makes certain that his audience recognizes a major part of his purpose in creating his character. Mrs. Pickle cannot bear even to hear Perry's name mentioned; she delights in believing he is ruining himself in his romance with Emilia. So devastating is Smollett's portrait that he must have his narrator remark on the grotesque caricature, and he does so in a manner that suggests what audiences expected in novelistic depictions of motherhood:

I am afraid the reader will think I represent a monster that never existed in nature, and be apt to condemn the oeconomy of my invention; nevertheless, there is nothing more true than every circumstance of what I have advanced; and I wish the picture, singular as it is, may not be thought to resemble more than one original. (107)

The last comment suggests how Smollett's fiction depends, in part, for its effect on his readers' interest in real-life affairs. Surely Smollett alludes to the contemporary curiosity about Richard Savage's claims about his rejection by his "mother" and to the circumstances of the Annesley affair that provides an inset for his novel.

No mention of Perry's mother fails to describe her conduct as unnatural. Hers is a "monstrous prejudice," a "distemper" void of "maternal regard" (108). By the time of Grizzle's death late in the novel, Mrs. Pickle has become "more determined in her rancor, that which was originally a sudden transport of indignation, being by this time settled into a confirmed inveteracy of hate" (584). On Perry's return to take over his deceased father's estate, she behaves like a madwoman, first trying to assail him with her nails and then verbally assaulting him. So uncontrolled is her hatred that she rejects his every offer of generosity.

By using grotesque caricature of mother hatred, Smollett has undermined the stereotypical idea of maternal love and concern. Mrs. Pickle plays her role in Smollett's satiric scheme in the novel even as she provides an important element in plot development and characterization of his hero.

Coming from the ugliness of Perry's mother to the lighter atmosphere of *Humphry Clinker*, the reader must find that even the caricature of the grotesque Tabitha Bramble, let alone the comedy of Win Jenkins, must come as a relief. That is saying a great deal in the case of Tabby, who has few redeeming features apart from the humor that she provides. In Tabby, however, the avaricious, selfish, mean-spirited, and sex-starved sister of Matt, the novel's central character, Smollett, in the fullness of his talent, takes a stereotypical character, exaggerates it to grotesque extremes, and manages to create a figure who remains one of the most memorable portraits in his fictional gallery.[33] As noted earlier Tabby's type was well established prior to the appearance in Smollett's novel. At least as early as her comic parading on the Restoration stage, the old maid or spinster was a target for ferocious wit. In seventeenth-century France Molière found ludicrous the pathos of the unmarried woman whose greatest sin was her inability to find a man to satisfy her sexual needs. Such eighteenth-century writers as Defoe, Richard Steele, and Henry Fielding, in varying but always stinging terms, mocked her situation and laughed at her desperate efforts to find a comfortable place in society—one that would elevate her from dependency on others and relieve her from the condition of unwanted sister or aunt. As Smollett's earlier use of the stereotype for Narcissa's aunt in *Roderick Random* and Grizzle Pickle in *Peregrine Pickle* reveals, he found great humor in the conventional view of the hopelessly unmarried woman.

For the eighteenth-century audience generally, the idea of the old maid, whether in fiction or on stage, evoked a response as stereotypical as the character itself. After all, accepting as they were of the gross portraits of Irishmen, Scots, and Jews in drama and in prose, audiences could be expected to respond automatically to the anticipated humor in appearances of the spinster with her given set of characteristics. Remarkable, then, was the reaction of someone like Mrs. Griffiths in the *Monthly Review* to Arthur Murphy's play *The Old Maid*.[34] For Mrs. Griffiths Murphy's treatment of the character was a "cruel insult, not upon vice or folly, but upon misfortune" as it assailed a woman for "her homely person and stale virginity," the very characteristics that mark Tabby in Smollett's novel. But hers was not only a lonely voice of protest at the time, but one that failed to echo through the years. As late as the mid-twentieth century a critic of Murphy's drama could denigrate Mrs. Griffiths's comments by dismissing them as a "petticoat view."[35]

Smollett, then, could feel secure in the stereotype, which had already gained such acceptance that the *Old Maid* stood as the title of a periodical essay-sheet (1756) edited by a woman at the very time that he was engaged in a journalistic career. Yet Smollett does not merely accept the stereotype; he breathes new life into it and invests the character with such fictional credibility that whatever its exaggerations it has become a memorable figure in the history of the eighteenth-century novel. Through what has been described as his "vigorous dramatization," the name "Tabby" was to become not only the appellation for an old maid, but in turn that of the striped cat and ultimately the female cat,[36] a kind of tribute to the characteristics identifiable with Miss Bramble in his novel. In *Humphry Clinker*, through Smollett's adept caricature and shrewd use of his epistolary technique, Tabby comes alive as a real person. She is a pivotal figure in his work, serving his purposes in a comic romance and reinforcing his theme of the vices of luxury.[37] Smollett employs her to draw forth the essential features of Matt Bramble; he uses her to provide necessary cohesiveness to his narrative;[38] and he sets her to work as an important element in his social satire.

While Smollett's use of the epistolary technique has been credited with providing him with the ability for the first time in his work to establish

convincing structure, it has not been emphasized enough as a device for
enhancing his characterization. If the reader comes to know a character
through what the character says and does and what others say about the
character, the epistolary narrative certainly is the best means of offering
characterization. It is far more convincing to present the multiple point of
view that Smollett's letters offer than to have a single narrative voice attempting to convey the same information. Whatever else Smollett's
method does, in defining the character of Tabby through her own words
and by the observations of her companions on the journey that carries the
narrative of *Humphry Clinker*, the method turns the flatness of the grotesque caricature into a rounded portrait of Tabby's character.

Anyone coming to the novel for the first time after having read about
it may be surprised to discover that Tabby's total epistolary contribution
amounts to only six letters. Moreover, only one runs to as much as a single
page; most of the rest are no more than a paragraph in length. While
much has been made of Tabby's malapropisms and their sexual innuendoes, these, too, are naturally limited by the amount of space that Smollett
affords them. Yet they are sufficient to suggest the qualities that Smollett
hopes to establish in the character through her own person. The malapropisms, if somewhat surprising for someone of her social status,[39] indicate her limited education and suggest the affectation in her attempt to
impress her even less educated housekeeper, Mrs. Gwyllim, to whom they
are addressed.

Despite the limited number of letters, Smollett manages neatly to represent the sexual repression that drives Tabby's character. Her malapropisms—frequently indicative of her pronunciation—suggest to the reader
the sexual preoccupations of her mind. Smollett's audience could not have
missed the point of her repeated rendering of *accounts* as *accunts*. It may
be no more than a matter of orthographical transcription of speech when
she replaces *shut* by *shit* or describes the maid Mary Jones as a "hussy
[who] loves *rumping* [rather than *romping*] with the men" (6). Still these
all indicate the anatomical fixation of Tabby's psyche. Hired *hands* are
invariably *hinds*, and her contemptuous reference to Matt's friend, Dr.
Lewis, who has shunned her advances will deny him any access to her
"though he beshits me on his bended knees" (156).

Best of all, though, is the sexual imagery she employs unconsciously in
her description of how Humphry, Matt's illegitimate son who later marries
Win Jenkins, her maid, will impress himself not only upon Win, but also
the other servants of the household: "Our new footman, a pious young
man, who has laboured exceedingly, that [Win] may bring forth fruits of
repentance [through this Methodist preaching]. I make no doubt but he
will take the same pains with that pert hussey Mary Jones, and all of you;
and that he my have power given to penetrate and instill his goodness,
even into your most inward parts, is [my] fervent prayer" (274–75). Not

only does Smollett comment here on Tabby's voracious sexual appetite, but by uniting her words to religious fervor, he satirizes at the same time her Methodist convictions. For Smollett, the unbalanced sexual drive reflects the same excesses in the Methodist faith and explains the appeal of the latter to women.

Five of Tabby's six letters are addressed to her housekeeper, and, of course, that helps somewhat to account for their tone and content and limits what she can say. Their brevity and tone are consistent with her relationship to her servant. Not only can she not reveal her feelings about men to Mrs. Gwyllim or recount her experiences with them, but she is hardly likely to tell her housekeeper about what is going on within her family. Closed-mouthed about her niece Lydia's affair—one of the reasons for the Brambles' journey—she has warned Win Jenkins, her maid, to remain the same. As Win informs Mary Jones, her correspondent—after she has revealed the secret—"Mistress bid me not speak a word of the matter to any Christian soul" (7). Tabby's tactiturnity, of course, extends to her own "romances." Even when, close to the end of the adventures, she foreshadows her marriage to Lismahago, her hints of the event come only in her orders to Mrs. Gwyllim. Telling her that she wants the bed and mattress "well haired," she cannot bring out the facts, but merely suggests, "because, perhaps, with the blissing of heaven, they may be yoosed on some occasion" (274). The very manner in which she accounces her marriage suggests the relationship between Tabby and her housekeeper. She distances herself from the action by ascribing it to "HEAVEN, [which] for wise purposes, hath ordained that I should change my name and cituation in life" (351), and then continues to give orders for household management.

If Smollett is suggesting that the very nature of Tabby's correspondent indicates her alienation from the rest of society—all her traveling companions address their letters to friends—it is to establish the coldness of her character. Smollett does nothing to mitigate the savagery of his portrait of an old maid whose only expression of feeling for another being throughout much of the novel is her concern for her miserable and intemperate dog Chowder, a monster who shares her meanest characteristics,[40] and even he is replaced in her fervor for Humphry's Methodist preaching. Whether writing to Mrs. Gwyllim or Dr. Lewis, Tabby displays her vanity and absurdity and exhibits a stinginess not only financial, but of ordinary human affection. The closest that Tabby comes to warm expression is in her closing of her final letter when she signs off with "Your loving friend" (352). But that is the extent of her generosity. Whereas Win Jenkins repeatedly sends small gifts to her friend, Tabby offers nothing to Mrs. Gwyllim or others, but instead finds excuses for not doing so, even when it comes to saving their souls: "If I had a private opportunity, I would send them [the servants] some hymns to sing instead of profane ballads; but, as I can't, they and you must be contented with [my] prayers" (157).

Everywhere in her limited number of letters, Tabby indicates her suspicious nature along with her stinginess. From first to last she expresses her distrust of her servants and her desire to give them as little as possible. She is overly concerned about their sexual proclivities and determined to keep them from enjoying each other. In particular, she distrusts Win's friend, Mary Jones, who for her is a hussy. She wants the maids kept busy and declares the wine-cellar off limits to the men. Complaining about Matt's generosity, Tabby watches every detail of the household that she has left behind, insistent that her brother's good nature takes "another good penny out of my pocket" (44).

Even in her happiest moments, she remains conscious of expenses at her expense. Anticipating her marriage to Lismahago, she has not mellowed in her attitude toward her servants, accusing them of laziness and wishing that she could do away with meat for their meals. Her letter accouncing her marriage carries a request for a maid to replace Win, now Humphry's wife, but warns: "she must not expect extravagant wages.... I must be more eoccumenical than ever" (351–52). As she earlier told Mrs. Gwyllim, Tabby's servants must not expect grace from her: "If you are found a good and faithful servant, great will be your reward in heaven" (156).

Tabby's single letter to Dr. Lewis underscores the same qualities in her character, particularly her affectation and lack of charity. Smollett appropriately contrasts her attempted sense of conveying her own authority with the slew of malapropisms that undercut the very image that she hopes to present. Angered by his earlier rejection of her advances, as her imperious letter to Mrs. Gwyllim indicates, Tabby gruffly takes him to task for what she regards as his responsibility for having given a lambskin to one of the hands. Its vituperation, sense of privilege, and selfishness mark it as one of her nastiest letters. Berating Lewis for "encourag[ing] servants to pillage their masters," she suggests he "mought employ your talons better" (78). The letter, filled as it is with sexually suggestive malapropisms and innuendoes about her not being taken advantage of by him as a man, reveals not only the underlying sexual drives that power her behavior, but the meanness with which it manifests itself in her conduct.

One last point that emerges from Tabby's letters suggests greater subtlety in Smollett's art than he has been credited with. Despite the full account of Tabby's personality that comes through much of the early letters by the various correspondents in the novel, Smollett holds off a physical description of her until the narrative is well along. Still, Tabby's appearance is suggested in her very first letter as she gives instructions to Mrs. Gwyllim for packing her trunks. Be sure to include, she directs her housekeeper, "my rose collard neglejay, with green robins, my yellow damask, and my black velvet suit, with the short hoop; my bloo quilted petticoat, my green manteel, my laced apron, my French commode ["tall head-dress"], Macklin head and lappets ["Mecklin head-dress with streamers"], and the litel box with my jowls" (6). Not only does the catalogue suggest Tabby's vanity; it offers the reader the opportunity to envision her appearance well before she has been described in full. Well before her nephew Jery has provided a detailed description of Tabby's grotesque appearance, Smollett has foreshadowed it with an account of her taste and anticipated it with the exaggerated account of her wardrobe.

The fullness of Smollett's characterization of Tabby's character comes, of course, in the comments of her fellow travelers, who offer both general views of her and the detailed account of her pursuit of a husband. Although limited, Win's and Lydia's general comments indicate Tabby's overall unattractiveness. It is largely through Tabby's tutelage that Win Jenkins takes on airs about herself, unfortunately mimicking Tabby's sense of self-importance, although never to the point of becoming as obnoxious as her mistress. Win's remarks to Mary Jones about Tabby's warnings to keep silent about family matters, something she is unable to do, suggest her mistress's demanding manner. That Win understands Tabby's sexual situation becomes clear in an anecdote that she relates to her friend. Attending the zoo with Tabby and being informed that the lions will carry on when approached by a young woman who is not a virgin, Win recounts the wild effect that Tabby's presence has on the animal. But in all innocence she declares to her friend, "but I'll go to death upon it, I will, that my lady is as good a firchin, as the child unborn" (108).

Lydia's views of her aunt are more serious, and while she is too proper to declare to her friend Letty her real feelings about Tabby, she repeatedly contrasts her with her uncle Matt. Much of this she conveys by her emphasis on her uncle's kindness, while either ignoring Tabby or suggesting the hardness of her character. When she describes to her former schoolmistress Mrs. Jermyn the familial reactions to her romance with Wilson (young Dennison), she knows that she will have her uncle's forgiveness, but she notes, "My aunt continues to chide me severely when we are by ourselves" (9–10). She recognizes Tabby's narrow-mindedness when she reports on her aunt's objection to her attending a coffeehouse for ladies in Bath because "young girls are not admitted, inasmuch as the conversation turns upon politics, scandal, philosophy, and other subjects above our capacity" (40). It is not without a hint of censure that Lydia writes about the "cordial, which [Tabby] always keeps in her pocket" (91), presumably for medicinal purposes. Although not weighty, Lydia's general comments on Tabby are a precursor to her condemnatory remarks later in the novel about her aunt's quest for a man.

Far more severe and denigrating are observations on Tabby made by Matt and Jery that clearly reflect Smollett's own attitude on the grotesque old maid whom he is ridiculing. From the very outset, in a letter to Dr. Lewis, who knows her well enough, Matt expresses his exasperation with his sister. For him she is "that fantastical animal," and "so intolerable, that I almost think she's the devil incarnate come to torment me for my sins. . . . I an't married to Tabby, thank Heaven!" (12). When she torments him about the lambskin he gave to one of his hands, Matt calls her "a domestic daemon" and again blesses God that "she is not yoked with me for life, in the matrimonial waggon." He describes her quarrels with servants about the gratuities that they expect and then pleads with Lewis, "Can't you find some poor gentleman of Wales, to take this precious commodity off [my] hands" (77–78). Even when he has dressed her down because of her conduct in the initial meeting with Humphry, he does not trust her reformation to last. Describing her as a "changed creature," he surmises that her "smile [is] like Malvolio['s] in the play—I'll be hanged if she is not acting a part which is not natural to her disposition, for some purpose which I have not yet discovered" (107). Unwilling to deny his responsibility to her and even protecting her from what he knows would be marriage only for her fortune, Matt dislikes the stereotypical spinster and longs to unburden himself of her.

The most devastating commentary by far comes from Jery in his exposition and narration. Unhampered by the kind of responsibility that Matt has for Tabby, Jery can freely describe her vices. He constantly compares her ill-nature with Matt's pretended harshness and marvels at his uncle's bearing up under the burden of caring for her. In doing so Jery provides an insight into one of Tabby's major functions in the novel. Useful for the structural unity of *Humphry Clinker*, serviceable as an instrument for Smollett's satire, and a vehicle for comic humor in herself, Tabby offers a means through which the fullness of her brother's character may be developed. Particularly in Jery's observations, Matt Bramble emerges as a type of the good-natured man who protects himself by offering a tough exterior. He is the benevolent misanthrope,[41] and nothing demonstrates this better than his tolerance of a harping and harrowing old maid.

In his very first letter, Jery informs his friend that "My aunt, Mrs. Tabitha Bramble, is a maiden of forty-five, exceeding starched, vain, and ridiculous" (8). Doing so, Jery becomes Smollett's mouthpiece for ascribing the difficult Tabitha's conduct to her sexual deprivation. This woman, he says, is "a perpetual grind-stone" for Matt,, "a striking contrast to her brother (28). And why? obviously because she is "declining into the most desperate state of celibacy" (32). In his letter from Edinburgh on 8 August, when the rest of the company has been soothed by the pleasant environs of Scotland, Jery savagely records Tabby's preparation for a ball and her conduct when she has failed to attract a man. "[She] had entertained hopes of being able to do some execution among the cavaliers of this assembly—She had been several days in consultation with milliners and mantua-makers, preparing for the occasion, at which she made her appearance in a full suit of damask, so thick and heavy, that the sight of it alone, at this time of year, was sufficient to draw drops of sweat from any man of ordinary imagination." Unsuccessful, "she became dissatisfied and censorious," commenting nastily on men and women. Jery then concludes: "Tabby herself was the most ridiculous figure, and the worst dressed of the whole assembly—The neglect of the male sex rendered her malcontent and peevish" (224–25).

Jery's letters substantiate the picture that comes through in Tabby's. When she mistakes Matt's charitable treatment of a widow for his payment for his personal misconduct, Jery attacks her suspicious nature and calls her "of all antiquated maidens the most diabolically capricious—Ever prying into other people's affairs" (22). He compares her conduct to "one of the sister Furies that guard the gates of hell" (79). He contrasts Matt's response to Humphry's pathetic poverty with Tabby's objection to the "filthy tatterdemalion," and when the poor fellow has made his first appearance in his bare posterior, she, in her false prudishness, reacts by being affronted by "his naked skin . . . he had insulted her with his obscenity." She comes off even worse when her vanity is gratified by his "compliment and [self-] humiliation" and by his ludicrous address to her as a "good, sweet, beautiful lady," of "noble countenance," and "handsome" (81–82). For Jery Tabby is a figure of fun, attractive only as an object of ridicule.

In the process of supporting these general observations of Tabby's character by her fellow travelers' running commentary on her desperate pursuit of a husband, Smollett bolsters the rhythmical device that provides the structural cohesiveness in his novel. *Humphry Clinker*, unlike his other works, has been praised for achieving a sense of unity in its narrative. As Tabby repeatedly fashions her sights on every man who crosses her path, each incident reinforces the impression of her character and, by recalling earlier episodes, holds the whole together. At the same time, the growing impatience and sense of desperation in her conduct allow for a development and progression in understanding her emotions and advancing the action of the novel. Smollett achieves the rhythm of *Humphry Clinker* by using the idea of a quest in the adventures of each of its characters: Matt's search for health; Jery's for maturity; Lydia's for romance; and Win's for social status. However, Tabby's insistent seeking out a husband marks a major portion of the novel's comic action.

Whether in his minor or major episodes, the pattern Smollett employs remains the same: Tabby's desperation; the unavailability of her objects of desire, whether young or old, whole or infirm, socially superior or inferior; and the old maid's final frustration—with the ultimate exception of Obadiah Lismahago, whose conquest resolves a major portion of the narrative. In each instance, even the resolution through Lismahago, Smollett presents Tabby's actions as ludicrous. Only with the modern use of

the word *pathetic* as *absurd* can her situation be so described. Seen mainly
through Jery and Matt's eyes, her behavior offers material for laughter
and mockery. In none of the commentary does the conduct of the spinster
suggest the novelist's sympathy for her plight. Even prior to the action of
the novel, as Jery reveals, Tabby has vainly pursued a recruiting officer,
curate, lieutenant of a man of war, and even Dr. Lewis. For Jery it is more
laughable than pitiful to recount her conduct emanating not only from her
natural temperament, but from "disappointment in love; for her long celibacy is by no means owing to her dislike of matrimony: on the contrary,
she has left no stone unturned to avoid the reproachful epithet of old
maid" (60).

While three of the episodes in *Humphry Clinker*—those with Sir Ulic
Mackilligut, Mickelwhimmen, and Lismahago—suggest serious possibilities for a match, Tabby's inordinate desire also creates a host of minor
misadventures, which even for the modern reader, likely to be more sympathetic than Smollett's contemporaries to his stereotype, are comic in
themselves. When Tabby believes that young Barton's pursuit of Lydia is
directed at her, Jery caustically notes her voracious appetite for a man
and lack of discretion. After suggestively questioning whether she "mistakes, or affects to mistake," he recounts her ludicrous performance: "she
returns his compliments with hyperbolical intent, she persecutes him with
her civilities at table, she appeals to him for ever in conversation, she sighs
and flirts, and ogles." Unsympathetic to her foolish behavior, Jery summarizes his aunt's conduct as "ludicrous affectation and impertinence"
(96).

With an equal lack of sympathy, Matt's letter to Lewis offers the cul-
minating scene of Tabby's farce—one that certainly was familiar to eighteenth-century readers experienced in the theater. Barton accompanies
Tabby to a meeting with Matt believing that she is championing his suit
for Lydia's hand rather than her own. Interrupting Barton's appeal to
Matt, Tabby stridently and pompously declares that the decision belongs
to her and not to her brother: "If I pay him the compliment of making
him acquainted with the step I intend to take, it is all he can expect in
reason. . . . I have been prevailed upon to alter my resolution of living a
single life, and to put my happiness in his [Barton's] hands" (142). Poor
Barton faints, but the scene continues. When Lady Griskin, their distant
relative, arrives to argue on Barton's behalf for Lydia, she and Tabby
almost come to blows. Matt delights in his description: "Lady Griskin's
face was like the full moon in a storm of wind, glaring, fiery, and porten-
tuous; while Tabby looked grim and ghastly, with an aspect breathing
discord and dismay" (143). For Matt and Smollett the event, whatever it
may do to Tabby, is the material for Restoration comedy or, as Matt puts
it when the two ladies terminate their exchange by bowing to each other
in exaggerated gestures, "the expression of the two faces, while they con-

tinued in this attitude, would be no bad subject for a pencil like that of
the incomparable Hogarth" (144). Matt provides a final touch in his next
letter to Lewis when he reports the reconciliation of the two women and
guesses that Tabby's conduct is dictated by the knowledge that the mar-
riage-brokering Lady Griskin may "provide an agreeable help-mate for
our sister Tabitha, who seems to be quite desperate in her matrimonial
designs." Still, Matt cannot believe that "any man in his senses . . . will
yoke with Mrs. Bramble from motives of affection or interest" (154).

But Tabby's desires are insatiable. Both Jery and Matt recount her pre-
occupation with Martin, gentleman highwayman who has rescued them
along the road. Although Tabby does not know his profession, she is taken
by his manners. Jery notes that she is "very full of praise of Mr. Martin's
good sense and good breeding, and seemed to regret that she had not a
further opportunity to make some experiment upon his affection" (159).
In a long report on "Tabby's progress in husband-hunting, after her disappointments at Bath and in London," Matt recalls her attempt to entrap
Martin, but he scoffingly declares that the highwayman "had been used
to snares much more dangerous than any she could lay, and escaped ac-
cordingly" (202).

Even after her meeting with Lismahago, who has left the company with
the promise of meeting them again, Tabby's mad pursuit continues. Smollett's pages on Scotland are strewn with the record of her vain endeavors
there. From Argyleshire on 3 September, Jery reports on her silly attempt
to lure Maclellin through their shared religious interests and her failure to
get beyond his spiritual concerns. Jery's letter from Carlisle on 12 September details her defeats in Scotland: "At every place where we halted, did
she mount the stage, and flourished her rusty arms, without being able to
make one conquest." She fails with Sir George Colquhoun despite her
best efforts: "She was grave and gay by turns—She moralized and meth-
odized [a pun on her religious beliefs]—she laughed and romped, and
danced, and sung, and sighed, and ogled, and lisped, and fluttered, and
flattered" (262). Unfortunately Sir George's defense proved impregnable.
No more successful are her efforts with the laird of Ladrishmore, who
saves himself in a meeting with her in the woods by bringing along the
parson of the parish.

Only briefly does Tabby reconcile herself to the hope of a reunion with
Lismahago. With the opportunity presented by Captain Brown, recently
returned from duty with Lord Clive, she recaptures her courage to pursue
the immediate prey. Thwarted by the fact that he intends to marry his
childhood sweetheart, Tabby can only console herself with the observation
and "with the toss of her nose" that, although he "was a civil fellow
enough, considering the lowness of his origin [he had been a journeyman
weaver] . . . Fortune, though she had mended his circumstances, was incapable to raise his ideas, which were still humble and plebeian" (265).

In Tabby's three major satiric romances in the novel, not only is she held up to ridicule, but the objects of her affection receive the same comic treatment from Smollett, particularly in their physical appearances. Spaced out in the novel so that they rhythmically reinforce each other, the episodes begin early on at Bath with the courtship of Tabby by Sir Ulic Mackilligut, a fortune-hunting Irish baron. It is here that Smollett—through Jery—offers the first physical description of Tabby, one that intentionally sets up the ludicrousness of her affairs:

she is tall, raw-boned, aukward, flat-chested, and stooping; her complexion is sallow and freckled; her eyes are not grey, but greenish, like that of a cat, and generally inflamed; her hair is of a sandy, or rather dusty hue; her forehead low; her nose long, sharp, and, towards the extremity, always red in cool weather; her lips skinny, her mouth extensive, her teeth straggling and loose, of various colours and conformation; and her long neck shrivelled into a thousand wrinkles—In her temper, she is proud, stiff, vain, imperious, prying, malicious, greedy, and uncharitable. (60)

Presented as the antithesis of the romantic heroine, Tabby in her major attachments attracts, for whatever their reasons, equally grotesque cavaliers to complete Smollett's parody of romance.

Sir Ulic certainly deserves the classification. As Jery remarks, he is certainly an "original." Taking lessons from a dancing master and annoying Matt in the apartment below him, Sir Ulic comes on as a comic figure, eccentric in his conduct. Jery places him "about the age of three-score, stooped mortally, . . . tall, raw-boned, hard favoured." When he removes his night cap in apologies to the ladies, he uncovers "his bald-pate." Jery's appropriate word for his bizarre appearance and conduct is "preposterous," which indeed he is (29–31). While it is difficult to imagine any woman interested in this specimen of declining manhood, it does not surprise Jery that his aunt, suffering from her own decline "into the most desperate state of celibacy, had formed some design upon the heart of Sir Ulic Mackilligut, which she feared might be frustrated by our abrupt departure from these lodgings [as Matt proposed]" (32–33).

Matt reports ironically and somewhat angrily on what he regards as a "connection [that] is exceedingly ridiculous." He recognizes at once that even an aging, "much out at elbows" suitor can be interested in Tabby only because he "has received false intelligence with respect to her fortune." For Matt the "flirting correspondence" that Tabby has established with Sir Ulic, preposterous in itself, presents an improper example for their niece Lydia, and he is determined to put an end to it (48). Tabby's determination, however, to capture the antique baron appears in the measures she takes to be his partner at the next ball at Bath, measures that include spending "some days furbishing up an old suit of black velvet to wear" (53).

Like all Tabby's alliances, with the exception of that with Lismahago, the affair with Sir Ulic concludes in comic disaster as foolish and grotesque as Tabby herself. Having been informed about Tabby's fortune, the Irish knight seeks a means for courting her "displeasure" (63). His opportunity comes when Chowder, her vicious dog, attacks Samuel Derrick, the master of ceremonies at Bath. Sir Ulic kicks the animal in her presence, and although he falsely pleads not knowing the dog belonged to her, Tabby is unforgiving. In a very real sense her identity, as Jery notes, is bound to that of the animal: "One would imagine she had distinguished this beast with her favour on account of his ugliness and ill-nature, if it was not, indeed, an instinctive sympathy between his disposition and her own" (62).

For Jery the incident—indeed the affair—affords an opportunity for merriment. Calling Sir Ulic "an old hound, that, finding her [Tabby] carrion, he quitted the scent," Jery turns her tragedy into comedy (60). His summary of the event displays delight rather than compassion. Nothing seems funnier than the desperate plight of an old maid. Jery looks forward to her next prospect for "nothing in the shape of man can come amiss. ... Though she is a violent churchwoman of the most intolerant zeal, ... she would have no objection, at present, to treat on the score of matrimony with an Anabaptist, Quaker, or Jew; and even satisfy the treaty, at the expense of her own conversion" (64).

As Tabby's pursuit of the Scot lawyer Mr. Micklewhimmen demonstrates, Jery can correctly predict his aunt's behavior. Jery describes the meeting of the pair at an inn where a company of originals is gathered, and he notes that anywhere "where there is such an intercourse between the sexes, can[not] be disagreeable to a lady of her views and temperament" (162). Toothless and so disabled that he must be waited upon (although the latter is a ruse to gain compassion from the ladies), the old Scotsman nevertheless receives Tabby's full attention. He plies his wiles upon her—wiles that Jery notes to foreshadow the disastrous outcome of the adventure. As Micklewhimmen appeals to her with "fulsome compliments, upon her piety and learning" (162), he gains her full attention.

Jery lays out the entire affair in the 1 July letter from Scarborough (173ff.). After their arrival there, Tabby employs her best efforts to captivate the Scotsman's heart by waiting upon his every need. He, in turn, continues his appeal by playing upon her Methodist beliefs. He has conned all the ladies, but Tabby stands out in her treatment of him, conveying him into the dining room, setting him up at the table, and providing him with all the delicacies he can desire. When Jery, suspecting that he is a fake, attempts to get him drunk to reveal the truth, Micklewhimmen turns the tables on him. However, the game is exposed in the course of a fire during which the lawyer miraculously regains the use of his limbs and casts

aside every obstacle, including Tabby, in making his escape from the
flames. Despite his ability to restore the good humor of the rest of the
company, "he could not regain the good graces of Mrs. Tabby" (178). For
her it is another of the unsuccessful attempts to rid herself of her unwanted
virginity.

Success finally comes with Obadiah Lismahago. Although happy in its
outcome, Tabby's ultimately gratifying relationship conveys all the comic
features of her earlier romances and points to the ludicrous figure of the
sex-starved old maid. In both physical appearance and conduct, Lismahago
displays Smollett's exaggerated grotesque characteristics sufficiently capable of matching those of Tabby. Smollett does provide Lismahago with
enough qualities to make it feasible for Matt to approve of his marriage
to Tabby, essential to demonstrating genuine feeling between brother and
sister, however much Matt finds her a burden and she resents her dependency upon him. It is a relationship that a still immature Jery does not
understand, but that he recognizes as early as the affair with Sir Ulic: "He
really has an affection for this original; which maintains its ground in defiance of common sense, and in despite of that contempt which he must
certainly feel for her character and understanding. Nay, I am convinced,
that she has likewise a most virulent attachment to his person; though her
love never shews itself but in the shape of discontent; and she persists in
tormenting him out of sheer tenderness" (62). Still, whatever Smollett's
need to provide Lismahago with positive characteristics to account for
Matt's acceptance of him, the novelist creates a comic character to match
Tabby's grotesque needs.

Smollett quickly and repeatedly establishes Lismahago's outlandish appearance, generally with an account of his odd behavior. The combination
is present in Jery's first description of the Scots lieutenant. Consistent with
his role in a comic romance, Lismahago appears "A tall, meagre figure,
answering, with his horse, the description of Don Quixote mounted on
Rozinante" (188). Jery later makes the same comparison with Cervantes's
knight of the sad countenance (283). Here he itemizes the articles of Lismahago's wornout clothing. Then, as the lieutenant attempts to dismount
his horse and accidentally comes tumbling off, "his hat and periwig falling
off, displayed a head-piece of various colours, patched and plaistered in a
woeful condition." With what proves to be his characteristic behavior, he
responds furiously to the laughter occasioned by his comical appearance.
For Jery the details are too rich for him not to complete his caricatured
portrait: Lismahago would have been six feet, "but he stooped very much;
was very narrow in the shoulders, and very thick in the calves of his legs.
...As for his thighs, they were long and slender, like those of
a grasshopper; his face was, at least, half a yard in length, brown and
shrivelled, with projecting cheek-bones, little grey eyes on the greenish
hue, a large hook-nose, a pointed chin, a mouth from ear to ear, very ill-

furnished with teeth, and a high, narrow fore-head, well furnished with wrinkles" (188). Even after Lismahago has recounted his Indian warfare and his captivity, his having been scalped by his captors, and his unfair treatment by the military that has discarded him with small recompense for his service, Jery, "without pretending to judge of his military merit, [says], I think I may affirm, that this Caledonian is a self-conceited pedant, aukward, rude, and disputatious" (190).

In later letters both Jery and Win elaborate on the bizarre image Lismahago presents, although Jery also suggests the lieutenant's intelligence, an important point if Matt, whatever his desire to marry off his sister, is to permit a wedding beneficial to her. Jery describes Lismahago's ludicrous figure as he makes his escape from a fire "in his shirt, with a quilted night-cap fastened under his chin, and his long lank limbs and posteriors exposed to the wind" (299–300). Win, too, focuses on his physical oddity as she expresses amazement at Lismahago and Tabby's "huggling and flurtation." For her the "ould Scots officer, called Kismycago ... looks for all the orld like the scarecrow that our gardener sets up to frite away the sparrows" (220). Win attributes Tabby's feelings for him to bewitchment. Regarding him as an infidel, bemoaning his lack of civility, and suggesting his roving eye, Win marvels at her mistress's interest in him: "Who would have thought that mistress, after all the pains taken for the good of her prusias sole, would go for to throw away her poor body? that she would cast the heys of infection upon such a carrying-crow as Lashmihago! as old as Matthewsullin, as dry as a red herring, and as pore as a starved veezel" (306). Win's malapropisms in themselves underscore her attitude toward the romance.

Despite Matt's willingness to find qualities in Lismahago to justify his allowing a marriage to Tabby and despite Smollett's willingness to provide the lieutenant with pro-Scottish arguments that comically support Matt's and Smollett's own views,[42] Matt finds the "old weather-beaten Scotch lieutenant" (202) no less ridiculous in appearance and conduct than Jery does. For Matt, Lismahago stands as "one of the most singular personages I ever encountered." He speaks of a "manner ... as harsh as his countenance." Matt ridicules his "knowledge made up of the remnants of rarities"; deplores "his pedantry and ungracious address"; and scoffs at his "self- conceit" (203). In his later account of Lismahago's refutation of any Scottish benefits from the Union with England, Matt clearly sympathizes with the arguments, but creates a portrait of a man so disputatious that only a most determined old maid could ever consider marrying him (275ff.).

That, of course, would have to be Tabby as Smollett clinches her absurdity in a narration of her maneuvers to capture the grotesque prize that is Lismahago. Both Jery and Matt caricature her behavior. Jery immediately notes and characterizes Tabby's designs at the first encounter with

Lismahago: "that indefatigable *maiden* [italics added] is determined to shoot at every sort of game, certain it is she has begun to practice upon the heart of the lieutenant" (190). For the entertainment of his friend, Jery provides a picture of her in action, fawning over Lismahago's name, praising his modesty for not celebrating his noble lineage after he has done so, and seeking his favor with abject adulation. She goes so far as to offer "ecomiums on his own personal address, his gallantry, good sense, and erudition" (194)—all of which Smollett has ridiculed. Utterly absorbed in Lismahago's account of his life among the Indians, when he comes to the point of his marriage to an Indian women, Tabby "*did seriously incline her ear*; indeed, she seemed to be taken with the same charms that captivated the heart of Desdemona, who loved the Moor *for the dangers he had past*" (194). Jery relentlessly pursues what he regards as Tabby's outlandish behavior here through to her later efforts to persuade Lismahago to remain in England rather than return to America.

Matt has equal fun with Tabby's romance. Remarking on her attentiveness to Lismahago's every word and her forwardness in the affair, he reports to Dr. Lewis, "Whether our sister Tabby was really struck with his conversation, or is resolved to throw at every thing she meets in the shape of a man, till she can fasten the matrimonial noose, certain it is, she has taken desperate strides toward the affection of Lismahago" (206). He notes her open invitation to him to accompany them to Scotland. With great amusement Matt later informs Lewis of the couple's seeking approval for their marriage, and he delightedly tells his correspondent, "and you shall give away the bride.—It is the least thing you can do, by way of atonement for your former cruelty to that poor love-sick maiden" (280–81). When Tabby has a momentary lapse from attention to her beloved because the newly widowed Baynard, Matt's friend, has joined the company, Matt seems not unduly worried, ascribing its cause appropriately: "These must be the instinctive efforts of her constitution, rather than the effects of any deliberate design" (344). An old maid's habits die hard.

Smollett's coup de grace to the most ludicrous if solely successful of Tabby's romances comes naturally with an account of the wedding couple. As Jery promises his correspondent, the prospect of viewing the pair in their connubial bliss would be worth a cross-country journey: "Two such original figures in bed together, with their laced night-caps; he, the emblem of good chear, and she, the picture of good nature" (281). As Jery describes her wedding attire, *outlandish* would be a charitable word. The best that can be said for it is that it is thirty years out of fashion. Jery smirks at her behavior following the wedding night: effusive about her lover's arts, coy in her unique imitation of a blushing young bride, she "giggles, and holds her hand before her eyes, affecting to be ashamed of having been in bed with a man" (349). But the final word is left to Win, whose perceptions as she describes the bride and groom take on a final dimension of ridiculousness in the maid's garbled language:

As for madam Lashmiheygo, you nose her picklearities—her head, to be sure, was fintastical; and her spouse had rapt her with a long marokin furze cloak from the land of the selvidges, thof they say it is of immense bally.—The captain himself had a large hassock of air, with three tails, and a tumtawdry coat, boddered with sulfur.—Wan said he was a monkey-bank; and the ould bottler swore he was the born imich of Titidall. (352)

In every way Smollet's comic tale of an old maid in quest of sexual gratification serves the purposes of his fiction. Not only does Tabby offer the kind of satirical humor on the stereotype that satisfies the taste of his particular audience, but it provides, as well, a series of the novel's needs: a way for making the irascible Matt a more appealing character; a contrast with the more wholesome affections of Lydia, the romantic heroine; a rhythmical device for helping achieve the structural unity of the work; and an instrument for both social and religious satire. The last point is evident in Tabby's conversion to Methodism after the appearance of Humphry Clinker in the novel.

Identifying Methodism in its effect particularly on women allows Smollett, from his point of view, not only to denigrate the religion that he had earlier mocked in *Ferdinand Count Fathom*, but to underscore the weakness in the female sex. It is a sign of Lydia's superior sense that, having been "persuaded to go" with Tabby and Win to a Methodist tabernacle (135), she is unaffected by the services and expresses some amazement that her companions "sometimes speak as if they were really inspired" (136). That Win should respond with fervor is not surprising—she, after all, follows her mistress's practices, displays extraordinary superstition, and, most important of all, represents the lower classes to whom Methodism most appealed. For Tabby to yield to the faith reveals, for Smollett, her lack of common sense and demonstrates her silliness. Despite her great concern for social status and her affectations of social privilege, her emotional imbalance blinds her to the fact of the religion's leveling effect. As the real-life Duchess of Buckingham pointed out to the fervent believer, the Countess of Huntingdon, the Wesleyans undermined the social structure by appealing to "the common wretches that crawl on the earth" and suggesting that they were equal to their superiors.[43] Matt, Smollett's chief voice in the novel, expresses precisely those sentiments to Lydia: "I don't think my servant [Humphry] is a proper ghostly director, for a devotee of your sex and character" (137).

Naturally superstitious, Tabby is easily drawn to the fervor of religion that proves both an outlet for her pent-up emotions and an offering of further opportunities for her husband hunting. Her attachment to Methodism proves as serviceable to her as any instrument for tyranny. She uses the faith to upbraid Win for what she regards as inappropriate behavior. She employs it to draw an image of superiority to her brother when Matt denounces Clinker's religious beliefs. But mainly it is a convenient access, she believes, to finding a man. Matt sees her conversion as an attempt "to ensnare the heart of Barton" and engage the interest of her co-religionist Lady Griskin "in providing matrimonial prospects" (140). She suffers disappointments with Mr. Moffat, who satisfies neither her spiritual nor sexual needs. Becoming entangled with Maclellan, she discovers to her dismay "that his attachment was altogether spiritual, founded upon an *intercourse* [italics added] of the devotion, at the meeting of Mr. John Wesley" (238).[44] Both Jery and Matt point out the shallowness of her religious beliefs and associate them with her desire for a man. Jery describes her willingness to renounce her religious passion for that of sexual gratification when Lismahago, evidently an atheist, appears on the scene. Matt, noting Tabby's continued Methodist practices, nevertheless observes that with the coming of Lismahago, "I believe the passion of love has in some measure abated the fervour of devotion" (207). Even Lydia, innocent as she is, links her aunt's religious hysteria with her going "to market with her charms" and declares, "but all this seems to be downright hypocrisy and deceit" (259–60). Tabby's religion provides yet another opportunity for Smollett to mock the sex-starved old maid, even as he uses her to further the more general satiric aims of his novel.

Like Tabby, her servant Win Jenkins displays Smollett's ultimate comic mastery in *Humphry Clinker*. Moreover, the juxtaposition of the pair demonstrates the range of his humor. If in Tabby he offers comedy through the grotesque, with Win, despite her similarities to her mistress, he manages his comedic effects without slipping into the nastier, less amiable territory of grotesquery. Indeed, comparison of the two characters provides by example a definition of the distinction between the comic and grotesque. It requires a generous-hearted reader to warm up to the crabby spinster that Smollett presents in Tabitha Bramble, a willingness to reach behind the prickliness associated with her family name in order to be understanding of her odd and bizarre qualities. Win, for all her faults, is never less than loveable. Forgiving her pretensions and dismissing her airs that mimic her social superiors demand nothing of the reader. If laughing at the grotesque leaves a slightly queasy feeling, responding to comedy itself brings a sense of good humor born out of fun.

But whatever the feelings toward the two characters, they further illustrate the difficulties in separating out Smollett's attitude toward women, whatever their social class, from the functions of fictional characters with multiple purposes in his novels. At her simplest, Win surely represents the stereotypical young servant woman as depicted in the various literary genres of the eighteenth century. Her illiterate malapropisms, earthy sensuality, and mimicking of her social "betters" characterize the type as it appears in the dramatic and fictional works of Smollett's contemporaries. Yet Win plays a significant role in *Humphry Clinker*. For Smollett she is an important amplification of his themes of the burlesque of romance, the attack on luxury, and the relationship of appearance and reality.[45] Through their responses to her, Smollett's other characters reveal aspects of themselves that permit the novelist to expand their development. Her romance with Humphry—like Lydia's affair with Wilson/Dennison and Tabby's lusting for a husband—provides Smollett with a further means for rhythmic development and plot resolution in his novel. In various ways she offers the novelist an opportunity to enlarge his satiric targets: Methodism, vanity, suppressed human sexuality, and social affectations.

Whatever her traits as a "sympathetic caricature of . . . a servant girl,"[46] for Smollett's purposes, he must go beyond mere stereotype to develop a credible and more rounded character, one who embodies a great deal of woman's sexuality, especially as Smollett identifies its availability with its origins in her social class.[47] Thus Smollett reveals something of his personal responses to women of the class he describes. The epistolary technique of *Humphry Clinker* that permits a more fully developed Win than might otherwise have been expected, however, also complicates the problem of discerning Smollett's own view. Most of what the reader knows about her comes from ten letters to her friend Mary Jones. Despite their brevity they speak to her fundamental character, her social attitudes, her basic nature, and her relationships to her fellow travelers in England and Scotland. At the same time, a good deal comes through in the comments on her from Lydia, Jery, and Matt—comments that tell us much about the commentators as well.

The limited treatment, however revealing, of Win by her social "superiors" suggests something of their—and, no doubt, Smollett's—views of the underclass. Win exists either to serve their needs or to provide amusement for them. Smollett's class-consciousness is clearly reflected in how she appears in the eyes of others. For Lydia, who has made Win her confidante out of necessity, Win otherwise is a poor creature whose conduct is viewed from on high with an evident air of snobbery. As a servant Win plays a useful function in enabling Lydia to carry on her covert correspondence with her friend Letty about her clandestine affair with Wilson. At the same time, any suggestion of Win's romantic actions is subject to Lydia's censorious comments.

As might be expected from the fact that she has chosen Win as a confidante (not an altogether wise move as Win's gossipy letters reveal), Lydia, overall, regards the maid with kindly affection. It does not hurt, as Lydia writes to Letty, that Win "has been kind to me in my affliction." Still, her observation, almost dismissively, that her "aunt's maid . . . is a good girl" (10) suggests that Smollett's heroine perceives what it is that she wants to see in someone whom she has little choice but to trust as there is no one else for her to turn to. Win here, as elsewhere, exists for Smollett as a character partly to throw light on Lydia's character. The point becomes apparent when Lydia notes the difference between Win's and Tabby's response to a Methodist service and her own, ridiculing the two women's speaking "as if they were really inspired" and contrasting her own failure to be affected (135–36).

The contrast between the two characters becomes more starkly drawn when Lydia's views of the world come more closely to resemble her uncle Matt's—and thus Smollett's own—as the novel progresses. Noting that "the poor creature is weak in her nerves, as well as in her understanding," Lydia goes on to describe Win's romantic behavior, her capriciousness, in a manner intended to underline her own steadfastness in her love for Wilson. Lydia begins sympathetically enough, but in patronizing fashion by declaring, "she herself is really an object of compassion—Between vanity, methodism, and love, her head is almost turned." But the tone changes as Lydia describes her actual conduct: "I should have more regard for her, however, if she had been more constant in the object of her affection; but, truly, she aimed at conquest, and flirted at the same time with my uncle's footman, Humphry Clinker, who is really a deserving young man, and one Dutton, my brother's valet de chambre, a debauched fellow" (259). Together with Tabby, Win becomes the object of Lydia's scorn as she recounts the behavior of the two women as they attempt to snare a man. Detailing the various ways in which Win and Tabby throw out their lines, Lydia, sounding remarkably like Matt, abjures their use of religion and false charms for their purposes. While focusing particularly on Tabby, Lydia does not allow Win to escape her wrath: "As for Jenkins, she affects to take all her mistress's reveries for gospel—She has also her heart-heavings and motions of the spirit . . . but all this seems to me to be downright hypocrisy and deceit" (259–60). More acute than her earlier views on Win, Lydia's comments, however, are intended less to analyze the maid's character than to provide Smollett with a means for contrasting the lesser morals of her shabby aunt and an unsophisticated maid behaving according to her class instincts with the well-developed moral sense of his heroine.

Jery, Lydia's brother, presents a more free-wheeling and comic description of Win, one that apparently offers Smollett's own satirical view of the servant class. In Jery's account Win comes through as a truly sensuous young woman, full of airs and affectation, but nonetheless likeable and tolerable because not too much more can be expected of her. It is not until near the close of the second volume that the only full description of Win appears, and then it is in Jery's perceptive and detailed picture of her, a balanced, though critical portrait that supports Lydia's view but goes deeper:

Nature intended Jenkins for something very different from the character of her mistress [the acerbic, sex-starved Tabby]; yet custom and habit have effected a wonderful
resemblance betwixt them in many particulars. Win, to be sure, is much younger and
more agreeable in her person, she is likewise tender-hearted and benevolent, qualities for which her mistress is by no means remarkable, no more than she is for being of
a timorous disposition, and much subject to fits of the mother, which are the infirmities
of Win's constitution: but then she seems to have adopted Mrs. Tabby's manner with
her cast cloaths.—She dresses and endeavours to look like her mistress, although her
own looks are much more engaging.—She enters into her scheme of oeconomy,
learns her phrases, repeats her remarks, imitates her stile in scolding the inferior servants, and, finally, subscribes implicitly to her system of devotion—This, indeed, she
found the more agreeable, as it was in great measure introduced and confirmed by the
ministry of Clinker, with whose personal merit she seems to have been struck ever
since he exhibited the pattern of his naked skin at Marlborough. (208)

Indeed, it is around the adventures of Win's romance with Clinker that
Jery's remarks evolve. Without him, and the humor that the couple provides in their lower-class antics, Jery takes no notice of the maid. For Jery
Win's affectations, her brand of Methodism, and her sensuous desires provide hilarious material to entertain his college friend, Sir Watkins Philips.
He regales Philips with an account of Win's response to poor Humphry's
initial appearance with his bare posterior showing through his shabby
clothing. She appears enthralled with the sight of his "skin as fair as alabaster" (81). When Clinker is unfairly jailed and acts as a religious orator
in prison, Win is there, and Jery informs Philips of her "tears, [as she is]
overwhelmed with sorrow," and adds slyly, "but whether for her own sins,
or the misfortunes of Clinker, I cannot pretend to say" (151). Win's naked
beauty matches the glories of Humphry's naked backside in Jery's narration of the comedy accompanying a fire at Scarborough. When she throws
herself from the window, Humphry breaks the fall. With the wind blowing,
"none of Mrs. Winifred's beauties could possibly escape the view of the
fortunate Clinker" (175). It is worthwhile to note that Smollett's sensibilities that permit him to dwell upon this kind of episode with a character
of Win's social status do not allow him to offer similar treatment for his
heroines of superior birth—as they all are—or to do more than suggest
the sexuality in their physical charms.

Jery pursues Win solely through her romances right up to her marriage
to Humphry. Before she gets there, she provides Jery with material for a
humorous account that allows Smollett to comment on female vanity and
take another swipe at what he regards as the hypocrisies in the appeal of
Methodism. As Win succumbs to the false charms of Jery's man, Dutton,
Jery recalls the basis of her attraction to Humphry, but it merely sets up
her capitulation to Dutton in terms that clearly reflect Smollett's own
views as Jery ascribes her weakness to vanity that characterizes the entirety of her sex. At the same time, the incident permits Jery to convey

Smollett's theme about the clash between appearance and reality. He contrasts the simple honesty of Humphry with the deviousness of Dutton's
attracting Win with his "second-hand finery," fawning and flattering, and
plying her with cheap gifts (209). Despite Humphry's preaching and pray-
ing, Win chooses the allure of meretriciousness above merit. So much for
the efficacy of Methodism even in its lower-class adherents when the real
world intrudes on their desires!

Jery's description of the details of Win's affair with Dutton focuses upon
those characteristics that Smollett himself appears to attribute to female
behavior: vanity, submission to men, and emotional hysteria. Falling prey
to Dutton, Win permits him to remake her appearance and alter her conduct, all to ludicrous effect as Jery presents it. Appealing to her vanity,
Dutton Frenchifies her, teaching her the language and dances and rede-
signing her mode of dress. Jery draws the picture of her as she chooses to
attend a play rather than Methodist services with Humphry: "The lady
was all of a flutter with faded lutestring, washed gauze, and ribbons three
times refreshed; but she was most remarkable for the frisure of her head,
which rose, like a pyramid, seven inches above the scalp, and her face was
primed and patched from the chin up to the eyes" (209). As a result, she
is taunted by a crowd as they throw dirt at her and call her a *"painted
Jezabel."* The event derives Win to an "hysteric fit" (209), only exacer-
bated when Dutton runs off with another woman and leaves her "in a fit
of crying" (213). More tears ensue when the hypocritical, man-hungry
Tabby reproaches her. Coming out of a period in which she has been oddly
quiet after a dressing-down by Matt, Tabby returns to her usual conduct:
"She now opened all those floodgates of reprehension, which had been
shut so long. She not only reproached her with her levity and indiscretion,
but attacked her on the score of religion, declaring roundly that she was
in a state of apostacy and reprobation" (213). The mistress's own behavior
is intolerable only when it is replicated by her servant.

On the outcome of Win's romance with Humphry, Jery's comments
maintain the humor, but suggest again, finally, Smollett's own class-
consciousness. Jery neatly captures, in Win's response to discovering that
Humphry is Matt's natural son, the eighteenth-century sense of class decorum even as it is seen from the servant's point of view. Her words
appear humorous, but the sentiment is not: "extremely fluttered between
her surprize at the discovery, and the apprehension of losing her sweetheart, [she] exclaimed in a giggling tone,—'I wish you joy, Mr. Clinker—
Floyd [Lloyd]—I would say—hi, hi, hi—you'll be so proud you won't look
at your poor fellow servants, oh, oh, oh!' " (319). Although wrong about
Humphry's reaction, Win proves accurate enough in estimating the upper-
class attitude toward their union. As Jery reveals, in his brief account of
the couple's wedding and in his own discussion prior to Matt's consenting
to it, both he and Matt are dubious about the union. Whatever the merits

of a bastard child of the upper class, they should be rewarded by marriage to someone above the status of a serving maid.

Matt himself, as might be expected from their social relationship, pays scant attention to Win. He scoffs at her attachment to Methodism as he does at Tabby's. Yet, after all, it is no more than can be expected of superstitious and weak-minded women, and in Win's case, as he observes, it is encouraged by her emotional attachment to Humphry. When Matt finally acquiesces to the couple's marriage, although he believes that his natural son might have done better, it is because he cannot withstand Win's pathetically female behavior "as the nymph's happiness is at stake, and she has had already some fits in the way of despondence." Win, like the other characters, plays a role in demonstrating that within the heart of the ostensible curmudgeon there is a soft and tender spot. His humorous observation on their union acutely comments on the lusty nature of the servant and ties it, as well, to the appeal of Methodism to the class: "The fellow is stout and lusty, very sober and conscientious; and the wench seems to be as great an enthusiast in love as in religion" (345). He anticipates an extensive progeny from the union.

Win's own letters attest to the accuracy of the observations of her fellow travelers on her character and often expand upon their essential points. However, her words, naturally, frequently indicate the inadequacy of perceptions that come from their limited points of view or the prejudices of their class. More important, Smollett's epistolary technique permits him to advance insights that make Win more than the stereotype generally identified with such minor characters whose function is to provide humorous material for a novel. As a result of her letters, Win becomes a more living presence to the reader, a woman struggling to find status in a class-conscious society and consequently attempting to reassure herself of her own importance while adapting in order to rise in the world. Underscoring her consciousness of her position as a servant, Smollett is not blind to the fact that her social aspirations do not differ from those above her in the levels of society and thus her conduct becomes a comment on her supposed "betters."[48] Writing to her friend and fellow servant, Win can be far more open than Tabby, who writes to her housekeeper; still her relationship to her friend does not quite match that of Lydia's to her school chum for she is in a superior position, closer to the family she serves and striving to impress someone who has not the advantage that she does in seeing the larger world.

In many respects Win's letters support Jery's assessment of her and show him to be a keen observer who at least can be counted on as a dependable reporter of external events. He was correct to note that her superficial faults emanated from her mimicry of Tabitha. In her first letter she expresses her own distrust of servants she has left behind, and her concern for her kitten mirrors her mistress's attachment to her dog. Still, as Jery has noted, Win possesses an essentially good nature. She worries about her friend's education, wants to share her newfound religious enthusiasm with those she has left behind, and, like Lydia, expresses her friendship by sending small gifts.

Like Lydia, too, she is young and exuberant, thrilled by new sights and experiences. Smollett uses her letters, like those of Lydia, to contrast with Matt's and to suggest that the luxury he attacks through his valetudinarian's remarks has its appeal to those whose reasoning powers, particularly women, remain undeveloped.[49] Amid the gossip from the traveling family, the talk about her romantic escapades, and her comments on servant matters, there is the excitement of the new adventure. From Bath she boasts to the stay-at-home Mary: "Dear girl, I have seen all the fine shews of Bath: the Parades, the Squires, and the Circlis, the Crashit, the Hottogon, and Bloody Buildings, and Harry King's row; and I have been twice in the Bath with mistress, and na'r a smoak upon our backs, hussy" (42–43). Departing the place, she exudes: "We are all upon the ving—Hey for London, girl!" (70).

Win's letters from London and Glasgow, while reflecting the enthusiasm of Lydia, indicate the class differences from Smollett's heroine and give evidence of her naive, superstitious, and innocent nature as noted by Jery and Lydia. Despite her lack of sophistication and education, she responds as Lydia does to the sights and sounds of the places they visit. She, too, is overwhelmed by the activity, people, and edifices. In language that suggests her speech, she writes from London: "So many strange sites to be seen! O gracious! my poor Welsh brain has been spinning like a top ever since I came hither! And I have seen the Park, and the paleass of Saint Gimses, and the king's and the queen's magisterial pursing, and the sweet young princes, and the hillyfents, and pye-bald ass, and all the rest of the royal family" (108). But it is all too much for the superstitious and religious girl: "The pleasures of London are no better than sower whey and stale cyder, when compared to the joys of the new Gerusalem" (109). Through her analogies and illiteracies, Smollett, whatever else he does, maintains his satirical view of her social class.

A similar pattern marks Win's letter from Glasgow, but Smollett shifts the focus to her superstitious beliefs. He has already linked these with her faith in Methodism in her letter from London about her visit to Sadler's Wells where the company's performance becomes the basis for comparison with "witches in Wales fly[ing] upon broom-sticks" (108). That description is immediately followed by her account of having gone to a Methodist service. The Edinburgh letter marvels at the wonders of the places she has seen, but focuses upon her belief in visions and her willing acceptance of Scottish folklore. Writing to Mary about a visit to a graveyard, she declares, "O Mary! this is the land of congyration—The bell knolled when we were there—I saw lights and heard lamentations." She speaks of "a mischievous ghost" and "fairies" that steal pregnant women unless they take such precautions as employing horseshoes for protection. She visits a fortune-teller and follows her ludicrous advice. For her "Loff-Loming" (Loch Lomond) "has got ne'r a bottom, and was made by a musician; and, truly, I believe it; for it is not in the coarse of nature.—It has got *waves without wind, fish without fins, and a floting hyland*" (260–61). For all the likeness of the exuberance in Win's and Lydia's letters, they are of a different order, and Smollett uses them not only to contrast the simple country girl and his heroine, but to satirize the simple-minded beliefs of Win's class.

In great part Win's letters reveal those areas in which the other correspondents either know little of what she is truly like or have only a limited view of her character—not surprising considering the nature of their relationship and the class differences. The effect of her own writing, at any rate, is again to create both a figure through whom Smollett can play upon his theme of the disparity between reality and perception and, at the same time, permit him to give life to the conventional stereotype that his audience expected. As Smollett reveals throughout his work, he clearly understands class relationships, and in Win's character he shrewdly observes how the underclass recognizes its submissiveness in society while employing its wiles to survive. In some ways this sense of class relationships comes naturally to a picaresque novelist familiar with the genre's master-servant connections.

Win's gossipy letters help advance Smollett's narrative and permit him to reflect on the awareness necessary for a servant's survival. In her very first letter, even as she declares, "we servants should see all and say nothing" (7), she offers the first real account of Lydia's affair with Wilson. For all of her sympathy for Lydia when Wilson's appearance as a Jewish peddler causes the young heroine to suffer a fit of near hysteria, Win delights in offering the details to her friend even as she insists, "I was always famous for keeping secrets" (43). She knows full well that Lydia's small gifts to her represent tokens to buy her silence.

Neither Lydia's little bribery and Win's emotional attachment to her nor Tabby's tyrannical threats can still Win's gossipy comments. When she writes to Mary from Bath about Tabby's relations with Sir Ulic Mackilligut from the "cunty of Kalloway" (43), she knows well enough how the knowledge of her mistress's secrets protect her from the dreaded spinster. Repeatedly insisting that she is not given to tale-bearing, she relates fully Tabby's conduct with the grotesque Lismahago: "There has been a deal of huggling and flurtation betwixt mistress and an ould Scots officer, called Kismycago." But she concludes her report with, "it shall never be said that I menchioned a syllabub of the matter" (220–21).

Taken together with Lydia's confessional letters, Win's gossip may suggest Smollett's view that women cannot refrain from loosening their

tongues to pass on secrets. Still, Win's epistles reveal the complexity in
the servant's situation. As she informs Mary about her employers' secrets,
she seems constantly aware of the precariousness of her own position at
the same time that gathering such information works to secure her against
any reprisals. The very device of repetition, however, also allows Smollett—as Dickens managed to do later with his minor characters—to
breathe life into Win by reinforcing the characteristic. As she reveals to
Mary Jones Tabby's carrying on with Lismahago and Lydia's feelings
about Wilson, she gains dominance over the two women, even as she says,
"But I scorn for to exclose the secrets of the family" (307). As she looks
into Lydia's heart and Tabby's mind, noting the deleterious effects of love
on the one and the scheming designs of the other, Win seems in control
of both, but nevertheless must be circumspect enough to conclude that
"whatever I may see or hear, not a praticle shall ever pass [my] lips" (262).

   One aspect of Win's character and conduct that the others on her journey cannot know is what her being a servant means to her. Despite his
hierarchical values, Smollett displays his own understanding of the situation. Moreover, he neatly places her in a situation where she stands some-
where between those servants she has left behind and the family with
whom she travels. Win's aspirations, indicated by her misguided attempts
to mimic Tabby's airs and affectations, set her apart from her fellows, and
yet she must constantly be aware, as her denials of gossiping suggest, that
she is, after all, a servant, at the whim and disposal of those who govern
her. It is no small thing, as her 3 June letter from London makes clear,
that even her ability to communicate with Mary depends on the kindness
of superiors or even the better placed butler of Lady Griskin who provides
her with franking privileges. When the prospect of Tabby's marriage
arises, even as she expresses envy at the servants' pay and dress where
the company is staying with Matt's friend Baynard, Win worries about
what will happen to her for, after all, she remains at her mistress's disposal.

   Smollett plays cleverly upon Win's particular situation: that of a young
woman of pride and vanity, desirous of social advancement, but always
conscious of her servitude. The result is to make her more of a real person
than merely the caricature of her type. She seems uncertain of the class
to which she belongs. Criticizing the servants at Bath as "devils [who] lite
the candle at both ends," she still can say, "I don't blame them for making
the most of their market [demands on those they serve], in the way of
vails [tips] and parquisites" (70–71). Still, when they take advantage of
her, stealing from her or getting in the way of her romance, she behaves
like her social superiors, turning one in to Tabby and getting even with
the other. Not only does she have social aspirations of her own, but she
writes to Mary about the importance of good handwriting and spelling for
those who would rise above their origins. In a comic style belying her own
advice, she admonishes Mary, "O, voman! voman! if thou hads't but the

least consumption of what pleasure we scullers have, when we can cunster the crabbidst buck off hand, and spell the ethnitch vords without lucking at the primmer" (109).

Nothing makes clearer the torments of class conflicts—surely not apparent to the others—than her letter to Mary concerning the culmination of her romance with Humphry. Worried about the relationship because of her discovery of his new status as Matt's natural son, she expresses both her fears and spirited pride. When Humphry does not stand up to Matt's objections to their marriage, she points out angrily the circumstances of both their births: "Thof my father wasn't a gentleman, my mother was an honest woman—I didn't come on the wrong side of the blanket, girl—My parents were married according to the rights of holy mother crutch, in face of man and angles—Mark that, Mary Jones" (338). In a combination of emotions, she remarks disdainfully on Humphry's dallying, warning that there is always Jery's man, Mr. Machappy, somewhat worn by the years, but a "gentleman born" with "a world of buck larning and speaks French, and Ditch, and Scotch, and all manner of outlandish lingos." Still, as she confesses, she does not want him, and, "I scorn for to do, or say, or to think any thing that mought give unbreech to Mr. Loyd" (338).

Win's strongest emotions of class conflict come with her marriage to Humphry. She senses—and Smollett, of course knows—what the difficulties will be with the change in household circumstances. Even late in the novel, Win writes to Mary on fairly equal terms about their "fellow-sarvents" (307). Nevertheless, things will never be the same with her change in status, and here the reader can see that, for all the constancy in Smollett's description of her, Win proves more than the single-dimensional stereotype. Describing the marriages of the three couples—Lydia-Dennison, Tabby-Lismahago, and Win-Humphry—she speaks pridefully of her own husband: "Thof he don't enter in caparison with great folks of quality, yet he has as good blood in his veins as arrow privet 'squire in the county; and then his pursing is far from contentible" (352). Deferential, still, to the gentry, she has no compunctions about asserting her rights to her former servant-equals. She clearly expects some conflict with Mrs. Gwyllim, Tabby's chief housekeeper, but certainly recognizes where she herself stands: "I hope she and I will live upon dissent terms of civility." The use of *dissent* for *decent* foreshadows the conflicts to be expected. As for the remainder of the servants, Mary included, Win does not hesitate to set forth the ground rules: "Being, by God's blessing, removed to a higher spear, you'll escuse my being familiar with the lower servants of the family; but, as I trust you'll behave respectful, and keep a proper distance, you may always depend upon [my] good will and protection" (353). The word *spear* itself becomes a warning for Mary to keep her distance. In the very last letter of the novel, Smollett still expresses his satirical view of the former servant's affectations, but his depiction of her emerges as more than a simple stereotype.

On the matter of Win's sexuality, too, Smollett presents his hierarchical opinion of the nature of the servant woman. His portrait of those in her class invariably suggests an earthiness and sexuality that he customarily denies to his heroines. Jery and Matt recognize—expressing Smollett's view—what they regard as her strong sexual nature. Her own letters bring this forth more clearly than their surface impressions allow. In the incident when she and Tabby visit a zoo and a wag tells them that the lion will carry on when confronted by a young woman who is not a virgin, Win finds excuses for not approaching the animal: "Now I had no mind to go near him; for I cannot abide such dangerous honeymills, not I" (108). Win's amorous conduct throughout the novel provides a coda to Smollett's hints at what the real danger might be.

Matt's comment, cited earlier, about Win as a "wench [who] seems to be as great an enthusiast in love as in religion," is borne out in the interest expressed in her by a variety of men in the novel besides Humphry. His man, John Thomas (a name with sexual implications), becomes furious with O'Frizzle, Sir Ulic's servant, who asks her to dance with him. Before Win sends O'Frizzle packing, with his "tinsy and his log tail" because he has betrayed her "with a dirty trollop under my nose" (70), he has pressed his suit with her. With a fullness of expression to Mary, unlike the kind of tight-lipped silence that Tabby has followed in her correspondence with Mrs. Gwyllim, Win provides the details of her affair with Dutton whom she has foolishly permitted to come between her and Humphry. Even at the end, Win's conscious sex appeal is evident as she suggests that if Humphry does not want her because of his newfound status, Mr. Machappy finds her attractive enough.

But her response to Humphry displays Win's physical desire most fully. Jery correctly noted the effect of Humphry's first bare-bottomed appearance on Win. In her very first description of him to Mary that image clearly has most impressed her: "a good sole as ever broke bread; which shews that a scalded cat may prove a good mouser, and a hound be staunch, thof he has got narrow a hare on his buttocks" (107). The image recurs in the final pages of the novel when Win declares that Humphry's new mode of dress cannot hide what truly lies beneath: "he is now out of livery, and wares ruffles—but I saw him when he was out at elbows, and had not a rag to kiver his pistereroes [posteriors]" (338). Even when Win describes the effects of Humphry's preaching, her metaphor draws upon the image of sexuality, prophesying that its outcome will be "to produce blessed fruit of generation," words that foreshadow those of Matt that forecast the progeny to follow their union (155).

But it is particularly in her malapropisms that Win reveals the physicality of her nature, and a good many of these remind the reader of her concern for Humphry's posterior, so much so that Sheridan Baker, using them as evidence of Smollett's comic romance, terms it Win's "anal fixation."[50] Giorgio Melchiori, relating Smollett's love of language to that of James Joyce,[51] has demonstrated how Win's malaproprisms become more complex as the novel develops and increasingly take on sexual and physical meanings. *Palace* becomes *paleass* (108); *consternation, constipation* (155); *farthing, farting* (220); *third, turd*; and *asafetida, ass of etida* (338). She turns *repository* into *suppository* (7). Even more interesting is the suggestiveness of delivery in the phrase *mail sex* (42) or her account of her accidentally dropping her petticoat in public: "they mought laff, but they could see nothing; for I was up to the sin [chin] in water" (44). It probably means something that Win cannot properly spell *virgin* (108) and that she renders *whore* as *hoar* (219).

Of course, these hardly exhaust the catalogue of Win's malapropisms, intended by Smollett as by every sophisticated writer to poke fun at the ignorance of the lower classes. The term *malaprop* used here is anachronistic since its existence came only with Sheridan's Mrs. Malaprop in *The Rivals*, four years after the publication of *Humphry Clinker*. But the concept, an appeal to the smugness of an educated audience, predated Smollett's work. Fielding employed it in the character of Mrs. Slipslop in *Joseph Andrews* (1742), but even by then the device had been in use for a couple of hundred years. Always its intention was to make the audience feel superior to the character, depending as it does upon the reader's awareness of the correct form. Win's *sitty* for *city* and *sites* for *sights* (108); *suet* for *sweat* and *nose* for *knows* (109); *sole* instead of *soul* and *veil* in place of *vale* or *grease* for *grace* and *pyeball* for *bible* (155–56); her turning *right* into *rite* and *tale-bearing* into *tail-baring* (220)—all of these and the rest depend for their humor on the reader's superior knowledge to that of the character and represent a class-conscious approach to the so-called lower orders.

If Smollett uses, at his best, these malapropisms to better purpose in revealing Win's fundamental nature as well as a sign of her affectation, nevertheless he intends them as material to make her a humorous character. Despite his multiple use of Win in his novel—to contrast her with Lydia on one hand and Tabby on the other; to develop his themes of luxury and the opposition of reality and perception; to throw light on Matt's character; and to enhance the structure—her primary function as a character in herself remains to serve as the object of humor in Smollett's class-conscious audience. He clearly delighted in the anarchic linguistic havoc he created with her language. He took pains—whatever the failures, noted by scholars, in his consistency in creating her dialect or accounting for the literacy of an uneducated servant girl—to experiment with her language, to give it an air of credibility, and to relate it to her character.[52] But for Smollett's class-conscious audience Win, like all of the Mrs. Malaprops in literary history, appealed to their smugness and revealed the author's own social attitude toward the vanity and ignorance of women.[53]

Finally, however, like all Smollett's female characters, Win, too, demonstrates the difficulties in easy generalizations about the effects of the author's male sensibility. Unquestionably, Smollett's novels exhibit his overall strongly male point of view, reflecting the values of his eighteenth-century patriarchal society. Like most men of his social standing and writers representing them, he manages to combine idealized notions of womanhood with a concept of a weaker sex. He expresses fear of feminine domination at the same time that he scorns what he regards as the female frailties of addiction to fashion, foolishness, and luxury. For all his demands for women's chastity, he depicts the difficulties confronting the sex—particularly members of the lower classes—in maintaining the highest moral standards because of an inclination to romanticism and superstition and of natural emotional propensities.

Nevertheless, the dictates of his craft lead to the creation of a remarkable variety in his characterization of women, whether heroines, victims, comic, or grotesque. How they function within his fiction determines their development. To be sure, he cannot conceive of them as anything but minor characters, but still, like many of Smollett's attendants upon his heroes, they are often given a fullness and life wrought from the vivacity and intensity of his style. Ultimately, even his idealized heroines, whatever their shared qualities, because of the roles they play are distinguishable from each other, and certainly there can be no denying the individuality of an Emilia or Lydia. Not even the fates of his fallen women follow a single pattern; differences mark the outcomes and characters of Wilhelmina, Elinor, Miss Williams, and Lady Vane. For the fullness of Smollett's imaginative development of women, no category better displays his abilities, and even success in getting beyond the limitations of stereotyping, than his caricatures of comics and grotesques. Figures like Win, Tabby, Grizzle, and Perry's mother have enjoyed a long literary life because Smollett manages to invest them with verisimilitude that overcomes the exaggerations of caricature through the vitality of his style. It was this quality of his work that appealed to Dickens. Whether with his characterization of such women or their male counterparts in his novels, it was this particular achievement that, indeed, made him an "author of the first distinction."

Notes

Parenthetic textual references to Smollett's *Travels* and novels are to the Oxford editions, which follow the first printings, including that of *Sir Launcelot Greaves* as serialized in the *British Magazine* for 1760–61. References to the plays are to Smollett's *Works* (1824). In quotations from Smollett's work neither spelling nor punctuation has been modernized, but the long "s" of the eighteenth century has been eliminated.

CHAPTER 1

1. Linda Colley, *Britons: Forging the Nation 1707–1837* (New Haven and London: Yale University Press, 1992), p. 252.

2. Donald Bruce, *Radical Doctor Smollett* (Boston: Houghton Mifflin/Riverside Press Cambridge, 1965), p. 74.

3. Gilbert D. McEwen, *The Oracle of the Coffee House: John Dunton's "Athenian Mercury"* (San Marino, Calif.: Huntington Library, 1972), pp. 108, 141, 160.

4. Robert D. Spector, "The *Connoisseur*: A Study of the Functions of a Persona," In *English Writers of the Eighteenth Century*, ed. John H. Middendorf (New York and London: Columbia University Press, 1971), p. 121.

5. Elizabeth Bergen Brophy, *Women's Lives and the Eighteenth-Century Novel* (Tampa: University of South Florida Press, 1991), p. 11.

6. James Hodges, "The *Female Spectator*: A Courtesy Periodical by Eliza Haywood," in *Studies in the Early English Periodical*, ed. R. P. Bond (Chapel Hill: University of North Carolina Press, 1957), p. 153.

7. Brophy, *Women's Lives*, pp. 13, 33.

8. Janet Todd, *The Sign of Angellica: Women, Writing, and Fiction, 1660–1800* (New York: Columbia University Press, 1989), pp. 9–10.

9. Katharine M. Rogers, "Inhibitions in Eighteenth-Century Women Novelists: Elizabeth Inchbald and Charlotte Smith," *Eighteenth-Century Studies* 11 (Fall 1977): 64–65, 78.

10. See Todd, *Sign of Angellica*, pp. 121–22; Leland E. Warren, "Of the Conversation of Women: *The Female Quixote* and the Dream of Perfection," *Studies in Eighteenth-Century Culture* 11 (1982): 367, 374ff. My final image adapts Warren's commentary, p. 367.

11. Ruth Perry, "Colonizing the Breast: Sexuality and Maternity in Eighteenth-Century England," *Eighteenth-Century Life* 16, n.s. 1 (Feb. 1992): 190.

12. Colley, *Britons*, p. 261; Brophy, *Women's Lives*, p. 42.

13. Lawrence Stone, *The Family, Sex and Marriage in England 1500–1800* (New York: Harper and Row, 1977), pp. 4, 5, 7, 119; Jean H. Hagstrum, *Sex and Sensibility: Ideal and Erotic Love from Milton to Mozart* (Chicago and London: University of Chicago Press, 1980), pp. 1–2.

14. Stone, *Family, Sex and Marriage*, pp. 356–57.

15. Colley, *Britons*, p. 239.

16. Warren, "Of the Conversation of Women," p. 371.

17. Todd, *Sign of Angellica*, p. 101. Quotation is from *The History of Women* (London, 1779), II, 317.

18. Marlene LeGates, "The Cult of Womanhood in Eighteenth-Century Thought," *Eighteenth-Century Studies* 10 (Fall 1976): 21; Todd, *Sign of Angellica*, pp. 104, 108–9.

19. Todd, *Sign of Angellica*, p. 101; Sheryl O'Donnell, "Mr. Locke and the Ladies: The Indelible Words on the *Tabula Rasa*," *Studies in Eighteenth-Century Culture* 8 (1979): 152; Perry, "Colonizing the Breast," p. 192.

20. Warren, "Of the Conversation of Women," pp. 370–71.

21. Brophy, *Women's Lives*, pp. 31, 50; Todd, *Sign of Angellica*, p. 120.

22. For material in this and subsequent paragraphs on the topic, I have drawn on the following: Harrison R. Steeves, *Before Jane Austen: The Shaping of the English Novel in the Eighteenth Century* (New York: Holt, Rinehart and Winston, 1965), Ch. 6; Todd, *Sign of Angellica*, p. 109; Stone, *Family, Sex and Marriage*, pp. 501ff., and 543; Patricia Meyer Spacks, " 'Ev'ry Woman Is at Heart a Rake,' " *Eighteenth-Century Studies* 8 (Fall 1974): 27–28, 36; LeGates, "Cult of Womanhood," pp. 22–23, 33ff., 37–38; Perry, "Colonizing the Breast," p. 189; Brophy, *Women's Lives*, p. 67.

23. For details of the Thrales, see James L. Clifford, *Hester Lynch Piozzi (Mrs. Thrale)*, 2d ed. (Oxford: Clarendon Press, 1952), especially pp. 98–99, 144.

24. See E. P. Thompson, *Customs in Common: Studies in Traditional Popular Culture* (New York: The New Press, 1991), Ch. 7.

25. Brophy, *Women's Lives*, pp. 2–3; Rogers, "Inhibitions in Women Novelists," pp. 63–64; Mona Scheuermann, *Her Bread to Earn: Women, Money, and Society from Defoe to Austen* (Lexington: University Press of Kentucky, 1993), p. 2.

26. Alan D. McKillop, *The Early Masters of English Fiction* (Lawrence: University of Kansas Press, 1956); Lionel Kelly, ed., *Tobias Smollett: The Critical Heritage* (London and New York: Routledge and Kegan Paul, 1987), pp. 293, 322–23; Frederick R. Karl, *The Adversary Literature: The English Novel in the Eighteenth Century. A Study in Genre* (New York: Farrar, Straus and Giroux, 1974), p. 317.

27. Edward C. Mack, "Pamela's Stepdaughters: The Heroines of Smollett and Fielding," *College English* 8 (March 1947): 296.

28. William Bowman Piper, "The Large Diffused Picture of Life in Smollett's Early Novels," *Studies in Philology* 60 (Jan. 1963): 45.

29. Jerry C. Beasley, *Novels of the 1740s* (Athens: University of Georgia Press, 1982), pp. 74ff., 82–83; Paul-Gabriel Boucé, *The Novels of Tobias Smollett*, tr. Antonia White and Paul-Gabriel Boucé (London and New York: Longman, 1976), p. 257.

30. Lewis M. Knapp, "Ann, Wife of Tobias Smollett," *Publications of the Modern Language Association* 45 (1930): 1035–49.

31. *The Letters of Tobias Smollett*, ed. Lewis M. Knapp (Oxford: Clarendon Press, 1970), p. 2; Lewis M. Knapp, *Tobias Smollett: Doctor of Men and Manners* (Princeton: Princeton University Press, 1949), p. 38.

32. Knapp, *Tobias Smollett*, p. 285.

33. Knapp, *Tobias Smollett*, p. 42.

34. Knapp, *Tobias Smollett*, p. 149.

35. See Knapp, "Ann, Wife of Tobias Smollett."

36. *The Letters of Tobias Smollett, M.D.*, ed. Edward S. Noyes (Cambridge: Harvard University Press, 1926), p. 110.

37. Knapp, ed., *Letters*, p. 112.

38. Knapp, ed. *Letters*, pp. 117–18.

39. Howard Swazey Buck, *Smollett as Poet* (New Haven: Yale University Press; London: Humphry Milford/Oxford University Press, 1927), p. 60.

40. Knapp, "Ann, Wife of Tobias Smollett," p. 1038.

41. Alexander Carlyle, *Anecdotes and Characters of the Times*, ed. James Kinsley (London: Oxford University Press, 1973), p. 172.

42. For details here I am indebted to Knapp, *Tobias Smollett*, pp. 111ff. The quotation is from p. 219, a letter to John Wilkes in October 1759.

43. T. C. Duncan Eaves and Ben D. Kimpel, *Samuel Richardson: A Biography* (Oxford: Clarendon Press, 1971), pp. 518, 527, 533, 537. Quotations are from pp. 518, 533.

44. Knapp, ed., *Letters*, p. 128.

45. *Selected Letters of Samuel Richardson*, ed. John Carroll (Oxford: Clarendon Press, 1964).

46. Eaves and Kimpel, *Samuel Richardson*, pp. 120, 209, 175, 234.

47. Robert D. Spector, *English Literary Periodicals and the Climate of Opinion during the Seven Years' War* (The Hague: Mouton, 1966), pp. 30–32, 59–61.

48. Knapp, *Tobias Smollett*, pp. 213–14; P.-G. Boucé, "Smollett's Libel," *Times Literary Supplement* (30 Dec. 1965).

49. See Buck, *Smollett as Poet*, pp. 39–40, 42.

50. Robert Adams Day, "*Ut Pictura Poesis*: Smollett, Satire, and the Graphic Arts," *Studies in Eighteenth-Century Culture* 10 (1981): 310.

51. Bruce, *Radical Doctor Smollett*, p. 77.

52. Ronald Paulson, *Satire and the Novel in Eighteenth-Century England* (New Haven and London: Yale University Press, 1967), p. 182.

53. James P. Carson, "Commodification and the Figure of the Castrato in Smollett's *Humphry Clinker*," *Eighteenth Century* 33 (Spring 1992): 27.

54. Robert Day, "Sex, Scatology, Smollett," in *Sexuality in Eighteenth-Century Britain*, ed. P.-G. Boucé (Manchester: Manchester University Press; Totowa: Barnes and Noble, 1982), p. 241.

55. Carson, "Figure of the Castrato," p. 39.

56. James R. Foster, *History of the Pre-Romantic Novel in England* (New York: Modern Language Association; London: Oxford University Press, 1949), pp. 120–21; Beasley, *Novels of the 1740s*, pp. 35ff.

57. See Michael McKeon, "Genre Transformation and Social Change: Rethinking the Rise of the Novel," in *Modern Essays on Eighteenth-Century Literature*, ed. Leopold Damrosch, Jr. (New York and Oxford: Oxford University Press, 1988), especially pp. 167–68, 171, 176.

58. I am indebted here for details and even phrases to Albrecht B. Strauss, "On Smollett's Language: A Paragraph in *Ferdinand Count Fathom*," in *Style in Prose Fiction*, English Institute Essays, 1958, ed. Harold C. Martin (New York: Columbia University Press, 1959), pp. 26–33.

59. K. G. Simpson, "Tobias Smollett: The Scot as English Novelist," in *Smollett: Author of the First Distinction*, ed. Alan Bold (London and Totowa: Vision/Barnes and Noble, 1982), pp. 91, 102.

60. Bruce, *Radical Doctor Smollett*, p. 67.

61. McKeon, "Generic Transformation," p. 160; Michael Rosenblum, "Smollett and the Old Conventions," *Philological Quarterly* 55 (Summer 1976): 392.

62. For some examples, see Simpson, "Smollett: The Scot as English Novelist," pp. 91–92; Rosenblum, "Smollett and the Old Conventions," pp. 395–96, 399; Boucé, *Novels of Tobias Smollett*, p. 189; Beasley, *Novels of the 1740s*, p. 36.

63. Sheridan Baker, "*Humphry Clinker* as Comic Romance," in *Essays in the Eighteenth-Century Novel*, ed. Robert D. Spector (Bloomington and London: Indiana University Press, 1965), pp. 154–64.

64. McKillop, *Early Masters*, pp. 154, 156; Lee Monroe Ellison, "Elizabethan Drama and the Works of Smollett," *Publications of the Modern Language Association* 44 (1929): 842–62. My particular indebtedness here is to Thomas R. Preston, "The 'Stage Passions' and Smollett's Characterization," *Studies in Philology* 71 (Jan. 1974): 105–25. All quotations in the paragraph are from Preston, pp. 113 and 115.

65. For the fullest treatment of Smollett's use of the picaresque, see Robert D. Spector, *Tobias George Smollett*, updated ed. (Boston: Twayne, 1989). See George S. Rousseau, *Tobias Smollett: Essays of Two Decades* (Edinburgh: T. and T. Clark, 1982), pp. 55–79; Alice Green Fredman, "The Picaresque in Decline: Smollett's First Novel," in *English Writers of the Eighteenth Century*, ed. John H. Middendorf (New York and London: Columbia University Press, 1971), pp. 189–207.

66. Day, "Sex, Scatology, and Smollett," pp. 226–27.

CHAPTER 2

1. Kelly, *Smollett: the Critical Heritage*, pp. 286, 360; McKillop, *Early Masters*, p. 160; Mack, "Pamela's Stepdaughters ," p. 300; Louis L. Martz, *The Later Career of Tobias Smollett* (New Haven: Yale University Press; London: Humphry Milford/Oxford University Press, 1942), p. 14.

2. Rufus Putney, "The Plan of *Peregrine Pickle*," *Publications of the Modern Language Association* 60 (1945): 1057.

3. Boucé, *Novels of Tobias Smollett*, p. 293.

4. *Boswell's Life of Johnson*, ed. G. B. Hill and rev. L. F. Powell (Oxford: Clarendon Press, 1971), II, 56.

5. Steeves, *Before Jane Austen*, p. 131; Mack, "Pamela's Stepdaughters," p. 294.

6. LeGates, "Cult of Womanhood," pp. 26ff.

7. Felicity Nussbaum, " 'Savage' Mothcrs: Narratives of Maternity in the MId-Eighteenth Century," *Eighteenth-Century Life* 16, n.s. 1 (Feb. 1992): 166.

8. Mack, "Pamela's Stepdaugthers," pp. 293–95.

9. Jean E. Hunter, "*The Lady's Magazine* and the Study of Englishwomen in the Eighteenth Century," in *Newsletters to Newspapers: Eighteenth-Century Journalism*, ed. Donovan H. Bond and W. Reynolds McLeod (Morgantown, W.Va.: School of Journalism, West Virginia University, 1977), pp. 109–12.

10. Mack, "Pamela's Stepdaugthers," p. 297.

11. M. A. Goldberg, *Smollett and the Scottish School: Studies in Eighteenth-Century Thought* (Albuquerque: University of New Mexico Press, 1959).

12. Robert Palfrey Utter and Gwendolyn B. Needham, *Pamela's Daughters* (New York: Macmillan, 1936), p. 89.

13. See Spector, *Tobias George Smollett*, p. 5, for some views. For a strong estimate that does not go beyond reasonable praise, see Boucé, *Novels of Tobias Smollett*, pp. 14–15.

14. Buck, *Smollett as Poet*, p. 14.

15. Boucé, *Novels of Tobias Smollett*, p. 15.

16. Robert Alter, *Rogue's Progress: Studies in the Picaresque Novel* (Cambridge: Harvard University Press, 1964), p. 77, notes the relationship to chivalric romance.

17. Alter, *Rogue's Progress*, pp. 76ff.; Boucé, "Introduction" to *Roderick Random*, p. xxxv, and *Novels of Tobias Smollett*, pp. 116–17, 128. For further comment on Smollett's limitations in expressing "the subjects of beauty and virtue [in] his fiction," see George M. Kahrl, "Smollett as Caricaturist," in *Tobias Smollett: Bicentennial Essays Presented to Lewis M. Knapp*, ed. George Rousseau and P.-G. Boucé (New York: Oxford University Press, 1971), pp. 186–87.

18. Goldberg, *Smollett and the Scottish School*, p. 45; Susan Bourgeois, *Nervous Juyces and the Feeling Heart: The Growth of Sensibility in the Novels of Tobias Smollett* (New York: Peter Lang, 1986), pp. 54, 61.

19. Robert D. Mayo, *The English Novel in the Magazines 1740–1815* (Evanston, Ill.: Northwestern University Press; London: Oxford University Press, 1962), pp 282–83.

20. Boucé, *Novels of Tobias Smollett*, p. 186; Bourgeois, *Nervous Juyces*, pp. 118–19.

21. David Evans, "Introduction" to *Launcelot Greaves*, p. xv.

22. Bourgeois, *Nervous Juyces*, pp. 138–39.

23. Boucé, *Novels of Tobias Smollett*, p. 136.

24. Robert Giddings, *The Tradition of Smollett* (London: Methuen, 1967), p. 136.

25. Goldberg, *Smollett and the Scottish School*, p. 141.

26. Many of the points about Smollett's indebtedness to Otway are made in Jerry Beasley's "Introduction" to *Fathom* in the Georgia edition, p. xxx; George M. Kahrl, *Tobias Smollett: Traveler-Novelist* (Chicago: University of Chicago Press,

1945), pp. 52–53; Boucé, *Novels of Tobias Smollett*, p. 151, some of which suggest Smollett's parody of romance.

27. Thomas R. Preston, *Not in Timon's Manner: Feelings, Misanthropy, and Satire in Eighteenth-Century England* (Tuscaloosa, Ala.: University of Alabama Press, 1975), p. 92.

28. References are too numerous to detail, but see the chapter on the novel in Spector, *Tobias George Smollett*, and see Goldberg, *Smollett and the Scottish School*, p. 90.

29. Boucé, *Novels of Tobias Smollett*, pp. 161, 174; Robert Etheridge Moore, *Hogarth's Literary Relationships* (Minneapolis: University of Minnesota Press; London: Geoffrey Cumberlege/Oxford University Press, 1948), p. 178.

30. Knapp, ed., *Letters*, pp. 47–48.

31. Giddings, *Tradition of Smollett*, p 100; Mack, "Pamela's Stepdaughters," p. 297; Paulson, *Satire and the Novel*, p. 184; Steeves, *Before Jane Austen*, pp. 137–38; Utter and Needham, *Pamela's Daughters*, pp. 159, 179; Putney, "Plan of *Peregrine Pickle*," pp. 1054, 1056.

32. See Susan G. Auty, *The Comic Spirit of Eighteenth-Century Novels* (Port Washington, N.Y., and London: Kennikat Press, 1975), p. 110. Ronald Paulson, "The Pilgrimage and the Family: Structure in the Novels of Fielding and Smollett," in *Tobias Smollett: Bicentennial Essays Presented to Lewis M. Knapp*, ed. George Rousseau and P.-G. Boucé (New York: Oxford University Press, 1971), pp. 77–78, n. 15, describing Emilia as a "subordinate character," places her in the category of Restoration heroines of stage comedy and notes "the increasingly resourceful nature of such women."

33. See, for example, Mack, "Pamela's Stepdaughters," p. 295.

34. Cf. the feminist view of Bourgeois, *Nervous Juyces*, p. 67. See Boucé, *Novels of Tobias Smollett*, pp. 133, 135–36, 139, 296. For a male view of Emilia's weaknesses, see Bruce, *Radical Doctor Smollet*, p. 71. But for contrary opinions, see Giddings, *Tradition of Smollett*, p. 102, and Kelly, *Smollett: The Critical Heritage*, pp.: 261–62.

35. Foster, *Pre-Romantic Novel in England*, p. 121; Steeves, *Before Jane Austen*, p. 143; Utter and Needham, *Pamela's Daughters*, pp. 159, 292; Diana Spearman, *The Novel and Society* (New York: Barnes and Noble, 1966), pp. 176–78.

36. Putney, "Plan of *Peregrine Pickle*," p. 1057.

37. Eric Rothstein, *System of Order and Inquiry in Later Eighteenth-Century Fiction* (Berkeley, Los Angeles, London: University of California Press, 1975); R. S. Jack, "Appearance and Reality in *Humphry Clinker*," in *Smollett: Author of the First Distinction*, ed. Alan Bold (London and Totowa: Vision/Barnes and Noble, 1982).

38. See John V. Price, *Tobias Smollett: "The Expedition of Humphry Clinker"* (London: Edward Arnold, 1973), pp. 9, 23, 40ff.; Bourgeois, *Natural Juyces*, pp. 145–46; B. L. Reid, *The Long Boy and Others* (Athens: University of Georgia Press, 1969), pp. 83–84; Jack, "Appearance and Reality in *Humphry Clinker*," p. 226; Frederick M. Kenner, "Transitions in *Humphry Clinker*," *Studies in Eighteenth-Century Culture* 16 (1986): 150; McKillop, *Early Masters*, p. 174; Rothstein, *Systems of Order and Inquiry*, pp. 149–50.

39. Baker, "*Humphry Clinker* as Comic Romance," p. 157; and John Sekora, *Luxury: The Concept in Western Thought, Eden to Smollett* (Baltimore and London: Johns Hopkins University Press, 1977), pp. 249–56.

40. Surely, the letter to Mrs. Jermyn reveals more than "a contrite little ninny who has nearly [?] fallen in love and humbly begs her revered governess's pardon" (Boucé, *Novels of Tobias Smollett*, p. 194).

41. Rothstein, *Systems of Order and Inquiry*, pp. 125–26, offers perceptive notes on Lydia's role in the structure and theme of the novel.

42. Bruce, *Radical Doctor Smollett*, p. 53.

43. Jack, "Appearance and Reality in *Humphry Clinker*," p. 210.

44. For a comparison of Lydia and Richardson's heroine, see David K. Jeffrey, "The Epistolary Format of *Pamela* and *Humphry Clinker*," in *A Provision of Human Nature*, ed. Donald Kay (Tuscaloosa, Ala.: University of Alabama Press, 1977), pp. 144, 149, 153.

45. Boucé, *Novels of Tobias Smollett*, p. 62.

46. Reid, *The Long Boy*, p. 95.

47. Reid, *The Long Boy*, pp. 94, 96–98; Boucé, *Novels of Tobias Smollett*, pp. 238–39; Preston, *Not in Timon's Manner*, p. 117; Price, *Tobias Smollett: "Humphry Clinker,"* pp. 11–12, 47; Jerry C. Beasley, "Smollett's Art: The Novel as 'Picture,' " in *The First English Novelists: Essays in Understanding*, ed. J. M. Armistead (Knoxville: University of Tennessee Press, 1985), pp. 174–75.

48. Sekora, *Luxury*, p. 262.

49. For the autobiographical material in Smollett's portrait of Bramble, see Lewis M. Knapp, "Smollett's Self-Portrait in *The Expedition of Humphry Clinker*," *The Age of Johnson: Essays Presented to Chauncy Brewster Tinker*, ed. Frederick W. Hilles (New Haven and London: Yale University Press, 1949), pp. 149–58.

50. Boucé, *Novels of Tobias Smollett*, pp. 213–14.

CHAPTER 3

1. For some discussion, see Susan Staves, "British Seduced Maidens," *Eighteenth-Century Studies* 14 (Winter 1980–81): 109–34; Jean B. Kern, "The Fallen Woman, from the Perspective of Five Early Eighteenth-Century Women Novelists," *Studies in Eighteenth-Century Culture* 10 (1981): 457–68; Felicity Nussbaum, "Herocletes: The Gender of Character in the Scandalous Memoirs," in *The New Eighteenth Century: Theory, Politics, English Literature*, ed. Felicity Nussbaum and Laura Brown (New York and London: Methuen, 1987), pp. 144–67; Janet Todd, *Women's Friendship in Literature* (New York: Columbia University Press, 1980); Nancy K. Miller, "Novels of Innocence: Fictions of Loss," *Eighteenth-Century Studies* 11 (Spring 1878): 325–39; LeGates, "Cult of Womanhood."

2. Carson, "Commodification and the Figure of the Castrato," pp. 24–26.

3. Tom Scott, "The Note of Protest in Smollett's Novels," in *Smollett: Author of the First Distinction*, ed. Alan Bold (London and Totowa: Vision/Barnes and Noble, 1982), p. 107.

4. Utter and Needham, *Pamela's Daughters*, p. 65.

5. Sekora, *Luxury*, p. 246.

6. Ever careless with details, Smollett shifts back and forth between *Melville* and *Melvil*, and *Elinor, Elenor, Ellenor*, and *Elenore*.

7. Compare the views of Spector, *Tobias Smollett*, pp. 69–71, with that of Damian Grant, "Introduction" to *Fathom*, p. xvii, as to whether the preface may be trusted.

8. Bruce, *Radical Doctor Smollett*, pp. 68–70; Paul-Gabriel Boucé, "The The-

matic Structure of *Ferdinand Count Fathom,*" in *Smollett: Author of the First Distinction,* ed. Alan Bold (London and Totowa: Vision/Barnes and Noble, 1982), pp. 172, 176; T. O. Treadwell, "The Two Worlds of *Ferdinand Count Fathom,*" in *Tobias Smollett: Bicentennial Essays Presented to Lewis M. Knapp,* ed. George S. Rousseau and P.-G. Boucé (New York: Oxford University Press, 1971), pp. 146–47.

9. Boucé, "The Thematic Structure of *Ferdinand Count Fathom,*" p. 173.

10. Treadwell, "The Two Worlds of *Ferdinand Count Fathom,*" p. 150.

11. R. F. Brissenden, *Virtue in Distress: Studies in the Novel of Sentiment from Richardson to Sade* (London: Macmillan, 1974), p. 102.

12. Paulson, *Satire and the Novel,* pp. 187–88.

13. Bourgeois, *Nervous Juyces,* p. 43.

14. Bourgeois, *Nervous Juyces,* p. 3, attempting to demonstrate Smollett's attachment to sensibility, seriously underestimates his opposition to Shaftesbury's ideas.

15. Again, Bourgeois, *Nervous Juyces,* p. 48, while acknowledging what she regards as Miss Williams's "misguided romantic sensibility," suggests, contrary to the evidence, that Smollett responds favorably to genuine romantic sensibility. For a clearer view of the topic, see Bruce, *Radical Doctor Smollett,* p. 71.

16. See Preston, *Not in Timon's Manner,* p. 74; Goldberg, *Smollett and the Scottish School,* p. 44; Boucé, *Novels of Tobias Smollett,* p. 111; Bruce, *Radical Doctor Smollett,* pp. 88–89.

17. Francine du Plessix Gray, "Splendor and Miseries," *New York Review of Books* 39 (16 July 1992), p. 31.

18. Moore, *Hogarth's Literary Relationships,* pp. 167–68.

19. Scott, "Note of Protest in Smollett's Novels," pp. 114–15; Simpson, "Smollett: The Scot as English Novelist," p. 81.

20. *Monthly Review* 4 (March 1751): 356; *Gentleman's Magazine* 19 (March 1749): 126.

21. Steeves, *Before Jane Austen,* p. 136.

22. Kelly, *Smollett: The Critical Heritage,* pp. 78–79.

23. *The Complete Letters of Lady Mary Wortley Montagu,* ed. Robert Halsband (Oxford: Oxford University Press, 1966), III, 2–3.

24. *Monthly Review* 4 (March 1751): 362.

25. Knapp, *Tobias Smollett,* p. 120.

26. *Selected Letters of Samuel Richardson,* p. 173.

27. *Selected Letters of Samuel Richardson,* p. 202.

28. Knapp, *Tobias Smollett,* pp. 119–20.

29. Foster, *Pre-Romantic Novel in England,* p. 123; David K. Jeffrey, "Smollett's Irony in *Peregrine Pickle,*" *Journal of Narrative Technique* 6 (Spring 1976): 137.

30. Howard Swazey Buck, *A Study in Smollett, Chiefly "Peregrine Pickle"* (New Haven: Yale University Press; London: Humphry Milford/Oxford University Press, 1925), pp. 31ff.

31. Jeffrey, "Smollett's Irony in *Peregrine Pickle,*" p. 138.

32. Knapp, *Tobias Smollett,* p. 117; Rufus Putney, "Smollett and Lady Vane's *Memoirs,*" *Philological Quarterly* 25 (April 1946): 120–26.

33. James L. Clifford, "Introduction," *Peregrine Pickle,* p. xxvi.

34. Boucé, *Novels of Tobias Smollett,* p. 137.

35. David Daiches, "Smollett Reconsidered," in *Smollett: Author of the First Distinction*, ed. Alan Bold (London and Totowa: Vision/Barnes and Noble, 1982), p. 38.

36. Damian Grant, *Tobias Smollett: A Study in Style* (Manchester: Manchester University Press, Totowa, N.J.: Rowman and Littlefield, 1977), pp. 180–81.

37. Auty, *Comic Spirit of Eighteenth-Century Novels*, p. 117; Goldberg, *Smollett and the Scottish School*, pp. 67–68; John M. Warner, "The Interpolated Narratives in the Fiction of Fielding and Smollett: An Epistemological View," *Studies in the Novel* 5 (Fall 1973): 276.

38. Giddings, *Tradition of Smollett*, p. 114; Preston, *Not in Timon's Manner*, pp. 79–80; Warner, "Interpolated Narratives," pp. 277–78.

39. Knapp, *Tobias Smollett*, p. 124; cf. Jeffrey, "Smollett's Irony in *Peregrine Pickle*," p. 139.

40. Buck, *A Study in Smollett* pp. 20ff.

41. W. Austin Flanders, "The Significance of Smollett's *Memoirs of a Lady of Quality*," *Genre* 8 (June 1975): 157. See, too, Bruce, *Radical Doctor Smollett*, p. 74.

42. Nussbaum, "Heterocletes," p. 146.

43. Buck, *A Study in Smollett*, p. 26; Foster, *Pre-Romantic Novel in England*, p. 121; Bourgeois, *Nervous Juyces*, pp. 74ff.

44. Flanders, "Significance of Smollett's *Memoirs of a Lady of Quality*," p. 146.

45. Flanders, "Significance of Smollett's *Memoirs of a Lady of Quality*," pp. 146–47.

46. In this and the next paragraph I am indebted for details to Clifford's introduction to the novel, pp. xvi–xviii. See his notes on pp. 795 and 798. For Smollett's constant concern for his audience, see Spector, *Tobias George Smollett*.

47. Nussbaum, "Heterocletes," p. 160.

48. Jeffrey, "Smollett's Irony in *Peregrine Pickle*," p. 140.

49. Boucé, *Novels of Tobias Smollett*, pp. 136–37. See the discussion in the chapter on the novel in Spector, *Tobias George Smollett*.

50. Buck, *A Study in Smollett*, p. 23.

51. *Complete Letters of Lady Mary Wortley Montagu*, III, 2–3.

52. Paulson, *Satire and the Novel*, p. 185; Jeffrey, "Smollett's Irony in *Peregrine Pickle*," p. 145.

53. Scheuermann, *Her Bread to Earn*, p. 240.

54. Boucé, *Novels of Tobias Smollett*, p. 138.

55. Buck, *Smollett as Poet*, p. 46.

56. The quotation is from *The Laws Respecting Women* (1777), cited in Colley, *Britons*, p. 238.

57. Scheuermann, *Her Bread to Earn*, p. 3 and "Conclusion."

CHAPTER 4

1. Strauss, "On Smollett's Language," p. 35.

2. Day, "*Ut Pictura Poesis*," pp. 298–99.

3. For the fullest treatment of Smollett's relations with Hogarth, see Moore, *Hogarth's Literary Relationships*, Ch. 5. Moore, however, underestimates Smollett's general knowledge of art.

4. Arthur Sherbo, *Studies in the Eighteenth-Century English Novel* (East Lansing: Michigan State University Press, 1969), p. 184.

5. Giddings, *Tradition of Smollett*, p. 70.

6. Wolfgang Iser, *The Implied Reader: Patterns of Communication in Prose Fiction from Bunyan to Beckett* (Baltimore and London: Johns Hopkins University Press, 1974), pp. 73–74; Michael Rosenblum, "Smollett as Conservative Satirist," *English Literary History* 42 (Winter 1975): 563; McKillop, *Early Masters*, pp. 152–53; Kahrl, "Smollett as Caricaturist," pp. 170–72.

7. Cf. Grant, *Tobias Smollett: A Study in Style*, pp. 130–31; Auty, *Comic Spirit of the Eighteenth-Century Novel*, pp. 109–10.

8. Sherbo, *Studies in the Eighteenth-Century Novel*, pp. 198–99, 202, 206; Piper, "Smollett's Early Novels," p. 53.

9. Kelly, *Smollett: The Critical Heritage*, pp. 366–67.

10. Piper, "Smollett's Early Novels," pp. 47–48.

11. For a discussion of the relationship between Smollett's episode and Shaw's play, see E. S. Noyes, "A Note on *Peregrine Pickle* and *Pygmalion*," *Modern Language Notes* 41 (May 1926); 327–30.

12. Rosenblum, "Smollett as Conservative Satirist," p. 561.

13. Giddings, *Tradition of Smollett*, p. 115.

14. John Richetti, "Class Struggle Without Class: Novelists and Magistrates," *Eighteenth Century* 32 (Fall 1991): 203–5.

15. John V. Price, "Patterns of Sexual Behaviour in Some Eighteenth-Century Novels," in *Sexuality in Eighteenth-Century Britain*, ed. Paul-Gabriel Boucé (Manchester: Manchester University Press; Totowa, N.J.: Barnes and Noble, 1982), pp. 170–71.

16. Paulson, *Satire and the Novel*, pp. 182–83.

17. Kahrl, *Tobias Smollett: Traveler-Novelist*, pp. 56–57.

18. Frank McCombie, "The Strange Distemper of Narcissa's Aunt," *Notes and Queries* n.s. 18 (Feb. 1971): 55–56; John F. Sena, "Smollett's Portrait of Narcissa's Aunt: The Genesis of an 'Original,'" *Modern Language Notes* 14 (June 1977): 270–75. The quotation is from p. 274. See, too, Boucé, *Novels of Tobias Smollett*, p. 116.

19. Utter and Needham, *Pamela's Daughters*, p. 235; Kahrl, "Smollett as Caricaturist," p. 186.

20. Staves, "British Seduced Maidens," p. 118; Sylvia H. Myers, "Learning, Virtue, and the Term 'Bluestocking,'" *Studies in Eighteenth-Century Culture* 15 (1986): 279–81.

21. O'Donnell, "Mr. Locke and the Ladies," pp. 158–59.

22. Simpson, "Smollett: The Scot as English Novelist," p. 72.

23. Kahrl, "Smollett as Caricaturist," p. 193, Bourgeois, *Natural Juyces*, pp. 82ff.

24. George S. Rousseau, "Pineapples, Pregnancy, Pica, and *Peregrine Pickle*," in *Tobias Smollett: Bicentennial Essays Presented to Lewis M. Knapp*, ed. George S. Rousseau and P.-G. Boucé (New York: Oxford University Press, 1971), pp. 80ff.

25. R. G. Collins, "The Hidden Bastard: A Question of Illegitimacy in Smollett's *Peregrine Pickle*," *Publications of the Modern Language Association* 94 (Jan. 1979): 91–92, summarizes the critical response to Smollett's characterization of Perry's mother. Collins's own explanation follows below. Samuel Johnson's popular *Life of Savage* was published in 1744.

26. Paulson, "The Pilgrimage and the Family," p. 62.

27. Perry, "Colonizing the Breast," pp. 184, 165.

28. Perry, "Colonizing the Breast," p. 191.

29. Nussbaum, " 'Savage' Mothers," pp. 168–70.

30. Knapp, *Tobias Smollett*, pp. 5, 161, 294.

31. Collins, "The Hidden Bastard," p. 92.

32. Rousseau, "Pineapples, Pregnancy, Pica, and *Peregrine Pickle*."

33. For details in this paragraph, see Ian Watt, *The Rise of the Novel: Studies in Defoe, Richardson and Fielding* (Berkeley and Los Angeles: University of California Press, 1957), pp. 144–45; Utter and Needham, *Pamela's Daughters*, pp. 216ff.

34. *Monthly Review* 25 (Dec. 1761): 437–38.

35. Howard Hunter Dunbar, *The Dramatic Career of Arthur Murphy* (New York: Modern Language Association, 1956), p. 135.

36. Utter and Needham, *Pamela's Daughters*, pp. 217f.

37. Baker, "*Humphry Clinker* as Comic Romance," pp. 157–58; Sekora, *Luxury*, p. 258. See, too, Price, *Tobias Smollett: "Humphry Clinker*," p. 40.

38. Price, *Tobias Smollett: "Humphry Clinker*," p. 49.

39. Price, *Tobias Smollett: "Humphry Clinker*," p. 9.

40. Keener, "Transitions in *Humphry Clinker*," pp. 150–51.

41. See Preston, *Not in Timon's Manner*.

42. Whatever the limits to Smollett's autobiographical characterization in the figure of Matt Bramble, his fictional creation clearly embodies the novelist's own point of view. See Knapp, "Smollett's Self-Portrait in the *Expedition of Humphry Clinker*."

43. A. S. Turberville, *English Men and Manners in the Eighteenth Century* (Oxford: Clarendon Press, 1926), pp. 161–62.

44. For details and discussion, see Sekora, *Luxury*, pp. 236–37, which cites the various examples.

45. Baker, "*Humphry Clinker* as Comic Romance," pp. 163–64; Rothstein, *Systems of Order and Inquiry*, pp. 125–26.

46. Kahrl, "Smollett as Caricaturist," p. 197.

47. Price, *Tobias Smollett: "Humphry Clinker*," p. 9.

48. Price, *Tobias Smollett: "Humphry Clinker*," pp. 15, 51, 53; Karl, *The Adversary Literature*, p. 199–200.

49. Sekora, *Luxury*, p. 258.

50. Baker, "*Humphry Clinker* as Comic Romance," pp. 163–64.

51. Giorgio Melchiori, *The Tightrope Walkers: Studies of Mannerism in Modern English Literature* (New York: Macmillan, 1956). Among Arthur W. Boggs's many contributions on the language in *Humphry Clinker*, see particularly, "Win Jenkins' Malapropisms," *Jammu and Kashmir University Review* 4 (Dec. 1961): 130–40 and "Some Standard Eighteenth-Century English Usages," *Quarterly Journal of Speech* 51 (Oct. 1965): 304–6.

52. See Grant, *Tobias Smollett: A Study in Style*, pp. 60, 95ff.; Steeves, *Before Jane Austen*, p. 157; Arthur Sherbo, "Win Jenkins's Language," *Papers on Language and Literature* 5 (Spring 1969): 199–204; Preston, "Introduction" to the Georgia edition of *Humphry Clinker*, pp. xxxv–xxxviii; Price, *Tobias Smollett: "Humphry Clinker*," p. 14.

53. Boucé, *Novels of Tobias Smollett*, p. 314.

Bibliography

PRIMARY SOURCES

Miscellaneous Works of Tobias Smollett, M.D. 12 vols. London: Otridge and Rack-
ham et al., 1824.
Travels Through France and Italy, ed. Frank Felsenstein. Oxford: Oxford University Press, 1979.

Oxford English Novels

The Adventures of Roderick Random, ed. Paul-Gabriel Boucé. Oxford: Oxford
University Press, 1979.
The Adventures of Peregrine Pickle, ed. James L. Clifford. Oxford: Oxford Uni-
versity Press, 1964.
The Adventures of Ferdinand Count Fathom, ed. Damian Grant. Oxford: Oxford
University Press, 1971.
The Life and Adventures of Sir Launcelot Greaves, ed. David Evans. London:
Oxford University Press, 1973.
The Expedition of Humphry Clinker, ed. Lewis M. Knapp. London: Oxford Uni-
versity Press, 1966.

Georgia Editions of Smollett's Works

The Adventures of Ferdinand Count Fathom, ed. Jerry C. Beasley and O. M. Brack,
Jr. Athens and London: University of Georgia Press, 1988.
The History and Adventures of an Atom, ed. Robert Adams Day and O. M. Brack,
Jr. Athens and London: University of Georgia Press, 1989.
The Expedition of Humphry Clinker, ed. Thomas R. Preston and O. M. Brack, Jr.
Athens and London: University of Georgia Press, 1990.

SECONDARY SOURCES

Alter, Robert. *Rogue's Progress: Studies in the Picaresque Novel.* Cambridge: Harvard University Press, 1964.

Auty, Susan G. *The Comic Spirit of Eighteenth-Century Novels*. Port Washington, N.Y. and London: Kennikat Press, 1975.

Baker, Sheridan. "*Humphry Clinker* as Comic Romance." In *Essays on the Eighteenth-Century Novel*, ed. Robert D. Spector. Bloomington and London: Indiana University Press, 1965, pp. 154–64.

Beasley, Jerry C. *Novels of the 1740s*. Athens: University of Georgia Press, 1982.

———. "Smollett's Art: The Novel as 'Picture.' " In *The First English Novelists: Essays in Understanding*, ed. J. M. Armistead. Knoxville: University of Tennessee Press, 1985, pp. 143–83.

———. "Smollett's Novels: *Ferdinand Count Fathom* for the Defense." *Papers on Language and Literature* 20 (Spring 1984): 165–84.

Boggs, Arthur W. "Some Standard Eighteenth-Century English Usage." *Quarterly Journal of Speech* 51 (Oct. 1965): 304–6.

———. "Win Jenkins' Malapropisms." *Jammu and Kashmir University Review* 4 (Dec. 1961): 130–40.

Bold, Alan, ed. *Smollett: Author of the First Distinction*. London and Totowa, N.J.: Vision/Barnes and Noble, 1982.

Boucé, Paul-Gabriel. *The Novels of Tobias Smollett*. Tr. Antonia White and Paul-Gabriel Boucé. London and New York: Longman, 1976.

———. "Smollett's Libel." *London Times Literary Supplement* (30 Dec. 1965).

———, ed. *Sexuality in Eighteenth-Century Britain*. Manchester: Manchester University Press; Totowa, N.J.: Barnes and Noble, 1982.

Bourgeois, Susan. *Nervous Juyces and the Feeling Heart: The Growth of Sensibility in the Novels of Tobias Smollett*. New York: Peter Lang, 1986.

Brissenden, R. F. *Virtue in Distress: Studies in the Novel of Sentiment from Richardson to Sade*. London: Macmillan, 1974.

Brophy, Elizabeth Bergen. *Women's Lives and the Eighteenth-Century English Novel*. Tampa: University of South Florida Press, 1991.

Bruce, Donald. *Radical Doctor Smollett*. Boston: Houghton Mifflin/Riverside Press Cambridge, 1965.

Buck, Howard Swazey. *Smollett as Poet*. New Haven: Yale University Press; London: Humphry Milford/Oxford University Press, 1927.

———. *A Study in Smollett, Chiefly "Peregrine Pickle."* New Haven: Yale University Press; London: Humphry Milford/Oxford University Press, 1925.

Carlyle, Alexander. *Anecdotes and Characters of the Times*, ed. James Kinsley. London: Oxford University Press, 1973.

Carroll, John, ed. *Selected Letters of Samuel Richardson*. Oxford: Clarendon Press, 1964.

Carson, James P. "Commodification and the Figure of the Castrato in Smollett's *Humphry Clinker*." *Eighteenth Century* 33 (Spring 1992): 24–46.

Clifford, James L. *Hester Lynch Piozzi (Mrs. Thrale)*. 2d ed. Oxford: Clarendon Press, 1952.

Colley, Linda. *Britons: Forging the Nation 1707–1837*. New Haven and London: Yale University Press, 1992.

Collins, R. G. "The Hidden Bastard: A Question of Illegitimacy in Smollett's *Peregrine Pickle*." *Publications of the Modern Language Association* 94 (Jan. 1979): 91–105.

Day, Robert Adams. "*Ut Pictura Poesis*: Smollett, Satire, and the Graphic Arts." *Studies in Eighteenth-Century Culture* 10 (1981): 297–312.

Dunbar, Howard Hunter. *The Dramatic Career of Arthur Murphy*. New York: Modern Language Association, 1956.

Eaves, T. C. Duncan, and Ben D. Kimpel. *Samuel Richardson: A Biography*. Oxford: Clarendon Press, 1971.

Ellison, Lee Monroe. "Elizabethan Drama and the Works of Smollett." *Publications of the Modern Language Association* 44 (1929): 842–62.

Flanders, W. Austin. "The Significance of Smollett's *Memoirs of a Lady of Quality*." *Genre* 8 (June 1975): 146–64.

Foster, James R. *History of the Pre-Romantic Novel in England*. New York: Modern Language Association; London: Oxford University Press, 1949.

Giddings, Robert. *The Tradition of Smollett*. London: Methuen, 1967.

Goldberg, M. A. *Smollett and the Scottish School: Studies in Eighteenth-Century Thought*. Albuquerque: University of New Mexico Press, 1959.

Grant, Damian. *Tobias Smollett: A Study in Style*. Manchester: Manchester University Press; and Totowa, N.J.: Rowman and Littlefield, 1977.

Hagstrum, Jean H. *Sex and Sensibility: Ideal and Erotic Love from Milton to Mozart*. Chicago and London: University of Chicago Press, 1980.

Halsband, Robert, ed. *The Complete Letters of Lady Mary Wortley Montagu*. 3 vols. Oxford: Oxford University Press, 1966.

Hodges, James. "The *Female Spectator*: A Courtesy Periodical by Eliza Haywood." In *Studies in the Early English Periodical*, ed. R. P. Bond. Chapel Hill: University of North Carolina Press, 1957.

Hunter, Jean E. "*The Lady's Magazine* and the Study of Englishwomen in the Eighteenth Century." In *Newsletters to Newspapers: Eighteenth-Century Journalism*, ed. Donovan H. Bond and W. Reynolds McLeod. Morgantown, W.Va.: School of Journalism, West Virginia University, 1977, pp. 103–17.

Iser, Wolfgang. *The Implied Reader: Patterns of Communication in Prose Fiction from Bunyan to Beckett*. Baltimore and London: Johns Hopkins University Press, 1974.

Jeffrey, David K. "The Epistolary Format of *Pamela* and *Humphry Clinker*." In *A Provision of Human Nature: Essays on Fielding and Others*, ed. Donald Kay. University, Ala.: University of Alabama Press, 1977, pp. 145–54.

———. "Smollett's Irony in *Peregrine Pickle*." *Journal of Narrative Technique* 6 (Spring 1976): 137–46.

Kahrl, George M. *Tobias Smollett: Traveler-Novelist*. Chicago: University of Chicago Press, 1945.

Karl, Frederick R. *The Adversary Literature: The English Novel in the Eighteenth-Century. A Study in Genre*. New York: Farrar, Straus and Giroux, 1974.

Keener, Frederick M. "Transitions in *Humphry Clinker*." *Studies in Eighteenth-Century Culture* 16 (1986): 149–63.

Kelly, Lionel, ed. *Tobias Smollett: The Critical Heritage*. London and New York: Routledge and Kegan Paul, 1987.

Kern, Jean B. "The Fallen Woman, from the Perspective of Five Early Eighteenth-Century Women Novelists." *Studies in Eighteenth-Century Culture* 10 (1981): 457–68.

Knapp, Lewis M. "Ann, Wife of Tobias Smollett." *Publications of the Modern Language Association* 45 (1930): 1035–49.

———. "Smollett's Self-Portrait in *The Expedition of Humphry Clinker.*" In *The Age of Johnson: Essays Presented to Chauncey Brewster Tinker*, ed. Frederick W. Hilles. New Haven and London: Yale University Press, 1949, pp. 149–58.

———. *Tobias Smollett: Doctor of Men and Manners.* Princeton: Princeton University Press, 1949.

———, ed. *The Letters of Tobias Smollett.* Oxford: Clarendon Press, 1970.

LeGates, Marlene. "The Cult of Womanhood in Eighteenth-Century Thought." *Eighteenth-Century Studies* 10 (Fall 1976): 21–39.

McCombie, Frank. "The Strange Distemper of Narcissa's Aunt." *Notes and Queries* n.s. 18 (Feb. 1971): 55–56.

McEwen, Gilbert D. *The Oracle of the Coffee House: John Dunton's "Athenian Mercury."* San Marino, Calif.: Huntington Library, 1972.

Mack, Edward D. "Pamela's Stepdaughters: The Heroines of Smollett and Fielding." *College English* 8 (March 1947): 293–301.

McKeon, Michael. "Generic Transformation and Social Change: Rethinking the Rise of the Novel." In *Modern Essays on Eighteenth-Century Literature*, ed. Leopold Damrosch, Jr. New York and Oxford: Oxford University Press, 1988, pp. 159–80.

McKillop, Alan D. *The Early Masters of English Fiction.* Lawrence: University of Kansas Press, 1956.

Martz, Louis L. *The Later Career of Tobias Smollett.* New Haven: Yale University Press; London: Humphry Milford/Oxford University Press, 1942.

Mayo, Robert D. *The English Novel in the Magazines 1740–1815.* Evanston, Ill.: Northwestern University Press; London: Oxford University Press, 1962.

Melchiori, Giorgio. *The Tightrope Walkers: Studies of Mannerism in Modern English Literature.* New York: Macmillan, 1956.

Middendorf, John H., ed. *English Writers of the Eighteenth Century.* New York and London: Columbia University Press, 1971.

Miller, Nancy K. "Novels of Innocence: Fictions of Loss." *Eighteenth-Century Studies* 11 (Spring 1978): 325–39.

Moore, Robert Etheridge. *Hogarth's Literary Relationships.* Minneapolis: University of Minnesota Press; London: Geoffrey Cumberlege/Oxford University Press, 1948.

Myers, Sylvia H. "Learning, Virtue, and the Term 'Bluestocking.' " *Studies in Eighteenth-Century Culture* 15 (1986): 279–88.

Noyes, E. S. "A Note on *Peregrine Pickle* and *Pygmalion.*" *Modern Language Notes* 41 (May 1926); 327–30.

———, ed. *The Letters of Tobias Smollett, M.D.* Cambridge: Harvard University Press, 1926.

Nussbaum, Felicity. "Heteroclites: The Gender of Character in the Scandalous Memoirs." In *The New Eighteenth Century: Theory, Politics, English Literature*, ed. Felicity Nussbaum and Laura Brown. New York and London: Methuen, 1987, pp. 144–67.

———. " 'Savage' Mothers: Narratives of Maternity in the Mid-Eighteenth Century." *Eighteenth-Century Life* 16, n.s. 1 (Feb. 1992): 163–84.

O'Donnell, Sheryl. "Mr. Locke and the Ladies: The Indelible Words on the *Tabula Rasa.*" *Studies in Eighteenth-Century Culture* 8 (1979): 151–64.

Paulson, Ronald. *Satire and the Novel in Eighteenth-Century England.* New Haven and London: Yale University Press, 1967.

Perry, Ruth. "Colonizing the Breast: Sexuality and Maternity in Eighteenth- Century England." *Eighteenth-Century Life* 16, n.s. 1 (Feb. 1992): 185–213.

Piper, William Bowman. "The Large Diffused Picture of Life in Smollett's Early Novels." *Studies in Philology* 60 (Jan. 1963): 45–56.

Preston, Thomas R. *Not in Timon's Manner: Feeling, Misanthropy, and Satire in Eighteenth-Century England.* University, Ala.: University of Alabama Press, 1975.

———. "The 'Stage Passions' and Smollett's Characterization." *Studies in Philology* 71 (Jan. 1974): 105–25.

Price, John V. *Tobias Smollett: "The Expedition of Humphry Clinker."* London: Edward Arnold, 1973.

Putney, Rufus. "The Plan of *Peregrine Pickle.*" *Publications of the Modern Language Association* 60 (1945): 1051–65.

———. "Smollett and Lady Vane's *Memoirs.*" *Philological Quarterly* 25 (April 1946): 120–26.

Reid, B. L. *The Long Boy and Others.* Athens: University of Georgia Press, 1969.

Richetti, John. "Class Struggle Without Class: Novelists and Magistrates." *Eighteenth Century* 32 (Fall 1991): 203–18.

Rogers, Katharine M. "Inhibitions in Eighteenth-Century Women Novelists: Elizabeth Inchbald and Charlotte Smith." *Eighteenth-Century Studies* 11 (Fall 1977): 63–78.

Rosenblum, Michael. "Smollett as Conservative Satirist." *English Literary History* 42 (Winter 1975): 556–79.

———. "Smollett and the Old Conventions." *Philological Quarterly* 55 (Summer 1976): 389–402.

Rothstein, Eric. *Systems of Order and Inquiry in Later Eighteenth-Century Fiction.* Berkeley, Los Angeles, London: University of California Press, 1975.

Rousseau, George S. *Tobias Smollett: Essays of Two Decades.* Edinburgh: T. and T. Clark, 1982.

———, and Paul-Gabriel Boucé, eds. *Tobias Smollett: Bicentennial Essays Presented to Lewis M. Knapp.* New York: Oxford University Press, 1971.

Scheuermann, Mona. *Her Bread to Earn: Women, Money, and Society from Defoe to Austen.* Lexington: University Press of Kentucky, 1993.

Sekora, John. *Luxury: The Concept in Western Thought, Eden to Smollett.* Baltimore and London: Johns Hopkins University Press, 1977.

Sena, John F. "Smollett's Portrait of Narcissa's Aunt: The Genesis of an 'Original.'" *Modern Language Notes* 14 (June 1977): 270–75.

Sherbo, Arthur. *Studies in the Eighteenth-Century English Novel.* East Lansing: Michigan State University Press, 1969.

———. "Win Jenkins' Language." *Papers on Language and Literature* 5 (Spring 1969): 199–204.

Spacks, Patricia Meyer. " 'Ev'ry Woman Is at Heart a Rake.' " *Eighteenth-Century Studies* 8 (Fall 1974): 27–46.

Spearman, Diana. *The Novel and Society.* New York: Barnes and Noble, 1966.

Spector, Robert D. *English Literary Periodicals and the Climate of Opinion during the Seven Years' War*. The Hague: Mouton, 1966.

————. *Tobias George Smollett*. Updated ed. Boston: Twayne, 1989.

Staves, Susan. "British Seduced Maidens." *Eighteenth-Century Studies* 14 (Winter 1980–81): 109–34.

Steeves, Harrison R. *Before Jane Austen: The Shaping of the English Novel in the Eighteenth Century*. New York: Holt, Rinehart and Winston, 1965.

Stevick, Philip. "Stylistic Energy in the Early Smollett." *Studies in Philology* 64 (Oct. 1967): 712–19.

Stone, Lawrence. *The Family, Sex and Marriage in England 1500–1800*. New York: Harper and Row, 1977.

Strauss, Albrecht B. "On Smollett's Language: A Paragraph in *Ferdinand Count Fathom*." In *Style in Prose Fiction*, English Institute Essays, 1958, ed. Harold C. Martin. New York: Columbia University Press, 1959, pp. 25–54.

Thompson, E. P. *Customs in Common: Studies in Traditional Popular Culture*. New York: The New Press, 1991.

Todd, Janet. *The Sign of Angellica: Women, Writing, and Fiction, 1660–1800*. New York: Columbia University Press, 1989.

————. *Women's Friendship in Literature*. New York: Columbia University Press, 1980.

Utter, Robert Palfrey, and Gwendolyn B. Needham. *Pamela's Daughters*. New York: Macmillan, 1936.

Warner, John M. "The Interpolated Narratives in the Fiction of Fielding and Smollett: An Epistemological View." *Studies in the Novel* 5 (Fall 1973): 271–83.

Warren, Leland E. "Of the Conversation of Women: *The Female Quixote* and the Dream of Perfection." *Studies in Eighteenth-Century Culture* 11 (1982): 367–80.

Watt, Ian. *The Rise of the Novel: Studies in Defoe, Richardson and Fielding*. Berkeley and Los Angeles: University of California Press, 1957.

Index

About the Author

ROBERT D. SPECTOR is Professor Emeritus of English and Coordinator of both the divisions of Humanities and of Communications, Fine and Performing Arts at Long Island University–Brooklyn. He is the author of over 400 articles and nine books, many of them on Smollett or aspects of 18th-century English literature, including *Tobias George Smollett* (1989), *Tobias Smollett: A Reference Guide* (1980), *The English Gothic* (1983), *Backgrounds to Restoration and Eighteenth Century English Literature* (1989), and *Political Controversy* (Greenwood Press, 1992).

ISBN 0-313-28790-2

90000>

EAN

9 780313 287909

HARDCOVER BAR CODE